WOULD THEY WERE WITH US AGAIN!

ULTAN BRADY

WOULD THEY WERE WITH US AGAIN!

ISBN 1 872490 25 5

KELLS PUBLISHING CO. LTD.,
John Street, Kells, Co. Meath.
Tel: (046) 40117/40255. Fax: (046) 41522.

PREFACE

Brothers, sisters, friends and foe, clap your hands and jump for joy, for if this script goes for publication, you are all authors unknown to yourselves! When I saw Gay Byrne signing his autograph on his books "The Time of my Life" in "Days' Bazaar" Mullingar, I was given the desired drive to get this manuscript finished and try my luck at getting it published. What would a poor chap like Gay, a man who was born and reared in a city, with nothing only the four walls of studio surrounding his working area, have to tell compared to me, who was born and reared into wild country life that had no limit to its boundaries? I believe that there is one book in 99% of the people. English was my worst subject in school and my best academic qualification was an Inter-Cert with honours on my second attempt at the late age of seventeen! This book is my true life story from the age of two to my present age of fifty-seven. My late father farmed 57 statute acres of land and all seven of us his children were born in a thatched cottage down a half -mile long laneway. As my father had a bad back he was slightly restricted in his mobility from the age of 36 and it gradually increased until he died at the age of 60. As we lived so far in off the road, we had no playing neighbours and made all our own sport to the best of our ability. I could safely say that our genetic culture was not much removed from the time of Adam and Eve! This has completely changed with the next generation of O'Bradaighs, as they were all born and reared in towns. It is for this reason that I would not like this story to die with me.

My father's name was Páraic O'Bradaigh who was born in the parish of Boyerstown, Navan, a chapel-of-ease to Bohermeen parish, in the year 1892. Boyerstown is about three miles from Navan which is pretty well the centre of county Meath. At the age of 33 he married Áine O'Clearaigh from Balreask, Navan, the daughter of a farmer who farmed a good sized farm. My father was an only son and at that time lived with his mother, his father having died a young man. The honeymoon was spent in England and

1

Birmingham was the first place they visited. As Da had a motorbike, shotgun and rifle, a visit to the BSA factory there was a must for him. They crossed the Irish sea in the captain's quarters of a cattle ship. Da was shown all through the engine rooms. This travel arrangement was all fixed up at the north wall Dublin a few hours before the departure of the cattle boat. At that time, the late twenties, honeymooners went little more than the next parish and only for a couple of days. We had a workman, who spent his honeymoon in the caravan that went round with the threshing mill. He reared a fine healthy family of seven, all of whom did well for themselves in later life. There were seven of us born in the thatched cottage. One year and a couple of months separated the birthdays of the first six of us. The last girl born was six years younger than the youngest of us. Marie was the eldest. Then came four boys in a row Seán, Páraic, Micheál and I the author of this book, Natlú. Áine was one year younger than I and Maggie six years younger than Áine. My Da and Seán were very mechanicallly minded and I was a heavy drinker for 33 years, so it is on these two qualifications that I write this book. I will use Da and Ma for handiness' sake and most other names in Irish as a partial disguise. I will do my best not to offend anybody but if I do so in any way please forgive me. My brother Páraic who must have read a few thousand books in his life-time and was trying to get me into doing likewise could not understand me going to the local every night for a couple of pints and a game of rings. I who have read only three books in my life-time told him I would rather write a book than read one. So big brother, here goes!

(Sadly Páraic is no longer with us. He was laid to rest on St. Stephen's Day, 1991. May he rest in peace)

CHAPTER I

I was born on the 3rd of September, 1933. Looking at my birth certificate Da did not register me until the 22nd of September that same year. The delay was that he must have been very busy reaping the harvest and the weather was probably very good. The 22nd must have been a wet day. Being the fourth son of four boys in a row, my physical features must not have been too pleasing to my Ma. Máire was six years older than I, Seán four, Páraic 2½ years, and Micheál 1 year and four months. Áine, my younger sister, was a year and three months younger than I. She was born on the 1st of November, 1934 a day on which it snowed according to Ma and she should know! We were all born in the thatched cottage with the aid of a mid-wife, a Nurse Harte from Emmet Terrace, Navan. My first recollection is of collecting primroses and cowslips with my Ma. The primroses adorned both banks of our laneway for about 300 yards. The cowslips were got in a neighbour's field a short distance from our farm. Ferns were placed in a vase that was ¾ full of water. The wild flowers were inserted round the circumference of the inner vase. The only flowers grown in our garden were rambling roses that were grown from the slip of a rose bush, brought from Ma's maiden home place when she got married. These roses did not flower till mid September.

A maid was employed for three days a week - wash day, churning days and human wash day. The clothes were washed on a Monday morning in a large wooden tub with the aid of a wooden washboard and life-buoy soap. Rinso washing powder came on the market about that time and made the work much easier. The churning was done on Wednesday and Saturday in the early morning so that the butter was ready for the market in the afternoon. The maid gave us our bath on Saturday afternoon in the big wooden tub. We were put into the tub, two at a time in our younger days.

3

Ma would show us the birds' nests in the spring hedging. She would warn us never to touch the nest as the birds would forsake it. The blackbirds seemed very tame on their nests when hatching out the eggs and it was possible to get very close to them. With amazment we watched the mother and father feed the fledgelings. It was much harder to find the nests of the robin and wren which were nearly always in a mossy bank. The wren, although being the smallest bird, engineered the most elaborate nest.

Da had a Fordson tractor AI-4429 and I got plenty of jaunts on it during my pre-school days. He had a very old-fashioned camera and took our photos every year and on special occassions. He obliged the neighbours with it when they required it for first communion and confirmation days. Our kitchen had the open grate with a hob on either side. The cats cleaned, licked and had their naps on one of the hobs, especially when rain was on the way. The other one was entirely used for the big metal black pot with its crude "Potstick" that stirred the linseed gruel and other animal food mixtures. A small hand bellows hung from a nail in the wall of the chimney stack ever ready to fan up a dying fire. Sometimes in the Spring months the cats had to give way to a sick chicken that would be put into the top of a man's sock with the rest of the sock wrapped around the bird, or a weak lamb that would be put into a box and left on the hob for a bit of warmth to get it back to full health. Three or four times a year Da took on an *Al Jolson* image to clean the chimney. There was an old wooden form on one side and once I fell off it and burnt my side with a red coal that had fallen out of the grate fire. The mark of that burning is plain to be seen over fifty years later! The ceiling of the kitchen was the old fashioned, black rafter type. The clock had Roman numerals on its dial and two winding weights, one for the main drive and the other for chiming the hours. There was a much more refined marble clock in the parlour. This special room was used for visitors and the two yearly stations, Christmas and Easter.

The first car I remember at home was a *Morris Cowley*. Its registration number was IM3062. It had the side running board, and a bull crest on the radiator. It was a two-door model with a booth at the back, the door of which dropped down until two hinged stay-bars of iron brought it to resting position. Three or four of us sat in this lowered booth which had a very comfortable spring seat. It was a very nice way to travel on a hot summer's day! The smell of the polished leather upholstery of the cars' interior was lovely. Da would bring three or four of us to visit his first cousin about once a month and always on a Sunday or holy-day. There was often a lot of tears when the team was picked on a Saturday night. Seán was always chosen as he would be some help if a break-down should occur. He was driving the car at the age of seven, not sitting on cushions but standing on the floor! He would bring it out of Boyerstown chapel yard after mass, to the amazement of the men at the church gates. There was always a big chat there after mass each Sunday about the past week's activities, hurling and football fixtures, the pictures that were coming to the two local cinemas, the health of any sick neighbours and who got a new bicycle or trap. There was no danger of Seán crashing the car as the only other car in the vicinity was the priest's car. The horse and trap brought about $^1/_3$ of the people to mass, the bicycle another $^1/_3$ and the other $^1/_3$ walked. The pedestrians came from all directions to the church most of them using the fields which had planks for crossing ditches and stiles to help out also. This weekly encounter was a sight to behold! I wish we could see it again!

My very first visit to church that I remember was walking with Ma to a holy-hour on a sunny summer's Sunday afternoon. I could not have been much more than three years of age then, and was very excited about going in a new rig-out for the occasion. The ceremony took place in an old parish hall as the church was undergoing repairs. I was brought up to a front seat in the gallery and had a bird's eye view of all the proceedings. I thought I was on another planet when the choir started singing the *Hail, Queen of*

Heaven. My other unforgettable memory of that occasion was the lovely scent of the incense, as it filled the entire space of this not too big a hall. I often wonder what fraction of that congregation are still living now, fifty four years later! In all probability there are less than $^1/_4$ of them. As the song goes *I wish I could see them again.*

Da had a *Winchester* rifle and took great care of it. It had a peep sight in the back and a little bead in the front. A magazine held ten .22 bullets. He would bring us all for the walk when shooting on a fine summer's evening. During these farm walks, Seán had the job of running back to tell us to stay quiet as Da approached a gateway or gap in a hedge. We would be boxing and wrestling and other energetic exercises. Da would peep out the gateway to a new field and if he saw anything he beckoned Seán to go forward so that he could rest the rifle on his shoulder for a steady aim. We would freeze rigid, wondering what he was shooting at. It was usually a rabbit, crow or pigeon. We fought over the discharged cartridge as it hit the ground and loved the smell of the burnt powder. The cartridge would be inserted in between my lips, open end first and touching my tongue-top. With an inward suction it became imbedded into the top of the tongue. This was another teasing act among the youngest of us. Crows and pigeons were shot to hang up in corn fields as scarecrows. Neighbours were often glad to get some for the same purpose as the ripening corn fields and potato crops were at the mercy of these same birds. It was on one of these farm walks we came across a green plover's nest. The mother bird got up very slowly and with a loud screeching cry went off very slowly as if to get us to follow her. Her wing movements were also peculiar. Da told us to look round for a nest. There sure enough in the crop of winter wheat was a nest with five eggs in it. The nest was made of dead scutch grass and a very simple affair. Da told us that most birds act in this manner when hatching and it is most notable with the wild ducks. That was the one and only plover's nest I ever came across and I presume it is unusual for them to nest in this country. Another evening we came across a hare's nest. It was on the side of a hillock of fairly loose clay and the nest was only about one foot deep. Inside were four lovely young ones which we did not disturb. Da pointed out the mother to us, as she watched anxiously from some one hundred yards away. After an evening's shooting Da always cleaned and oiled the rifle. He had special oil and pull-through brushes for the job. We would often have a competition to see who could put the most cartridges one on top of the other. Our nerves were more steady then and Seán could go as high as 14. Da would give a reward to the winner but there was a handicap of 1 cartridge for every year of age over the age of the youngest of us. Ma said that when she got married there would be a shooting competition most Sunday afternoons, to be followed by a penny game of 25, after the tea, before we came on the scene. Judging from the score cards which I saw in the attic the shooting was a very high standard.

Rabbit stew was a common dish in our house. Meat was used two days a week, Wednesday and Sunday. Bacon and cabbage substituted any remaining days. I had many an accident in my pre-school days. Once I climbed up a ladder on to a semi-circular roofed shed, up to the top I went and sliddered down the far side which was a 14ft drop on to scrap iron and nettles. How I escaped without a broken bone still surprises me. I got a fierce stinging but was all right after Ma had rubbed me with docking leaves for a few minutes. Another time Máire was minding us while the rest of the family were at Sunday mass. My sister Áine and I went about lighting the kitchen fire while Máire was out. We put in the paper balls and light timber on top before fuelling it with parifin oil from a one-gallon tin. Having put on too much some of it leaked out of the fireplace on to the kitchen floor. As soon as we lit the paper in the fireplace a huge blaze gushed out to the middle of the floor. Only for Seán arrived on the spot our two lives could have been lost! He threw a sack on the blaze and then a bucket of water. Da gave us our first beating which we always remembered. Páraic was hospitalized for an appendix operation at the age of five. The nurses had to give him his way when he was put into a women's ward. He refused to stop crying until he was put into a men's ward!

I loved helping Ma to dig the new potatoes in the early summer. I picked them as she spread out the forkfuls on top of the ground to separate the potatoes and the clay. I would leave the poreens but Ma would send me back to put them into the bucket saying that only for them the free range hens would stop laying eggs! The spring cabbage was fit for use at this time of year also, so Ma had a big load to carry home. I heard a joke about picking potatoes which I thought was a good one. A strong city chap who was on his uncle's farm during the summer holidays was asked to go into the garden and dig out the potatoes for the dinner. Giving a Kerryman's answer, he replied with the question "Who planted them?" On being told Tommy Brown he replied "let him go and dig them, he knows where he hid them!"

When I was three years of age I slept in a cot in my parents' bedroom and Áine slept with them. We were put to bed at about 9 o'clock at night. I got up at about 10 o'clock one night and pissed in a grand new child's bedchamber that Má had brought home that very same day. Áine heard the noise and looking up she took into a fit of crying. Da added fuel to the fire by asking Áine what did I, the bloody devil, do? It took Ma the best part of an hour to calm her down and that with the promise of a new chamber especially for herself the very next day. Da christened that episode *The Battle of the River Po!*

We drank out of tin mugs as it was too hard to keep us supplied with delph mugs. These mugs were supplied by tinsmiths that would call to the house every now and then. They were also available in hardware shops. Ma always gave the tinsmiths a mug of strong tea, wheaten bread and jam. This was greatly appreciated by them and the reward of a prayer was always promised. One of these travellers always looked for buttermilk and often downed three mugs of it!

One of my Da's first cousins lived only four fields from our house. Three one-foot wide heavy planks joined the fields for easy crossing. Séamus Boccán was the cousin's name and he farmed about 120 acres of good land. He visited our house two or three nights a week. In the spring time of the year he would bring scallions and lettuce which he would have pulled freshly from his own garden. One of his three workmen dug and planted the garden with early potatoes and vegetables every spring. In the autumn he would bring us an odd bucket of lovely eating apples and rhubarb and gooseberries for jam making. His uncle Tomás Cain and sister Áine lived with him. Tomás used bring us a bag of sweets every now and then and he was the first man I ever saw with a moustache and walking stick. He sold a large sized farm of land and went to spend his retirement with his nephew Séamus. Áine was very clever but would not be accepted in a convent to go on to be a nun because of her poor health. She died when she was only about thirty years of age. Tomás Cain died one year later at the age of 84. Da's mother who was a sister of Tomás Cain died the year I was born. Seán remembered the waking in our house well and actually saw Da cry, a thing I thought him incapable of doing. Both our grandfathers died when our parents were young so we never had the pleasure of seeing them. Ma's Ma was the only grandparent we had the joy of seeing.

Séamus Boccán was a well educated man and his mother was a school teacher. He was educated in St. Finian's College, Mullingar which had been just newly built. He got his leaving certificate before staying at home to farm. Da had told us that apples and oranges, pears and plums grow on trees. I got hard to believe this till I saw the apple trees in Séamus Boccán's garden in the autumn. I was astonished to see how many lovely apples grew on one tree and was disappointed when Da told me that oranges did not grow in this country and Spain was the nearest place to us where they grew.

My Ma was a good singer and I remember her singing while she sat me on her knee. She knew all the lovely old songs of that time e.g. *Home, Sweet Home, Danny Boy, The Harp That Once, Oft in the Stilly Night, Little Grey Home in the West, Darling I Am Growing Old, My Darling Clementine, If I Were a Blackbird, Dublin's Fair City, Just a Song at Twilight, When I Grow Too Old to Dream*; it was on my Ma's knee that I learned some of the Christmas carols also e.g. *Silent Night* and *Adeste Fideles*. She was a good Irish step dancer and slow-time waltzer as well. Da employed one farm worker, a strong robust man named Christopher Ball. He milked the cows, fed the calves and cattle as well as helping with the general farm work. He too was a lovely singer and always sang while milking the cows. That was a very common practice in the old days and the old people believed it increased milk yields and that the cow let the milk down more readily. In the morning it was possible to hear Christopher whistling as he came to work and he still about a $\frac{1}{2}$ mile away. He played the trumpet or mouth organ with equal ease and it was a great joy for us listening to him in these pre-telly and almost pre-radio days. He helped Da at threshing contract work for about ten years previous to Da's marriage. The thresher was driven by a steam engine and I just remember the threshing mill before it was sold. Da told us that threshing was tough work and as you were in draughty areas in most places that you threshed, it was very easy to catch a head and chest cold. It was a dusty old job as well. My last memory of the threshing mill, was of it in the hay barn. The drum had been taken out of it and we used enter at that point, crawl on our hands and knees and come out at the straw shakers.

Aunt Rose, our Ma's sister, called to our house every second Sunday evening and always brought a large bag of sweets to us. She was good about a few coppers as well. I often went with my younger sister Áine, Ma and Rose, through the fields on summer evenings to view the crops. Wild flowers were always brought back to replenish the vases with fresh flowers. Sometimes we would walk to the head of our laneway, sit down on a mossy bank, have a chat and view the passing traffic. In a two-hour stay there, one or two cars might pass by. Pony traps and bicycles were the common means of travel then in the middle to the end of the thirties. Da always inquired whom we saw on our return home and if we saw any cars on that busy Navan to Athboy road. If we were talking to any of the passers-by he would inquire if they had any news. These were the days of hard work coupled with a leisurely "after work time" and the great gift of conversation which people freely used.

Every year in the month of June, Ma, Aunt Rose and one of us the children went to Skerries for a two week holiday; I was never lucky enough to go there on holiday but I went out with Da and Seán in the car to see them on a Sunday afternoon or to bring them home. Páraic went there a couple of times and had the enjoyment of seeing "Skerries 100" a famous motorbike race that was world renowned. You could bet your last penny on Ma bringing home one particular item on her return from holidays. It was an oil cloth for the kitchen table. She did not realise how worn and cut up the old one was till she saw a respectable one on the table of the hotel in which she was staying. On returning from holidays Ma always had a lovely tanned face and arms from the sea water and the sea breeze, as she was never very fond of too much sun.

We were a "born free" type of family and made all our own simple sport. We played "blind man's buff" in the kitchen at night. We wheeled old car tyres up a plank that was resting on a 40-gallon drum to see who could make the longest distance from the drum as the tyre flew off the plank into free air. This sport often lasted for an hour and was very energy-sapping. There was seldom any trouble getting us to sleep at night. Micheál was more interested in machinery than most of us and could be seen carrying a bucket with a few cogwheels in it very often. He would spend a lot of time meshing the cogs into one another and turned out to be very clever with all machinery in after-life. I gained my knowledge of diesel and petrol engines as a result of his teaching. He never talked about machinery or studied books about them but showed great interest in them at the Ballsbridge Spring show or if he saw an engine stripped down for repair in a garage. Seán and Páraic started to play draughts, a game we all got to know at an early age. Da would join in to provide fun for us at times. He would go down on his hands and knees to allow three or even four of us to mount his back. A couple of buckleaps would knock us off which was great fun for us. Seán and Páraic used make catapults for bird shooting. The "Y" shaped fork of a young ash branch was the main ingredient of this machine. The holding stem would be about 9" long and the two off shots about 6" long. Two 10" strips of a bicycle tube, about $\frac{1}{2}$" in width was firmly joined to the top of the two off-shoots. The loose ends were then connected to a half-tongue of a shoe, to act as a launching pad for a small stone. By pulling back the tongue in which there was a small stone inserted and taking aim it was possible to kill birds. We were chastised over this and so put empty bottles on top of a stick for a cock-shot. I will never forget the first catapult myself and Áine made when all were at Sunday Mass with only Máire to look after us. We failed to get any rubber tubing but my sister Áine told me where she could get some. She brought down Ma's knickers and told me to get the elastic out of one of the legs. I got a scissors and had it out in a jiffey. When Ma saw the catapult she immediately asked us where we got the elastic.

She brought down the knickers to show Da what we had done. We got our second well-earned flogging from Da himself. Ever after that Ma could keep correction on us by saying "If you don't obey me I'll tell your Da". Áine and I used tease each other over new clothes and sandals. I remember Áine with a new white dress that was dotted with blue and red circles. I was very jealous as she teased me with it and I with nothing new to show her. I would similarly tease her with my new corduroy shorts or new shoes. Boys did not wear underpants then but the shorts were lined with cotton. Shorts were worn until the age of fourteen or even fifteen. Jerseys were worn up to the age of confirmation when you received your first full suit which included a waistcoat also. The jerseys had a lovely decorative collar and cuffs. A lovely soft multi-coloured belt with an "S" hook fastener was worn around the waist to keep the shorts in position.

Our toilet was a small triangular wood a short distance from the house to be used by the three youngest. A much larger wood was used by the older ones. An outhouse was used on wet days. My Ma would allot a certain corner of the little wood to each of us, the three youngest. A small reward was given each week to those that kept to their own corner of the wood. I soon learned that this exercise was to determine whether it was worm powders, milk of magnisia, syrup of figs, cod liver oil or cascara pills you would get the following morning on a fasting stomach. These chemicals were kept on the top shelf of Ma's wardrobe. A jar of extractive malt, Sloan's liniment, antivegestion ointment, iodine, castor oil, a roll of lint, cotton wool and antiseptic ointment were kept there also. Worm powders were my greatest dread so I often played a rude game of draughts in the little wood to avoid getting them. How true the adjectival clause for mother's *Hearth of my cradle days.*

Maureen Potter's table cloth was used as our toilet paper. On a radio play some thirty years ago Maureen had a son called Christy. Once I heard her giving out to him thus "Christy don't spill tea on the table-cloth, your Da hasn't read it yet".

My Da was a heavy smoker. *Sweet Afton* and *Players* were his favourite choice. *Players* packets carried a picture card on the back of them inside transparent paper. They would show a picture of famous buildings, land marks, ships, wild animals and wild birds on them. They carried a story on the other side about the picture shown on the front. We saved hundreds of these *Fag Cards* as we called them and it was a pleasant pastime to go through the lot of them perhaps once a year. Each 10 pack of *Aftons* carried 1 coupon and for every 500 of these collected and sent to P. J. Carrolls Ltd., a lovely prize was given. A shaving set, leather school bags, our first Brownie 65 camera to replace a very large old type one that needed the tri-pod and blanket on a sunny day, and a football are some of the prizes we got. A football was a very welcome and a very valued item in the late thirties. We often made a ball out of rags or paper before that.

Da used set one field of meadow grass every year when we were very young. The one man got the option of taking it every year, on a friendly understanding and always gave Da a satisfactory price for it. He was one of four unmarried brothers who lived with their sister on a small farm and in a thatched cottage. All their work was done manually with the aid of two Clydesdale horses and horse machinery. They mowed the meadow, turned it with a horse drawn *Black Stone* swarth turner if it was a light to medium meadow and rowed it with the same machine by reversing the drive of one of the set of turning tyings, thus putting two swarths into one. If the meadow were a heavy one the four men turned it with hand forks and shook out the lumps in the process. It took about five hours for them to turn the entire field by this manual means and on a few occassions I saw the rain coming just as they had finished. They had to repeat the same process the following day if it looked anyway promising.

These brothers lived a very simple life and their only bad habit was that three of them had a grá for chewing tobacco. It did not look a nice thing to do and when the big black spit was ejected from the mouth, we were a wee bit disgusted. They were so gentle otherwise that we had great respect for them. They often put me up on the mighty big horse's back and held me there while coming and going to the field. They were great lovers of buttermilk and always brought a can of it to the field with them as Ma always had a plentiful supply. As these men had only a little farm the taking of the meadows helped to give them a decent living. During the winter and spring months they drove the loose hay to the Dubling hay market, a distance of almost 40 miles, with horse and cart power. They would load up in the early morning, start for Dublin at about

1 o'clock and land on the market at about 5 - 6 o'clock the following morning. Two horses were used each getting a rest after each ten miles of road. The return journey was completed at about 10 p.m. the same day as the sale day. The two horses were seasoned campaigners and were very quiet. While the horses were tied at dinner hour on our farm all six of us would go under the horse's belly and out the other side as he ate hay or grass. These Clydesdales were mighty big animals with huge strong legs. Three of these four O'Reilly brothers were humped men. The fourth was to become humped in later years. At that time, the late thirties, every parish had about 10% of its population over the age of fifty humped, be they male or female. The men got it from sheer hard work while in a stooped position. Using the scythe a lot, tying sheaves of corn on the ground, weeding and thinning root crops, turning and shaking out hay, picking potatoes and bog work all helped to leave men in this humped condition. The ladies helped at most of this work as well as washing clothes and scrubbing wooden floors which accounted for their disfiguration. Nowadays in the nineties humped people are almost a thing of the past.

I saw my first vision of a plane in the sky about the year 1937. Da pointed it out to us and told us that there were people in it. We thought that he was fooling us. By the time Sean got the telescope out, the plane had gone out of view.

There was an auction of the contents of a scrapped ship in the Dublin docks once and Da made a few very useful purchases at it. He bought the ship's telescope, the compass, the barometer, the ship's binoculars and a thermometer. We viewed the moon and distant landmarks from the top of the haybarn with the telescope. It was possible to see a crow in the window of an old stone building about seven miles away. The binoculars were handy for looking at a cow calving or a sheep yeaning in a field without upsetting them, if everything was going all right. The barometer was a rare instrument then and this one did the weather forecast for half the parish. Neighbouring farmers would come to see the reading of the dial hand during the hay and corn harvesting time. It was a very good guide and could be trusted especially when the indicator hand went up or down slowly. The dial gave the readings *Stormy, Rain, Change, Fair and Very Dry.*

Mice in my young days were a bit of a problem as the only way of keeping down their numbers was by trapping them. We had three types of traps at various times in use to catch them. There was the common little spring trap which is still available in 1991. This trap caught but one mouse at one setting. The second type was set with thread and had three entrance holes. The mouse had to cut the thread to get at the bait, thus allowing a circular wire $1\frac{1}{2}$ inches in diameter to take a decapitating position around the mouse's neck and thus choking it. The third type was the only one of its type I ever saw and I asked several travellers about it while I worked in two different hardware shops in later life only to be told they never saw one of them. I think Da must have got it while honey-mooning in England. The shape of this trap was an "L" shaped rectangular one. The upright rectangle was twice as high as the base rectangle. The mouse went into a little entrance chamber 3" x 3" x 4" to get the bait. Once he stood on a platform when in there, the entrance door shut behind him. Now the only place he had to go was up a $1\frac{1}{2}$ inch tubular gauze. When 9" up this tube he went on to a collapsable platform and fell into a box of water where he drowned. On leaving the last platform he automatically set the entrance door at the base ready open for the next mouse. I saw eight mice caught in this trap set in a corn loft, in one night.

Like all children we found Christmas a great exciting time. We had two holly trees on the farm and I always collected a few shillings by distributing small bundles of it to our near neighbours. The making of two large puddings was mixed in the largest crock. Six loaves of bread were crumbled up as there were nine mouths to be fed. Raisins, sultanas, orange peel, cloves, nutmeg, and spices were added to the bread crumbs and all mixed up with great care. This mixture was left so over night, but early the next morning bottles of porter and eggs were added to moisten the mixture into a sticky dough. Half the contents of the crock were put into a cloth that was well greased with flour and margarine. I will never forget the boiling of these puddings in a huge metal pot that hung over the kitchen fire. It was grand to hear the ploop-ploop-ploop of the slow boiling puddings and smell the scented steam that came from the pot. Ma would make sure that the water did not go off the boil as this would allow the pudding to soak the water with bad effects. Boiling water had to be added every now and then to keep the water level over the top of the pudding. The parlour fire was used for cooking the meals for these two special days. These two puddings were hung from the kitchen ceiling for the four weeks before Christmas to come to full maturity. The three youngest of us used to get up on a kitchen chair to smell them just like the older ones. The lungs were completely emptied of air and then a long slow suck in through the nose gave the required satisfaction. The longer the puddings hung the more enticing the smell got. By Christmas morning the bottom of the puddings had numerous small nose dents in them. Need I tell you Da put his mark there too. Not very hygienic, but no one complained when they were opened. The pudding cloth was air and water resistant, nothing getting in, only the smell that came out. Santa came of course and Da and Ma spent a day shopping in Dublin a few days before Christmas. Train-sets, cars, tractors, jig-saw puzzles, carpenters' sets, toy soldiers and small cap guns were got for the boys with dolls and toy delph got for the girls. Sometimes instead of getting what we wanted we were left wanting what we did not get. My belief in Santa came to a premature ending as Máire made a very clumsy Santa. Once my sister Áine got a doll whose eyes would close when left lying down. My brother Micheál and I had an argument as to how this performance was enacted and decided to investigate. The saw was got from Micheál's carpenter set and I did the decapitating. Having seen the works to our satisfaction, Micheál stuck back the head with glue. Later that day Áine let the doll fall and the head rolled off.

Micheál stuck it with glue again to the great gratification of Áine. We often had a good laugh over that act in later life. I once had a toy car that was not too remote in structure from the mighty selling German *Beetle* of the early fifties onward. I once got a capgun that was the envy of my bigger brothers. A few weeks after Christmas, as these toys got the worse for wear, bits of them were scattered all over the farm yard. As well as enjoying the wren boys in our young years we were shown the fox hunt which went through our farm in Boyerstown every St. Stephen's Day. We saw the horsemen and women and the hounds, but never saw the fox that was being pursued.

Halloween was another big day in my childhood life. We were all very anxious to get the rings in the bracks. We were all very fond of nuts especially hazelnuts which were easily extracted. That same night we all tried in vain to get a bite from an apple that hung from the ceiling. We had more luck in getting a sixpenny piece from a basin of water with our mouth. Pancake day which fell on Shrove Tuesday was another of our favourite days and we always got a half day from school in later years. Each of our birthdays was celebrated in a simple party, no great pomp attached to them.

Then there were outdoor events on the farm that excited us also. Sculling day was one of these days. There were no cattle crushes then or injections to ease the pain of that bloody operation. This was one of many *Swap Help* jobs that were the order of the day that time. About five extra men were procured for the job. The big bullocks, as we thought they were then, were about 6 cwt. in weight. One by one they were pulled out of the shed by a rope attached to a ring in the animals nose. Three men held on to this rope while another man *screwed* the animals tail to get him on the move. The animal was then held firm on the sculling ground, as four strong leather straps called *Hobbles* were attached to the ankle of each leg. Each of these hobbles had a strong "D" hook attached to it and from one of these hooks a strong chain about 8 ft. long was attached. That particular strap was put on to the left front leg of the animal. All four straps were made up of four $^1/_4$ inch leather strips which were stitched together to form a 1-inch thick end product. The chain was then put through the other three "D" hooks and finally through its own "D" hook. Then the men on the rope changed their pulling power to the chain while a man at the back shoved the animals rump away from him. Slowly the four legs came closer together and the animal toppled over. A horse shoe was then put through a link of the chain closest to the "D" hook to keep the legs firmly together. The ring rope was then tied round the top front leg a number of times to prevent slipping of the same. The heaviest man stood on this rope while the rest lay on the unfortunate's body. The saw-man then got to work on the top horn. A mighty roar came from the animal as the saw penitrated its way through flesh and horn. This was quickly toned down by the man at the animal's head, as he closed the bottom jaw up to the top one with half the bullock's tongue still out. All the animal's remaining energies were transferred to its rear end from where came dung and naughty noises. Finally the animal gave in and took all that was coming to it, in a more silent manner. At the end of the operation bleeding veins were plugged with pointed $^1/_2$ match sticks. Some men used plain pins with a few ribs of hair twisted round the head of it. All being well the ring rope was released, the animal's head was raised and brought back to the animal's body and the ring rope twisted round the animal's top back leg. The other horn was then taken off in the same fashion as the first one. All was now ready for the animal's resurrection. While the nose ring was held in position the four strap buckles were unfastened with caution. The ring was taken of the nose and the animal arose leaving all the gear on the ground. It was a much humbler animal that walked off than the one that came out of the shed. When the last animal was finished the men sat down for a good smoke and a few bottles of stout while the tea was being prepared. After tea a good inspection of the cattle took place before the farm help departed. Should any of them be bleeding they were immediately rehoused and the vein in question pluged.

Docking the lambs' tails was not one of our more pleasant days. My Da would cut them off with a penknife. Ma would ring them off when the lamb was about 1-week old. There was often an argument over which was the best method. Seldom did Ma and Da have a heated argument. If it was getting too heated Ma would go for a walk. On her return Da would greet her with "Come over here darling Nan, till I give you a big birdie". Ma would smile and put on the kettle to show that all enmity had ceased. When put to a vote as to which way was best to dock the lambs tails we the children voted for Ma's method. If a lamb was got dead in a field for no known reason a post mortem was carried out on him. This always revealed a certain amount of sheep's wool in the lamb's stomach and this was certified as the cause of death. We spent many a day collecting wool in the fields to rectify this. As there was wool in every second perch of the fields it took a lot of time and was a very monotonous job. It was the few shillings we got as a reward for this that kept our spirits up. It was discovered in later years that it was pulpy kidney or lamb dysentery that caused these unexpected deaths and that the piece of wool that got into every lambs stomach was not the culprit. Castrating bull calves and ram lambs was another job usually carried out by the sculler. The bull calves were done by a bloody operation using a sharp knife, two 5 inch x $^{3}/_{4}$ inch sticks qf an ash plant sliced in half and a few pieces of twine. During the operation pieces of red raw flesh were thrown on to the blood splattered straw. The poor animal did not object as one man held his nose while keeping him pinned to a wall at the same time. The poor calf went round for three days with the timber and twine intact. When taken off the bag healed up quickly and all was well again. Come to think of it now a pair of clothes pegs and two small pieces of twine could have done the job just as well. In the early 40's an Italian squeezers called a "Burdizzo" came on the market. This was then widly used to doctor male calves and lambs. A minute is all it took to do the job and the animal had no set backs.

Sheep shearing was done by contract men who charged a small price per head. The sheep shears clipped half the country's flocks, a hand twist clippers the remaining half. In the late thirties and early forties there was no perfect fly dip to keep the "Blue bottle fly", from laying eggs in sheep's soiled wool. This resulted in these poor, most timid animals of all, to be attacked by the white flesh-eating maggots. Sheep were examined each day during the summer and autumn months. Infected sheep were very restless and would try getting their head back to their rear end to relieve themselves. They were housed immediately and treated with cold water and "Jeyes Fluid". This mixture brought the maggots up to the wool surface when sapped on with cloth. The maggots were then brushed off and another sapping done to complete the job. All the sheep were housed once a week and the ones with dirty wool were brought out one by one and dagged with a hand shears. This prevented the sheep's droppings from clinging to the wool and as a result they were less likely to be attacked by the culprit the blue bottle fly. This same "blue bottle fly" worried more than the sheep. During my shop working years in later life, I once saw a grocer's apprentice washing maggots out of pieces of bacon that were for sale that very same day. He told me that he had to do this work very often, first thing in the morning during a heatwave. I also remember passing a butcher's shop in very hot weather and getting a very foul smell of meat that had "gone off" as a result of fly attack. There were no fridges except ice cream fridges and they were a very expensive item in the thirties and forties. House flies were another scourge and all thatched houses seemed to favour their larger numbers. Ma would get a few fly catchers and hang them from the kitchen ceiling. No sooner would one be up, when up to one hundred flies would have got stuck to this sticky strip of two foot by two inch paper. Da once got his head of hair caught in one and prepared the "Flit Gun" and "Flit Spray" mixture. The table and all the shelves in the dresser had to be covered with newspapers for the operation. It was a very successful way of getting these pests eliminated. During the month of July, men working in the hay field would have a 1-foot string of a mixture of plain house flies and horse flies, flying over their heads ready to attack all bare parts of humans especially if the victim had hair oil lubricating his hair.

Cattle too had their fly worries during the fly season. The noise of the warble fly, saw all animals put their tails switching on their backs and a full race to the nearest sheltered ditch followed. So much did they fear this fly that they spent most of the eight hottest hours of a summer's day in outhouses or sheltered ditches. This warble fly laid its eggs in the animals' hock. The larva of these eggs spent the next few months crawling under the animal's hide on their way to the animal's back. In th spring time of the year, marble sized lumps appeared on their backs. These lumps contained a beetle sized insect before its emergence as a warble fly. Luckily enough for the horse, the warble did not bother him, as his hide was much tougher than that of the domestic animals. A much smaller pest called the "horse fly" attacked both humans and horses.

Our greatest pleasure day of all during the year apart from Christmas was threshing day. We had the steam engine drive on a few occasions. The sound of a whistle made by a steam escape signalled the neighbouring helpers to come with forks on their backs. Each farmer supplied his own turf, coal or timber to fire the steam engine for his own work. A mixture of fuels was sometimes used. It was a full time job for one man to keep the water level of the boiler at the mark "full". Two buckets were used to draw the water from a "Jack pump". We always got the day off from school to help out. Seán and Páraic kept the boiler full and Micheál and I kept the chaff pulled back from underneath the mill where it piled up. Ma, Máire and the housemaid looked after meal preparations. Anything from sixteen to twenty men helped at this swap-job threshing. It took a large roast of beef, one and a half buckets of potatoes and about six heads of cabbage or eight turnips to fill the men at dinner hour. The potatoes were put out on two large "Willow pattern" carving plates. This was another day in the year that the parlour was used. The chat at mealtime was usually about sales of nearby land and its price per acre, who died during the year, who got married, how the war was progressing, men's ages and who got shook-looking, who was looking well and of course football and hurling as the senior finals would have been completed a short while ago. The voices and chuckle of the laughter of the men as they ate is still fresh in my ear's recording department never to be erased. Bottles of stout and minerals were supplied at 11 o'clock, 3.30 p.m. and before the evening tea. Great sport was enjoyed killing rats and mice as the reeks of corn were nearing completion. A lot of stick was given to a man that would let a rat escape passed him. *I wish they were with us again.*

After tea the men homeward plodded their weary ways to milk their cows and look after their stock. Ma would breathe a sigh of relief and thank God that all had gone well for her. The corn was usually loaded and lorried away to the merchant the following day. The bags of oats and barley for animal fodder were emptied on the loft. Reeks or pikes of straw were neatly headed and anchored down with twine and weights. The day of the threshing and the day after neighbouring children brought home bags of chaff to renew their make-shift matresses for another year. Things were fairly tough in the late thirties. The remaining chaff was left to rot till the following spring when it would be dumped on some waste land. Hens got no feeding for three weeks after the threshing as they filled their craws with grains of corn that failed to reach the sacking department, as they gently turned the chaff over. There was always two acres of oats grown for animal and hen feeding with the valuable straw being kept for thatching. If Da did not need any thatching done a good price was always available for oaten straw.

One room of the house was used as a dairy. One large table ran the full length of one of the four walls and it was well stabilized for carrying a good weight. It had to carry one very large crock, a medium sized crock, one enamel bucket, the three milk buckets and one large butter dish that housed the butter plate and the two butter clappers. A narrow shelf at the bottom of the same table was used to rest the three washed milk buckets and have them ready for the milkman the next morning or evening. Three buckets of milk were brought into the dairy after each milking. The remainder went to the calves and the cats. Being a strong man the milkman carried two buckets of milk on his left arm by putting one on his forearm and the other in his hand. The third bucket of milk hung from the forearm of his right hand leaving his right hand free for opening and closing doors. Ma would do the emptying into the two crocks and enamel bucket. She had her own way of doing this like every other dairy woman and would trust no one else to do it. She always finished up with the two crocks full of cream for churning twice a week. In the spring time of the year when the flush of grass came, extra enamel buckets came into use to cope with the extra milk. We had no separator so the cream was skimmed off the top of the milk with a saucer, after a twelve hour cooling period. All the skim-milk went for animal feeding. The crocks of cream had to be kept at a certain temperature. In very cold frosty weather they had to be cured in the kitchen. They were all right in the dairy in hot weather as the house was thatched which helped to keep down the temperature and the dairy was on the northern end of the house. The only other time the large crock was used was for catching the pigs blood for the making of the black puddings, and the steeping of mushrooms for a few days before making ketchup.

The churn was a large 20 gallon end-over-end type. In later years when I was left to do the churning from the start Ma would warn me to let go the steam after about 50 twists of the handle and again after fifty more. This was done by loosening up one of the three clamps that held down the churn lid securely. Not trusting me, Ma would rush up before the time and let go steam herself.

Whether it was some chemical change or just expanded hot air there would come a great gush of steam to relieve the internal pressure.

The very well clamped-on lid had a 1-inch diameter circular inspection glass, which showed to be clear when the butter was ready for making. The lid was then removed and a half bucket of cold water thrown into the churn. This my Ma maintained left the butter much more easily collected. The wooden butter plate collected all the churn's butter into the wooden butter dish. The 1-lbs of butter were made on the plate with the help of the wooden butter clapper which was corrigated to give a nice finish to the butter. Buttermilk was lovely to drink and made lovely bread. A few of our neighbours were regular customers for a $^3/_4$ gallon can or three quart can as it was called, full of buttermilk. It cost them 2d and Ma always gave it to the person that helped with the churning. Ma made the bread in the oven of an "Esso" oil cooker which was fuelled with parifin oil and heated by a 5" circular wick. One or two cakes of bread could always be seen on the coolest window of the house. It was lovely bread but still was not as nice as pot-oven bread which was made in a metal pot with legs, that hung from a crook over the open hearth fire and had red coals on its lid. A hard working man that followed a pair of horses ploughing all day had no shame on him when faced with a plateful of this bread, home made butter and home-made plum or damson jam.

Lighting in the late thirties was restricted to a lantern for the farm yard and sheds, a parafin wicked table-lamp and a similar wall lamp. The humble candle was used for the bedrooms. Ma always warned us to put out the candle as soon as we got into bed. The battery torch lamp was used in place of the storm lantern on occasions. A twin celled battery lamp was widely used on bicycles that had no dynamos on them. Seán and Máire remembered the gas lighting in the town of Navan. I do remember carbide lamps that were used on traps instead of the candle lamps. They were fueled by a white powder that got messy in damp weather. The light came from either a wick or wire gauze. We had a carbide lamp on the old

Fordson tractor which was sold for £10 in 1962 for scrap. The exhaust pipe was missing on the same tractor and a robin built its nest in its manifold for several years as it lay idle.

Da did a lot of reading at night so Ma had a lot of persuading on him to come to bed especially if he was properly dug into a good book. If he was not reading he would be playing draughts or chess with Seán or Páraic. Other times he would be experimenting or mending a tractor magnito, distributor or carburettor. I once saw him repair the barometer when its indicator hand failed to move. He tricked about with old wirelesses as well. Ma wasn't too pleased to see this stuff on the kitchen table but for peace sake tolerated it. Ma and Máire spent some time most nights knitting, sewing or darning. Many is the time I spent holding the wool yarn in my two lower arms as Ma wound it into convenient sized balls ready for knitting. Pullovers, socks and scarves were knitted. Socks with holes were darned with a darning needle, wool and the aid of a polish box. This box varied in size depending on the size of the hole. It was inserted into the sock directly under the hole and as well as covering the hole area it covered about 1 inch all round it as well. Darning started with a close row of up and down strokes until the whole of the hole area was covered. It was then completed by another close set of rows that ran under and over the first set of rows and at right angles to them. The seats of the boys' pants were patched as well as the elbows of coats. Missing buttons were replaced in whatever garment they were missing from. A large tumbler held an awful lot of assorted buttons which were cut out of clothes that were been discarded for the dump.

Saturday night was a very busy night in my younger days. All the wash had to be ironed with special attention given to the white shirts and the unattached collars. All white clothes were "blued" and then starched after washing. The iron was the same as the electric irons of today except that it had a hollow inside and an "up-and-down" door at its rear to allow the red hot iron to be inserted and kept there during ironing. Boots and shoes were polished and shined, all nine pairs of them and sometimes more. It was bath night for the older folk, the younger ones of us having got our bath in the afternoon. Da had a good wash and shave with an ever-ready razor that worked with a single edged blade with the trade mark of "Bohemian". On special occasions he used a "cut throat" open razor which he sharpened on two leather straps. We always enjoyed the faces Da made while he was shaving. Some of us used a shoe horn to help put on shoes and boots especially if they were in their first few weeks of life. Da always used it and there would be holy war if it were missing on a hurried Sunday morning. Usually Ma made sure that it was hanging from its crook on a Saturday night. A neighbour of ours used half the shell of a bullock's horn as a shoe horn to great effect. A neighbouring handyman was employed to cut our five heads of hair once a month. In later years Seán did that work.

My first visit to a blacksmith at the age of about three was to Harry Callaghan's of Ongenstown, Navan. Harry, a huge muscular man, shod all class of horses, put the shoeing on cart and trap wheels, made iron gates, turned scythe blades and many other types of iron work. I will never forget the ringing of his round-nosed hammer on the anvil as he shaped a set of shoes for a horse from the whitish red heated iron that showered sparks of all shapes and sizes into a lovely display of fireworks that sizzled out on the clay floor. He was a neat looking man dressed in his leather apron, had a huge hairy chest and a massive pair of black hairy arms. A few pulls on the rope from the bellows after putting on more coal and dampened slack kept the fire ready for firing more iron. The straight length of iron was then shaped round the nose of the anvil, hit and hit several times with the hammer until it was a perfectly shaped shoe. Re-heating and hitting was repeated several times. It was then fitted on the horse's foot, re-heated and altered if necessary. Some horses would lean over on the blacksmith when he raised one leg. This was remedied with a bit of gentle persuasion. The smell of the steaming hoof of the horse was a unique and pleasant one and no one cared at that time whether it was healthy or not. I thought at that time that this shoeing was very cruel on the horse. When the shoes were fitting perfectly the nails were driven in and clinched on the upper hoof. Blacksmiths were great men to chat and share jokes with. They are now a breed of the past, as mass produced light aluminium shoes in varying numbered sizes can be bought in most good hardware shops.

Da was a very tasty man at carpentry work and made a lovely easy-to-pull trailer for drawing behind his 1M 3062 Morris Cowley car. It conveyed bags of cement, bags of meal and bags of potatoes as required. The trailer was built on a car axle and had pumped wheels. It was easily pulled or pushed by one man to bring hay and straw to the various sheds. Balers were a very scarce item in the thirties. Da made a full sized tractor trailer shortly after the car trailer. It did all the general farm work and had 2-foot high easily detachable sides. With the sides off, it brought about eight cocks of hay from the meadow fields to the hay barn. In like manner the stacks of corn were brought in to be reeked. These two trailers were made in the barn on winters' nights. A good coal fire on the forge kept the shed quite warm. An oil engine was used to drive the lathe for boring holes in the iron and timber parts. Da fixed a car gear box and universal joint drive on to that same lathe. A circular sharpening stone on one end of the drive was used to sharpen the hatchet, slash- hooks, reaping hooks and the kitchen carving knife. As petrol got scarce in later years, 1939 - 45, the lathe had to be hand-twisted. We all took turns at this twisting, even my eldest sister Máire. A wooden wheel-barrow and a hand truck were manufactured with the help of the lathe also. Not too far away from the lathe was a circular saw. It was driven by the petrol engine also. All the timber for the two trailers, the barrow and truck were cut out on that saw. The timber came from trees grown on the farm which were left to season for six months after felling.

A large press in the corner of the barn housed all sizes of bits and augers for boring holes in iron, wood and galvanise. Other instruments kept in that press were large and small hand twist drills, a wood brace, a wood spokeshave, two wood planes, hacksaw, fret saw, two diston hand saws, a saw setter, a "T" shaped square, a bevel, a spirit level a few wood chisels one of them bevelled, chisels for iron work, a centre punch, two ordinary punches, blow lamp, soldering iron, flux, an instrument for taking the pressure off valves in cylinder heads, a hand twist valve seater, valve grinding paste, assorted copper rivetts and washers for repairing the binder canvasses, sections and rivets for renewing hay and corn mowing knives. Binder canvasses and mowing knives were repaired during winter days. Some of our neighbours got articles soldered and holes bored in iron and timber.

Another smaller press in the barn also housed nails of all description; nuts and bolts, sand paper, rectangular and round carborundum stones, an oil stone for sharpening chisels, spare fingers for meadow and corn mowing bars, points and wings for plough breasts, paint brushes of various sizes and a fair supply of paint for iron, timber and galvanise work. Da told us that most of the contents of the two presses were picked up at auctions at great value.

Hens, cocks, chickens, ducks, turkeys, guinea fowl and cats roamed freely about the farmyards and adjoining fields. We had no dog in my young days. I used to think the cocks were eating the necks of the hens and the buck cat doing likewise with the female cats, not knowing that they were performing their fatherly duties. I saw my younger sister Áine trying to push the buck cat off a female's back as Ma passed by. Ma told us to leave them alone and we would have grand little kittens in a few weeks' time. We did not believe her till we saw the proof of it as foretold. We marvelled at Ma's wisdom. Seán and Páraic would whisper into each others ears when they saw these mating acts which left me a wee bit suspicious. They would not dare give us the younger ones scandal having listened to a sermon relating to scandal and the fear of the millstone round the neck and the casting to the bottom of the sea, or much worse. Talking about cats Da had the laugh of his life one Sunday morning. Ma was trying to get a very reluctant cat down off her wardrobe. Having failed she got Seán to help. He managed after some persuasion. Ma pulled down her best Sunday hat only to find it contained four newly born kittens. Da put netting wire on the top half of that window to prevent a repeat performance of that episode. That story about completed my pre-school recollections except to tell of my promotion as an egg collector. Ma showed me all the nests which were to be found in very different places. Three or four nests were in the henhouse itself, two in an old trap, another few in the hay barn, three in the calves' manger and one in the nettles in the large wood. A delph egg was left in each nest to entice the hens to lay there and preventing them from laying in the wilds. Ma warned me not to bring in this egg at any time and put an 'X' pencil mark on each of them. I was warned also to put the eggs very gently into the collecting basket.. Many is the time I would come across a hatcher sitting on a nest. Instead of getting off it when pushed she would fan her tail, ruffle her feathers amid noisy forbidding chuckles. She would peck my finger at the first chance she would get. I would then resort to poking her off the nest with the handle of a fork. Of course I did have a few breakages at the start but soon became an expert at the job. I wonder do they use plastic eggs instead of delph eggs in the 1990's!

CHAPTER II

I remember well my first day at school which occured at the end of August 1937. I got a lot of lovely smells that same day from my lovely new leather school bag, sandles, the school chalk, the ink which was a special brew made up by the teacher herself and the apple and orange that Ma put into my school bag. I was the fifth member of the family to attend Boyerstown National School, leaving only Áine at home with Ma. We went across three fields to Séamus Boccán's yard. We then went up his avenue to the Ardbraccan road. At the head of the avenue Seán asked me what direction to the school. I looked to the right and saw a church spire in the distance. I guessed that way which was wrong. Little did I know that morning that this church was built in the middle of our family graveyard. Its foundation was only a few yards away from our burial plot. I was one of three first day pupils. The other two were girls which did not create a problem for me at that age. Our teacher was a large robust lady who was very strict and punished by pulling the bob of the hair up and down as well as slapping the hand with a ruler. I was equipped with slate, chalk and marla, i.e. putty. We were encouraged to draw a kettle, tea-pot and cup on the slate by copying the teacher's drawing on the blackboard. After a few days we made these objects with the marla.

The teacher had about 25 pupils in three different classes in the smaller room of this two-teacher schoool. The headmaster looked after all the classes from third to seventh. He happened to be my teacher's husband. They had three children attending school, one in infants, one in first class and one in second. The mother punished them more so than she punished the rest of the pupils. One picture I got and was retained in my eyes' photocopy department to this very day, when I was only on my third week at school, was that of my brother Micheál who was in Class I and erred in answering

31

some question and the teacher after slapping him on the two hands without the desired response, started pulling his bob of hair up and down with a vengeance. He started to cry fiercely and at the same time looked back at me. I don't know if it was for help he was looking or out of shame to see if I his younger brother was looking but I rose on my two feet, drowned out his crying with my crying while stamping my feet on the ground. The headmaster came into the class room and had a stern chat with his understudy. All went well after that for a few days. At that point the teacher had cause to punish Micheál again and was in the act of catching his bob when she looked down at me. I was in the act of standing up again ready for another outburst. She immediately told Micheál to sit down!

Her husband had to teach five classes. About 38 pupils comprised all these classes leaving a roll call of about 63 for the entire school. This head master suffered a lot with toothache and used the cane freely. He happened to be my godfather and he used often call to our house. Both these teachers transferred to a school in Garristown about six months after my starting school. We were presented with two quite young single lady teachers in their place. One of them Miss Helen O'Donoghue, the principal teacher, came from Tralee, Co. Kerry. The other a Miss Mary Smith a good, gentle teacher from Kells, Co. Meath was a sister of Kevin Smith the great Meath Senior football goalkeeper of the 1949 team that won Meath's first All Ireland Senior Championship. She rode a bicycle 9 miles to Boyerstown every morning and 9 miles home in the evening irrespective of the weather conditions. In wet or snowy weather she wore a cape and pullups to keep her dry. She used get me to pull the pullups off her. My younger sister Aine who had just started in infants class would tell Da that evening. He who would have left us up at school in the car the same wet morning would smile and say while looking in Ma's direction "Well the rip didn't call me in to pull them off". I looked in Mas direction also as she made bread and noticed a smile in her face's profile.

I was by now doing addition and substraction sums and transcription as well. The patience of the teacher as she got behind you, took your hand in which there was an N-pen, into her hand and got you to write a copy of the line above was marvellous. It took a lot of effort to teach three classes of 25 in their childhood years and hold your cool. That was the difference in the teacher that first taught me and this lady from Kells. After morning prayers we were put through our breathing exercises. All air was firstly exhausted through the mouth from the lungs. When completely emptied, intake of fresh air through the nostrils took place until the chest was fully expanded. We had arm and leg exercises as well. I suppose there was about 10 minutes drill in all. The first fine days of May we were brought out for teaching in the school yard. The teacher sat on the stump of a tree in a corner of the yard and we in a quarter circle around it. It was a lovely change for us from a darkish classroom. An odd horse and dray would pass the road-side alongside us. As that road was a stoney road just like most other bye-roads we could hear the dray coming when a mile away and then until it had gone another mile away from us. The teacher would have to raise her voice, as would we also until all was quite again. The same noise could be heard inside the school as well but of a lower decibel. Mentioning May reminds me of the lovely May altar, put into the southern window of the large class room by the junior school teacher, just as Ma made one at home for the month of May. One of the more senior girl pupils made a "St. Brigid's Cross" for the first day of February as well.

This school bye-road was a quiet one and travellers used it as a halting-site very often. One lot of them would be only after moving when another lot would arrive. We were somewhat scared of them for no particular reason. A dog, a couple of goats and a few hens could be seen under the dome shaped caravan. Sometimes we could see a tin- smith tapping with his hammer on the tinware he would be manufacturing. The plight of the bare-footed, badly dressed children in bad weather was something cruel. They were very poor and a few coppers, old clothes, a drop of milk, a few potatoes or a cake of bread would more than satisfy them. The old people would say that the travellers brought good luck to the area in which they halted. The first poem I ever learnt was about a traveller. It went like this and was followed by many workers of that time.

"Sing a song, a tinker-man,
Sitting in the sun,
Sing it, when the day begins,
Sing it, when it's done,
Be it hard or be it soft,
Here's a jolly plan,
Sing to make your work go well,
Like the tinker man".

My second poem to learn off by heart was short and sweet just like that one.

"Rain rain rattle pane,
Dont rain on me,
Rain on little nigger boys,
Far across the sea,
Rain in the night time,
Rain on the sea,
But don't rain on Ireland,
On poor little me."

At home on frosty mornings Seán would have to thaw out the ice in the jack pump before school. A few bundles of straw at which we too helped were piled round the stem of the pump. Seán then set it alight without any trouble as frosty mornings were always calm ones. This fire was fun for us younger ones and the heat was a welcome guest. As the flames died down the sparks would start flying about and we would have to keep back. When Seán heard the pump begin to make noises it was time to put in half a bucket of water to prime it and with a few strokes of the handle, cool clear water gushed forth. Our neatly trimmed hedge in its winter setting that ran the full length in front of the house had thousands of cobwebs on its front and top sides. Da used tell us that the spiders spun all these webs to keep themselves warm during frosty nights. On hard frosty mornings as on dry spring and summer days we went to school the shortest possible way. This took us across eight fields that had plank crossings and two stone walled stiles that had four steps up to the top of them and four more on the downward journey. Lots of fields were joined with planks and stiles in the thirties as they were used as "Mass passes" then. Any country church that time, would have up to 30% of its Sunday worshippers come there, through the fields and double ditches. During the winter and spring four pupils of our school were picked in turn to bring turf, coal, or timber to fuel the two small grate fires for the day. That meant that we had to bring our bundles one day in every two weeks, as infants class were exempt from this duty.

As there were six of us crossing the fields to school we had a well worn down path-way formed. Hares were plentiful and its often we got very close to them. Some one of us would say "Stop" and all the remainder would literally freeze rigid until we got a good look at a hare only a few yards away from us and usually in a tuft of grass or a rush. His head would be tucked into his body, ears sleeked backwards, eyes bulging in fright. The only sign of life was his pulse beat that was doing about three to every second. One of us would go to take a coat off to throw on top of him but before the act was completed, up would jump the hare and run away for about forty yards. Feeling safe at that distance he would stop, stand on his hind legs, survey the scene for a few seconds before going his way. Of course, we saw plenty of rabbits that scurried through the furzes. One low-lying field we crossed every time on our way to school through the fields, had a plentiful supply of curlews and snipe in it. The curlews always greeted us with their startled encore. Many a time we raised a pheasant or a full convey of partridges. It was on my way to school that I saw my first fox in the flesh. I had seen a couple of dead ones that Da had shot with the rifle. Da had told me a lot about the cleverness of the fox which left me more anxious to see one. Seán saw one coming and raising his hand he said "Fox coming". As we all stood still he kept coming towards us until about 20 yards from us. He then gave one quick look, changed his course and trotted off in no huge hurry. Da had told me that the fox was so clever that he would know whether you were armed or not. He also told me that to rid himself of fleas and other vermin, he clasped a wad of sheeps' wool in his mouth, gently walked into a stream until all was submerged except his head. He then took a deep breath, slowly disappeared under water for a few yards before coming up after leaving the wool with all the vermin behind. When the vixen had her cubs she would not allow the dog fox that fathered them into the den as he would kill all the male young ones. Instead he foraged for them and piled up food for them near the entrance to the den.

Coming home from school and at a drinking hole was where I saw my first stoat. I had longed for a long while to see this member of the weasel family from what I had been told about him. He had a quick glance at us, up a bank and then hurried away. I believe that once he gets hold of a rabbit or hare, he will ride on his back and keep drinking his blood until the animal collapses. In later years and not so long ago I spotted a stoat, just starting to eat a rabbit that had been killed by a blow of a car. He immediately ran up a bank and disappeared. I guessed that if I let the car up very close to the rabbit with the engine turned off that he would reappear and get on with his job. I was right and it was wonderful to see this rat sized animal pull a rabbit at least five times his weight up a bank that was about thirty times his height and all the time in reverse gear. This was the equivalent of a sixteen stone man pulling a ten cwt. bullock up a small mountain. I noticed that all the time while he was towing the rabbit his back worked in a telescopic manner.

A story I forgot to tell about the fox when I was on that subject was the method they used to catch a crow. One fox keeps circling the crow while the other takes on a "creeping-in" action just like the Wicklow collie dog. When this last fox gets within twenty yards of his prey he takes one desperate dive at him and nearly always succeeds. I would like to have a video of that hunt. I love watching nature films on the telly. The best hunt I ever saw was on the telly. It was taken in African marsh land and showed a jaguar catching a pheasant. The bird rose about twenty yards ahead of the animal but with one fierce dive and leap he pulled the bird down when he was about ten feet off the ground. That same animal had a leap of about eight feet ground clearance from a standing position.

Another clip of a nature film that impressed me and showed some of the cruel action of wild animal life was that of a lioness separating a half sized zebra calf from its mother and driving it home for her half sized cubs to have rough play with and finally have their first kill.

One morning on our way to school we came across a dead turkey about one hundred yards away from the house. On examination we found the bird had a snare around its neck. My brother Micheál had set it to catch a hare that had a pass way through a hole in the hedge. We enjoyed a premature Christmas dinner but Ma was not too pleased as it was going to lighten her "Pin Money" at the Christmas turkey market. Another morning we saw our good neighbour Seán Devine in trouble with a newly born lamb. The lamb was taken over by a mare ass who would not let the mother sheep or a human near it. The man that owned the sheep was obliging a neighbour with the grass for the ass. We watched for about ten minutes as Seán tried to rescue the lamb but without success. The ass would turn her rump to the intruder and lash out with the two back hoofs and all the time making sure that the lamb was directly under her. Time was against us and we failed to see the successful conclusion to that story. Going to school by road, the two Dunderry school teachers a Mrs. McCabe and a Miss Brennan both from Navan, would pass us in their pony and trap. Our own Headmistress Miss O'Donoghue, would pass us as she cycled her way to teach. We were well trained to say "Good morning Miss", to her.

Each of our school bags had a good lunch and a bottle of milk in them. In the cold wintry weather we had the milk heated and cocoa or ovaltine made by a grand old lady, a Mrs. Dolan who lived right opposite the school. She always managed to have a Kerry cream biscuit for each of us as well. I suppose this work was paid for by barter as Da had done hire work for her husband. Her son got married during the war years and Da gave him a present of two petrol coupons. This left him with a full tank of petrol for his BSA motorbike. He brought his wife down to Killarney on the honeymoon on the back of this noisy machine. Motorbikes at that time could be heard coming from two miles away. In the months of May and June we went to school in our bare feet. This was common practice then. The last day before our summer holidays we had a school party which was at the expense of the school teachers. Sweets, biscuits and home brewed lemonade did the job.

Once we all got the measles and the school was closed down for two weeks. Election day was another free day for us. Boys were allowed two weeks in the month of May to help with bog work. We were exempt from this two weeks as we did not use turf. Young lads got good money for catching turf, footing it and giving a hand at the clamping. These were poor times and some of the pupils would wear their top coats all day in school. The teacher would ask them to take them off but the reply was "Mammy said I am to keep it on". God only knows what was under these little coats. A labouring mans wage was £2 per week and some of them had from six to ten children in the family and no children's allowance at that time. The same sad story of the coats on all day was very pronounced in the De La Salle school in Navan in my new school of later years. Navan, I was told by a very knowledgable Irish teacher priest, was arrived at from the Irish for the "Meeting of the rivers". Navan was the meeting point of the rivers Boyne and Blackwater. After some time the "meeting of the waters" was shortened to "of the waters" or "na-habhann". So from "na habhann" a few middle letters were dropped, the resulting proper noun NAVAN was formed. "bh" in Irish is pronounced as "v" in English.

The two priests of Bohermeen parish lived in Bohermeen parochial house which was half way between Boyerstown and Cortown, the two parishes of ease to Bohermeen. One of the two priests attended our primary school, Boyerstown, at least once a week. He would get some of the pupils to notify the homes of old people of his coming the following morning, to hear their confessions and give them the "Blessed Sacrament". I would be assigned to notify a William Reilly, a few fields away from our house. I always got a 6d piece from the old lady of the house, a cup of tea, pot oven bread and plum jam. They had the fire on the hearth in this thatched cottage and it was here I heard the chirping of the crickets for the last time. The pot oven bread I got in this house was by far the nicest bread I ever ate since or before.

Our games in Boyerstown school were very simple. We kicked football with a ball of paper or cloth tied with twine. Sometimes we had the luxury of a worn down tennis ball. We played a game of "Towns" sometimes. This was a crossbred game of cricket and handball. It was the only game played by both boys and girls. Once we were playing it when our C.C., a Rev. Fr. McLoughlin, came on the scene. He let a roar at us, the boys, to go off to the back of the school and play on our own away from the girls. That poor man "Lord rest him" finished up as P.P. in the parish of Duleek where his suspicious bones were laid to rest. I don't think the more learned pupils of the 1990's would respect his reqest as obediently as did we. Sometimes we brought our catapults to school and would have a cock- shot at a bottle. With six or seven boys shooting at the one time the bottles got little rest time on the stick on which they were put, upside down. We had our own home-made bow and arrows at home but they were too encumbersome to bring to school. In the spring time of the year we brought our marbles and spinning tops to play with at lunchtime. We were the only pupils with unbreakable marbles as there was always a pleniful supply of ball-bearings, which we got from cast away ball-races. Seán used make spinning tops for himself and the rest of us. He would saw the required 4-inch pieces off a broken fork or shovel handle and finish them by turning them out on the lathe. After getting a coat of paint and a bootstud for a point, they were every bit as presentable as the shop bought ones. Unlike the spinning tops which every boy scutched on his own the game of marbles created a lot of arguments, especially if some boy was losing a lot of them. Every time your marble was hit by an opponent's marble you had to surrender one. In the Autumn we played another game with chestnuts called "conquers". There was a wee bit of skill attached to this game in trying to break your opponent's nut that hung from a 2-foot piece of twine. Other times we spent the lunch break jumping ditches in a field joining the school. The girls played with their skipping ropes and another game called "Hop Scotch". This was played by jumping and hopping into and out of squares which were marked by chalk. In the month of September we collected mushrooms on our way to school for the school teachers and on our way home we collected them for Da. The teachers would give us sweets and Da would give us a few coppers. Wrestling was a common game of ours and Dan O'Mahony was our idol being the Irish Champion at that time. Tempers often rose high at this sport and we would finish up with bare fisted boxing until a nose bleeding or black eye caused the end of the match. That reminds me of my one and only fight with my brother Micheál. Páraic took on to train me for a few days and he guaranteed me that I would be able for my senior by one year and four months. He had me punching a bag of sand, ducking and weaving at imaginary blows, repeating quick straight lefts in rapid succession and of course the right swing which would guarantee my success.

When Páraic thought I was good enough he told me to have a go. I walked up to Micheál and started with my straight lefts and right swing while my feet did a merry dance. Micheál came in with one right swing and broke the bridge of my nose which is still broken now, fifty years later. There was no going to a doctor as we were afraid to tell Da. It never gave me any trouble in after life but Seán and Páraic had one good long heck of a laugh over the same episode!

There was an old Council jack pump about 50 yards from our school. It was a welcome guest to us on hot summer days. Six local houses got their entire water needs from that pump except for clothes washing and human washing which came from a forty gallon barrel, that collected rain water from the roofs of their houses. Ma maintained that rain water was much better for washing than spring water. It was much easier to get the soap to lather. Two of the houses were a full half mile away from the pump and the mothers of these houses drew at least four buckets of water in two shifts each day. The other four houses were quite close to the pump. The chapel joined the grounds of our school. Its grounds contained a lawn each side of the driveway in. On these two lawns there grew about twenty trees. These trees were used to tie horses during Mass, holy hour, stations of the cross, funerals and even weddings. A bell hung from a tower at one end of the church. I never heard that bell as there was a bigger bell erected on a fourteen foot high iron frame when I was one year old. The church had a gallery that held the choir and about sixty worshippers as well. The entire chapel looked after the spiritual needs of about four hundred parishioners. The sand martins came to the church every year and their screeching could be heard in the school very plainly. As the chapel had about ten right-angled corners on its perimeter walls the strong winds gave off overtures, depending on the direction of the wind. When the outer vestry door was opened on a windy day, there came a whistling music through the key hole of the inner vestry door that no musical instrument could compare with for low and high notes, for sharp and flat ones, and soft and hard ones. You would think that every cubic inch of wind in the twelve statute acre field opposite these southern faced doors, was trying to get through the key hole at the same time! I loved the musical wind and at home in our thatched cottage when the March wind blew its music through the rafters in the attic, it was good to be sitting at a good coal fire in the parlour. Telly, radio and family arguments have drowned out these godly tunes as well as better finished roofing. Sitting on the back seat in Mullingar Cathedral, on the right hand side of the main porchway, a door there gives off that musical whistling through its key hole when ever a strong southerly wind blows. That key hole has been covered over with a wall of timber that was erected for the selling of tapes in the baptistry without any respect for old men that had sat on that back seat for over forty years. The good news I got a few weeks past is that the same key hole music can be heard on the corresponding left hand corner of the cathedral. Men who sit on the right hand side back seating would dare not intrude on the people on the left hand side during their usual Sunday mass. The lonesome hush of the wind that is mentioned in the poem *An old woman of the road*, is only near equalled by the howling of distant wolves at a full moon, an American wake or the banshee. Looking at Mullingar cathedral reminds me of the Rennicks and Bennet families of stone masons at the White Quarries, Ardbraccan, Navan about three miles from our home place in Boyerstown. They are the direct decendants of "Head Stone" cutters, grave side kerbing manufacturers and ornamental stone work operators from many generations past. Some of their lovely hand work can be seen round all the doorways of Mullingar Cathedral and likewise some of the more refined work of masonary on that elegant building, Trinity College, Dublin. Ken Rennicks is a member of the said gifted families, the man who gave all his best to the Meath Senior Football team that were only a middling lot of lads at that time. He was by far their key man and the star man of a game against Kerry in an All-Ireland semi final.

Every school has its own flock of crows that visit it during and after lunch hour, and our school was no exception as there were a couple of woods nearby. The neighbouring farm workers knew that it was 1 o'clock when they saw the crows swooping down for bread crumbs that the children had left after lunch or else they experienced the silence of the had been playing school children.

In the Spring of 1938 Da made a visit to a neighbour who had a wind charger in operation. He decided that it was a "must", when he saw that it could light the house, sheds and farmyard as good as any ESB. It was decided to erect it on top of the 30 foot-high hay barn. The stand for holding the charging unit was another fifteen feet high. It was made in two sections to simplify its erection. Lengths of angle iron were bought, cut into proper lengths, altered on the anvil where necessary and all the holes were bored on the lathe. An oil engine powered the lathe drive. This petrol engine had to be started by hand twist, just like the old Fordston tractor we had, as neither had a battery to create the spark, but a magnito. When all the iron pieces of the stand were shaped and bored they were coated with two coats of aluminium paint. One half sheet of galvanize had to be taken off the roof of the haybarn to allow the stands to be erected. Two five foot long lengths of 4 inch x 3 inch timber were secured underneath the roof. Two legs of the first stand were bolted on to each of these two timber lengths. When the four legs were secured all the angle iron cross sections were bolted on. The legs of the second stand were then bolted on to the legs of the first stand and its angle ironed stabilising pieces bolted on. This completed the stand which was tapered from 4 foot at the base to 1 foot at the top. This tapering took a bit of engineering at ground level, to leave the erection handy. The holes on the angle iron were numbered with the corresponding holes on the stand legs. A dynamo with a tailpiece at one end to keep the rotating blade of the other end facing the wind at all times was firmly bolted on to the top of the stand. The blade which was six feet high was cut from a length of a special picked tree on our farm. It was then planed down, with reverse taperings on the two half lengths which were then tipped with sheet zinc on the driving side of the blade to prolong its working life. All this work was done by Da in the barn at night and rainy days. The blade speed was controlled by a governor which slowed it down in very windy weather. There was a braking device on the dynamo drive to bring the charging system to a complete standstill in stormy weather, for fear of overcharging the batteries, that powered the lighting system. A two stone weight was hung from a hook at ground level for the brake to be engaged. The hook was the lower end of bull wire that came from the charger and hung about two foot from the ground. The blade when driving during low winds was creating the very same swish as that of helicopter blades when idling after landing. Two coloured rubber covered wires came from the windcharger to a switch board in the barn that had an amp-meter among other readings. Da had a hydrometer for testing the acidity of batteries. He charged wireless batteries for our neighbours as well as our own batteries. He often charged eight batteries at the same time by joining them "+" to "-" to "+" to "-" etc. One of our neighbours had a large English made wet battery that showed three coloured dots, red + white + blue, at the base of the batteries front side when fully discharged. These coloured dots rose to the top of the battery one by one and when all three got to the top the fully charged battery was disconnected.

Wiring the house, sheds and farm yard took some time as it had to take second place to the usual farm work. A day's shopping in Dublin was spent buying the indoor and outdoor wiring, ceiling roses, adaptors, switches, connectors, bulbs and lamp shades. While wiring in the darker areas a torch and candle light was used. Seán worked from the attic or loft as we called it. Da bored the required holes for the switches and adaptors to allow Seán to lower the power line when required. I took turns with Micheál and Páraic to hold a candle that was anchored in a lovely enamel candlestick for Da's work and Seán used a torch. I would be told to raise and lower the light to suit the level at which the work was being done. It was monotonous work and one's arms tired when holding up a light at a height for a few minutes. A narrow strip of boarding was removed from some of the partitions to conceal the wiring that came down to the switches. They were neatly replaced when that part of the wiring was completed. All instructions during work had to be shouted from the attic to ground level and vice versa. During the tea after work Ma would inquire if the work was nearing completion and then say that "It will be a God send when it is". The light in the parlour had a lovely decorative circular ceiling rose that was 2 feet in diameter. Out of the centre of that ceiling rose came a three pronged copper, swan necked adaptor. There was no wire to be seen from the ceiling down and three strong bulbs and coloured shades completed that room. The sheds and yard were wired much quicker as they had not to be as detailed. There was a great celebration on the day of the switch on and Da blew a good party. The lighting system was as good as any ESB and there were no two-monthly bills to be paid! It was now a pleasure doing our home studies and both the candles and storm lantern became reduntant. All that work was done in the year 1938.

Sometime during all that wiring work there came a telegram to Ma to say that her brother Dan had died. He got a heart attack after returning from the stations of the cross in Navan the night before. Ma burst out crying and was very annoyed that she had not gone to visit that family the previous Sunday. After some consoling words, Da got to calm her down. Dan was only 43 years of age and left a widow and two teenage children.

The spring of 1938 was one of the coldest I ever saw. It freezed so hard that the river Boyne which is a fast flowing river freezed over from bank to bank. A large portion of the population of Navan and the adjoining countryside took to sliding, some of them with roller skates. There was a sudden upsurge into the two adjoining hospitals with people that had broken an arm or leg. Our own workman, Christopher Ball, broke his leg while crossing a street in Navan. The frost was so severe that drinking places for cattle had to be broken up each day with a sledge. That hard frost took place in the first three weeks of January and was followed by a few weeks of snow which caused large drifts at the windy side of hedge rows. All during that hard weather Da would get us to feed the birds. We took advantage of this hard weather to trap birds.

To do so we got a sand-riddle which we raised at one end with a 4-inch piece of timber. A length of twine was tied to the bottom of that timber and then stretched gently into the nearest out-house. Making sure that there were no domestic birds about, a fistful of oats was laid under the riddle. It wasn't long until a lot of birds started feeding and the twine was pulled to trip the 4-inch piece of timber leaving the birds trapped underneath. We examined the catch through the $\frac{1}{2}$ inch wire mesh and admired the lovely colour of most of them before releasing them again. We noted the different breeds of birds and our favourites were the blue tits, the bull finches and the yellow hammers. Anyone catching birds in this manner would want to put the bait in the centre area of the riddle, avoiding the wooden circumference area as this would kill or injure the birds when the timber piece was tripped. Seán trapped a couple of rats under the same riddle, before the hens were let out in the morning. These were rats that were used to coming when the hens were feeding. We had a special rat trap for catching rats in the out houses. The main grain loft had two tempting inlets for rats but once in there was no possible outlet. I saw a few rats heeled over from a belt of a .22 bullet. Da and Seán were deadly accurate within thirty yards. I saw both of them shoot down a hawk from the barn door as they idled in search of prey, with the same rifle. Owls are famous for catching rats and mice. That is why a large circular hole was left in the gable end wall of a grain loft in estate farm sheds built many years ago.

The Summer of 1939 was a beautiful one as were all the summers in my very young days. During the long evenings we would go out hurling or kicking football. Other times we had 50 yards or 100 yards sprints, high jumping, the long jump, frog leaping and, to finish up, a bout of wrestling. The winner of the wrestling would thump himself in the chest and say "I am Dan O'Mahony". Our two sisters Máire and Áine would sometimes join in the running games and Ma would call them "tomboys". Learning to ride a bicycle was a bit of a problem for us all. Unlike now when there are all sizes of bicycles in every homestead, the only bicycle we had to learn on was Ma's bicycle. Usually an older brother helped out in this learning by holding the back of the saddle until the student got in on the balancing act. This took several training sessions but patience was duly rewarded.

There was a timid ass in a neighbour's field and we tried our hand at riding him bareback. On most attempts the ass would do the rodeo act and the rider would part company with him. This greatly added to our enjoyment. I have a hunch that the poor ass enjoyed it also as he never objected to any of us walking up to him and catching him by the head.

In the end of Summer evenings, especially if our long shadows were willing partners, we mostly finished up eating cherries off the two trees of them that grew on our farm. It was a miracle some of us did not get killed by falling off the trees as we often went too far out on a branch to get the ripest cherries. The fall would be eased by the branches on the way down. We always jumped the ditches when going to and coming from fields. Some of these jumps were big but with a bit of a sprint to them an "Arkle feat" would be performed. Once to our regret we took a notion to chase a horse which belonged to our next door neighbour. It was in a six-acre field adjoining the cherry trees. The six of us would try to corner the horse but with a clatter of hooves off he would go making nasty noises from the rear end as he released some form of carbonic gas from his grassy filled stomach. This caused us to double up laughing so we repeated this act about six times, when we heard a roar "Stop - Home". It was Da who had heard the clattering hooves of the horse. We strolled home like dogs with their tails between their legs, knowing well that we were in for a flogging. Da sat with an ash plant in his hand, on a chair in the garden. We were called in one by one for our flogging. Putting us across his lap he gave each of us six of the ash plant on the backside.

times. The culprits he told us all died in peculiar circumstances, and a curse fell on their families. The economic war years were told to us, when farmers could not get sixpence for a suck calf. We enjoyed listening to these true stories and took them all in.

On the Saturday before our school return after summer holidays Ma would have a lot of clothes and footwear to buy. New school bags were got for the older ones and their bags were passed on to the younger ones. The announcement of our school return was made at Mass the previous Sunday and all our spirits would sink to a low ebb after a pleasant long hot summer. Micheál did not like school and it was not unusual for him to hide his shoes or school bag. An all-out search by the five of us would reveal the lost property much to Micheál's dismay. We were only back in school one week when Da told us that World War No. 2 had broken out. It was on Sunday, 3rd September, 1939, on my sixth birthday. Even though Ireland remained neutral the war had a big bearing on our changed life style for the following six years. There was a large map of Ireland on our kitchen wall and now Da put on another large map of Europe. The two maps took up one entire wall and Ma did not object. As well as using it to follow Hitler's marches Da used it to teach us the rivers and capital cities of the European countries. He already had us well up in the counties, mountains, large towns, rivers and lakes of Ireland. We had a few geographical rhymes that helped us. *Dublin on the Liffey, London on the Thames, Rome on the Tiber, Paris on the Seine, Berlin on the Spree and Constantinople on the Bosphorus.*

Long legged Italy kicked poor Sicily into the Mediterranean Sea!

Hungry Germany took a lump of Turkey and dipped it in Greece.

With the aid of a sugar bowl as a substitute for the sun, a tennis ball for the moon and the world globe for the earth, Da showed us the reasons for night and day, the four seasons of the year, and the reason for the eclipse of both the sun and moon. He also told us that all eclipses of the moon showed the arc of a circle thus proving that the earth is round.

We would have an odd family question time on Irish and European geography. It was chaired by Da who asked the questions and kept the score. The toughness of the questions depended on the age of the answerer. Seán and Páraic were quite knowledgeable by now. We all listened to Joe Linnane's Sunday night question time. We were amazed at Da's general knowledge answering while Ma excelled in the musical ones. Very few houses had a "wireless" then and for a broadcast of hurling and football semi-finals and finals a few of our neighbours would come to hear the commentary. At the start of the war Kerry, Cavan and Roscommon were the football leaders while Dublin, Cork, Tipperary, Kilkenny and Limerick were to the fore in Hurling. I remember Mick Mackey playing, who along with Christy Ring must be the best hurlers ever. Micheál O'Heir singles out Tommy Murphy of Leix as the undisputed leader with the bigger ball.

Around the fire was another wireless programme we enjoyed. It was a light hearted musical with an odd recitation thrown in. A very useful programme for the war years was *Making and Mending* by Peadar O'Connaire. Listeners sent in their carpentry, plumbing, painting, building and decorating troubles among others, that were expertly answered. Da tuned into the BBC for the English news and other European stations that gave such a poor reception that he had to hold his ear to the speaker. I well remember Lord Haw Haw's Germany propaganda news that started always the same way *Germany calling, Germany calling*. Da always had a smile on his face when listening to the man whose surname was Irish "Joyce". The propaganda news was aimed at the British.

As well as the wireless we had an old type gramophone and a selection of John McCormack and Delia Murphy records. The turntable was powered by a large spring that was hand wound. The

CHAPTER III

The house roof was renewed with a new coat of thatch every third year provided the oaten straw was of the proper length and quality. There were three thatchers in our area and they were all kept busy. All three of them enjoyed a few pints a night. It was mostly in the pub that their working contracts were finalized. They were well fed and got about double the wage of a farm labourer. The first few days were spent pulling, scutching and tying fistfuls of the finished thatch into bundles that were easily carried up a ladder. If the depth of thatch was too great an appropriate amount would be taken off before the job proper started. That done, the first bundle of thatch was brought up the ladder by the thatcher himself and rested on his two knees. Starting at the eve he neatly pushed a small fistful of the new thatch into the old thatch with his thatching fork. He took a 3-foot scribe at a time, right up to the top. A good day's work was about five of these scribes. For the last half hour in the evening the thatcher threw about six buckets of water on top of his day's work. It was then beaten down with the back of an iron hand rake and then to finish a small amount of raking was done. Every four days work was neatly trimmed at the eve with a hand shears. When all the thatching was completed, which usually took about four weeks, a single line of bullwire was erected along the thatch about two foot from the top. This line was stitched into the thatch with 8-inch lenghts of bullwire that were shaped like small walking sticks and inserted every two foot along the line. Another similar line was imbedded into the thatch about two foot up from the eve. Our house had a galvanized ridging on top and so did not require the twisted rope pieces that finished off other houses. The outer walls of the house and sheds got a fresh coat of whitewash three times a year. This took place at Christmas and just before the two house stations. No modern bungalow looked as well as a newly thatched and whitewashed farmer's cottage and they blended into the background much better.

Early in 1940 a couple of mud-walled sheds were pulled down and replaced with concrete ones. Eight to ten calves were housed in one of them and the other was used for wintering the yearlings. Almost all farmers used gubbáns to keep calves from eating straw or even hay for the first four weeks of their life. A gubbán was a small basket that covered the calfs lower half head and was held in place with twine that went round the calf's neck. Its only good point was that it created employment for a few gifted men. Just as the sheep's wool was blamed for killing lambs, straw that showed up in a dead calfs stomach got the blame for the calf's death. This was a false verdict and for the past thirty years gubbáns are not used at all.

Timber and coal were used in the fire-grate in the kitchen and parlour. We got great pleasure watching big trees fall. Using the two-man crosscut saw was a slow labourious job. After setting the teeth of the saw with a saw-setter Da would sharpen them with a three cornered file. Seán would climb the doomed tree and attach a long strong rope to a strong branch about $^3/_4$ way up as directed by Da. The other end of the rope was attached to the draw-bar of the tractor. A large wedged shaped piece of the tree was cut from its trunk on the side that it was meant to fall. This was usually on the southern side as the heavier branches grow on the sunny side of any tree. Having removed the wedge the sawing proper started on the other side of the tree. The purpose of the wedge of timber taken out was that it prevented the tree from kicking back on top of the saw- men when almost cut through. Da was very careful with his instructions and said an awful lot of men died felling trees. A steel wedge was driven into the cut behind the saw to keep the tree from sitting down on the saw. This wedge got an odd tap of the lump hammer. When the tree was cut out to the last couple of inches we were ordered to stand well back. A gentle pull of the tractor while the men kept on sawing brought it down with one hell of a mighty crash. The tractor was then stopped and Da would always say *Poems are made by fools like me, but only God can make a tree!* As we were now into the war years about three trees per year were felled. The tree was cut into suitable lengths for putting up on the tractor trailer. These lengths were then sawn into 1-foot lengths on the circular saw. Commercial lengths of the tree were left out for six months to season. To get the heavy lengths of commercial timber up on the trailer a tripod and pulley blocks were used. Every bit of the tree was put to use except the very small tops which were piled up and burnt. Even the saw-dust from under the saw was used to heat the barn. A five gallon drum that had its top taken off was put sitting on four fire bricks. It was then filled with saw dust and packed. A 4" tubular bar was put down through the saw dust and the bottom centre of the drum. The sawdust was packed hard again and the bar was withdrawn. A small amount of parafin was then sprinkled on the top and set alight. It burnt all day and kept the barn quite warm. The commercial timber was used for paling posts, sheds partitions, flooring and loft boards. There was a couple of nice gates made out of home grown timber as were the roofing timber and wall plates for the two new concrete sheds that were built. One of the many good workmen we had once, would spend the long summer evenings from 6 p.m. - 10 p.m. laying a hedge after a hard day's work. His reward apart from good fresh air was all the timber he could salvage for himself. He drew it the two miles home and was as happy as Larry in doing so. Yes, times were tough in the early forties.

One of our house stations was celebrated in March and the second one in the month of September. Preparations would be worked out on the Monday after the Sunday mass announcement. A samll little woman named Rosie Bray from Dunderry would be notified and commence working two days before the station morning. This little woman was always highly charged with working power. No work was too hard for her, not even scrubbing wooden floors with a scrubbing bursh while down on her knees. Why she hadn't a deck-scrub I do not know. The delph tea-pot and china tableware were taken from the china cabinet, freshly washed and shined. Shirts and collars had to be washed, blued, starched and ironed. Furniture was dusted, mansion-polished and shined. The fire grate, fender companion set and coal scuttle were all black-leaded and shined. As there were eight of us in the family our cousin, Seamus Boccán, Rosie Bray and the farm hand were the only others invited to the celebration. The vestment box which was 4 foot long, 2 foot wide and 2 foot high looked like a small coffin. The chalice, curcifix, bell, missal and altar cloths were carried in it as well. It was collected in the chapel vestry the day before the station. Da would collect it in the car at about 3 p.m. and give us a welcome lift home from school. If a neighbour had a station the previous day to ours, it was the practice for that neighbour to deliver it to our house after his station. All cattle in the fields along the laneway were removed and the three gateways left open the previous evening to the station. We all got up at 7.30 a.m. on the big morning and it would be very little later when "Rosie" as we called her would arrive. It was she made sure that we the childer were looking spick-and-span. She would look after the putting on of Da's collar that had a centre back stud as well as a front stud. Rosie was no threat to the "Ozone Layer" as she had to use a chair for this work. Da used ask Rosie "What do you think about this hairy chest". Ma would say "Don't mind him Rosie". Rosie would give him a good slap in the back and say "None of your bad talk, Pat, or I will tell the priest on you". It was we the young ones that enjoyed the chat. Ma prepared for the breakfast and aired the priest's vestments, on the backs of chairs round the parlour fire. Seán always set the altar table in the manner that Da had trained him. Ma escorted the priest in on his arrival. She stood in the parlour with him until it was time for our confessions to be heard. All confessions were heard in a near face-to-face manner so we always made sure that we would not have much to tell coming near station time. That reminds me of two priests who were great friends and happened to be in a plane crash scare. The pilot came out and told the passengers to fasten their belts and prepare for a crash landing. The two priests who had being living a fairly high life heard each others confessions. The pilot came back out and said you can undo your safety belts, as everything is ship-shape again. One priest looked at the other and said "Isn't it horrid how you can exaggerate when you are in a tight corner!" The other priest fully agreed with him. Our confessions were heard with the youngest first and up the ladder until Da called us, when all was ready for mass. Seán served the mass under the watchful eye of Da. Like mass on the radio it was more easy to concentrate as there were less distractions and the responses were loud and clear, as are the masses in the smaller country chapels. I think one amplifier among the congregation in the larger churches would increase the quality of the mass in such big churches. I will always cherish the sound of the little bell during the station as it had a very unique sound. It has gone into my ears recording department never to be silenced, in my lifetime.

After mass we all returned to the kitchen. About ten minutes was allowed for the priest to take off his vestments and say his communion prayers. Seán would then pack the vestment box and Ma would set the dining table. My parents, Seán and Séamus Boccán shared the meal with the priest. I never saw in my time any one priest who would have a fry. Grape fruit, boiled eggs, toast bread and marmalade was taken by all. Cubes of sugar that were about 1cc in size were used on that morning. They were handled by means of a forceps that had two small spoons at its tips. These cubes were tempting to children and Ma would say "they will fill you with worms". A long chat about current affairs, the goings on in the parish and war news would last for about two hours after breakfast. Séamus Boccán would wait on for his dinner. Rosie Bray looked after our breakfast and packed us off to school. Sometimes Da and Séamus would visit their first cousin Tomás

Fagan and do some shopping coming back through the town of Navan. On Da's return home he would put Rosie Bray's bicycle in the back of the car and leave her home. Rosie lived with her brother Mick on a small "unlivable upon" farm. They farmed what they had very well, tilled every square inch of the garden and Rosie planted the two small lawns in front of the house with all classes of flowers. It was Rosie that supplied the flowers for our two stations. Rosie did a lot of part-time work and got good money as she had no equals. As well as Rosie supplementing the farm income Mick fulfilled thatching contracts. He was a hard man to get as he always had a long string on his waiting list. It was he who did all our thatching except he was desperately busy. Mick wore his cap at a full 45% angle to the line of his ears. The Dunderry boys used say that he wore it that way to get a better view of his work and to blind his eyes to all that had to be done!

Thomás Fagan lived with his sister Áine on a large farm of first class land in the town land of Antylstown, Navan. He visited our house about six times a year for a good chat with Da. He might have a machinery, tractor or car problem and trusted in Da to solve it. Farmers with tractors, men with cars, of whom there were very few in the war years, and even garage men were very helpful to each other and shared their knowledge freely. Da knew the works of an engine from magazines he purchased and the motor-bike he had in his twenties. Garage owners were only learners themselves in the 30's and early 40's. These were the days when men spent up to a day and often more helping out an neighbour with a mechanical problem with no value whatsoever on their own time. They were men that valued the knowledge they got in fault finding. Tractors had a magnito with a built-on distributor on one end instead of the dynamo-battery system to cater for the ignition of the vapourized fuel. I often saw three men take turns twisting engines to get compression built up again after a re-bore. Da and Seán got their share of that work and the threat of a back-fire of the engine that was responsible for wrist, hand, knuckle and finger breakages, was always there. A rest would be taken for a smoke and discussion, every now and then with perhaps a mug of tea. Distributor wires would be checked as the firing order of the engine was called out, the points and plugs would be inspected and the spark advanced or retarded depending on when the back-fire came. These men had great patience and had great pride when they got an engine purring again no matter how long it took. A near neighbour of ours who lived on the Commons Road, Navan, whose name was Patrick Lightholder, was in his glory when helping out with a reluctant starter. He was another monthly visitor to our house and as he had a tractor and other farm machinery he had no trouble chatting with Da. Like Da, Pat Lightholder had a motor bike in his early twenties. At that time engines were re-bored and fitted with larger piston rings. Nowadays engines are re-sleeved and fitted with a set of the original sized piston rings. A reconditioned engine has to get a new set of big end bearings also. Da had nothing to pay for to get an engine reconditioned except for the engine rebore and a new set of rings. He stripped the engine in the barn and took it out with pulley blocks. He took the head off and did the valve grinding himself. The engine was sent off to some engineering works and rebored. On its completion the right sized piston rings were got and a set of gaskets. The crankshaft was refitted with a new set of bearings. Da made these bearings himself with wooden moulds and white metal. He had a special pan with a small spout for handling the smelted metal that was rendered so, on the forge fire. Any alterations that had to be done on the bearings was done on the lathe. Another money saving device Da used sometimes was to buy the special paper for making gaskets and cut them out himself. All major tractor repairs were done from Christmas to the end of February so as to be ready for the busy Spring work.

Ma's busiest day of the month was the Sunday we went to visit Tomás Fagan. She had the job of getting the two young ones that were going with Da and Seán ready. She would give our faces an immaculate cleaning and dress us in our very best clothes. Our shoes would get a renewed shining. Our handkerchiefs were neatly folded and put into our breast coat pocket with the reminder not to forget to use them. The next query was did you all do your No. 2? This was a code word for the major call of nature. Our biggest worry now was would the car start. Ma would take a final inspection on us and having been satisfied she would turn her attention to Da. She would straighten his tie, bring out the clothes brush and give his coat a few final brushes. The loading then started and the two young ones were lifted into the booth at the back. There was a nice leather cushion seat to sit on and it was possible to lie back against the booth door that opened up the reverse way to the modern booth doors. Da then got in and after a few gentle swings of the starting handle by Seán the Morris Cowley started and a great hurrah from all would be heard. Ma gave us in the back a final warning not to forget to tap the back window if any of us wanted to get out. Then with a raised hand for Da not to go yet she rushed into the house brought out a bottle of holy water, sprinkled the car and then made each of us dip a finger in the neck of the bottle and bless ourselves with the holy water. The drop outs watched with saddened faces as the lucky ones broadly smiled and waved their hands in a final goodbye.

On entering the kitchen Ma would plop down on a chair bless herself and say "thank God that gang are gone out of our way". The trip down to Tomás Fagan's place was six Irish miles and it took a full half hour as Da was in no hurry and took in the country side on both sides of the road. It was not at all uncommon for him to stop the car, go to a gateway to admire a field of potatoes, corn or beet. Going through the town in the summer Seán would be sent into a shop for a lot of ice-cream. The two inch thick of this lovely solid white block was sandwiched between two very nice flakey wafers and it held its solidity down to the last mouthful. During one of these stops which is about fifty five years ago, we noticed every one on the town's square including the corner boys looking in the one direction. They were looking in disgust at a lady dressed in slacks, with a cigarette coming from her lips that were plastered with lipstick. Da with a big smile told Seán, who was after coming out with the ice-cream, to have a look at the English woman. He asked us "How would you like to have a mother like that one?" Big hand salutes were given and taken by passers-by and lads on the street corners of the town who did point duty the seven days of the week. Corner boys were part and parcel of every town and Navan had its supply of them in plenty. They pitched their bodies at Loughrans Corner and at three different sides of the town's square. They drew the dole and some of them got occasional work in bottling stores, helping farmers on fair days and during the hay and corn harvest. Half of them had their little flutter on horses each day. The result of that betting, determined whether or not there would be a pint or two in the evening. Their equivalents in the 1990's can afford to play pool, cards and bet on horses and still have a few pints each day, be they married or not.

The car was at its level best to climb the hill at Proudstown, known to all who ever attended Navan races. On our arrival at our destination Tomás would come out to give us all a big handshake and escort us into his kitchen. He was a large man, with a neatly trimmed mustache, a huge warm big heart and wore a gold chained pocket watch in his waistcoat pocket. His sister Áine who lived with him would have a big handshake and was delighted to see us. Her first question was "How do you think the war is going, Pat". Da knowing that she was an ardent allied forces supporter would emphasize Hitler's great marches and victories.   If she was kneading bread at the time she would rub her two hands on the hips of her apron and get into a serious discussion about the war for a few minutes. She would bring down a few tumblers and serve up a drink to us all while still war talking. Da would get a large tumbler of Power's Whiskey and a large box of assorted biscuits went well with our red lemonade.

Tomás Fagan was a very up to date farmer and at those early years of machinery he was fully mechanized. All his machinery was cleaned, shiney parts oiled and neatly housed during the winter months. He even found room for his huge big threshing mill and elevator. During the months of October, November, December, January and February there were always about six pikes of unthreshed corn that would be neatly thatched round the top $^1/_3$ of the way down and 6 foot high $^1/_2$" mesh netting wire to keep rats and mice out surrounded the perimeter of the stack's base. These pikes were threshed in the month of February and a premium price got for the grain that was sold to a local seed merchant.

Tomás Fagan was well known throughout Meath and even parts of Louth as a first class cattle breeder. He had a roomful of trophies that he won at Summer shows and pre-Christmas fat stock shows and sales. It was a glorious sight to see in the month of December the ten to twelve Hereford cattle that were getting the finishing touches before the Christmas fat stock show and sales. These jewels were kept perfectly clean and their coat of hair was currycombed night and morning. Special attention was paid to the lower brush of the tail which was plaited and currycombed on alternate days. There would be a shine on their coats from the good feeding they were getting. As these animals were bedded down in one foot of straw their dewlaps touched the straw. They looked the picture of contentment and showed no ill effects of their couple of months confinement. As the emphasis in the 30's and 40's was for fat I don't think these handsome animals would win prizes in the 1990's.

Even though this farm was highly mechanized two Clydesdale horses were kept as well. The female of them had to carry a foal as well as do light work. Visiting there in the summer always entailed a farm walk to view the sugar beet, turnips, mangolds, kale, potato and corn crops. If the day looked showery the Clydesdale horse was yoked into the trap on which was fixed a canopy that could be folded back when not required. On viewing each crop Tomás with his two thumbs stuck in his waistcoat pockets and chest stuck out would ask Da "Well, Pat, what do you think of the field?" Da would have to admit that his crops which were immaculate in every way were better than Da's own crops. An odd time the reverse verdict was given. A big discussion took place on the tilling, manuring and management of the various crops. On our return to the house at about 6 p.m. Áine would have a great meal ready. A large helping of roast beef was nearly always part of the menu and it was mostly from a Hereford heifer that was reared on the farm and sold to James Duffy, a Navan butcher. About four farm hands were employed on this large farm as well as a nephew of their who was the heir apparent. Nicholas McGuire was the nephew's name and he was reared with his uncle and aunt from the time he left school. His mother Elizabeth, a sister of Tomás and Áine Fagan was married to a Mr. Nicholas McGuire from Braystown, Rathkenny, Slane, Co. Meath. He was a large farmer and they reared a family of four, two boys and two girls. Our departure time after another drink and big handshakes all round was always about 8 p.m. Our return home would be sometimes greeted with "I thought you were going to stay the night, come along childer or you won't be able to get up for school". We always got a half crown from Tomás Fagan which was quite a nice gift at that time. It was always painful getting up for school after such an enjoyful Sunday like that.

In the Spring of 1940 Da announced a prize for the best plot of vegetables planted in the garden. We showed great interest in it and all six of us soon had our plots marked up. The two girls were in a separate category as they wanted to sow flowers. It was that Spring I got to know the different breeds of flowers as they grew. Pansies, wallflowers, antheraniums, white and red carnations and tulips were planted in the inner flower bed, while white-centred blue forgetmenots' bordered it.. Ma who had enough work looking after six of us would give an odd small helping. The only gardening experience we had was from looking at the well kept garden of Séamus Boccán and a garden right beside our school. It was from the latter we took our cue and kept a good eye on it and the man as he worked it from day to day.

Seán settled for three ridges of potatoes, Páraic for a bed of shallots, Micheál for a bed of lettuce and I chose three short drills of scallions. Sean helped me to sow my three drills. Páraic and Micheál were well able to do their own work. It was a very dry Spring so the watering can got plenty of work. Da said he would not look into the garden at all until the 10th of June, when he would announce the winner after a good inspection. This we believed at the time but what about the times when we would all be at school and Ma would look in each evening and help out with the weeding? Páraic's shallotts were first to show signs of growth as quarter of the seed bulbs were over ground. Micheál's lettuce was up second and Seán's potatoes shortly after. I was beginning to lose heart and to add to my disappointment Páraic would insist that I planted the scallion seed upside down. I had just got my first communion rosery beads and having great faith at that time, one evening I drew my beads up and down each of the three drills as I prayed a few Hail Mary's to Saint Job the "Patience Saint" as my Ma had advised me. In about two days time I rubbed down a small amount of clay off one of the drills and to my great satisfaction the onion plants were about to surface. The ladies' flowers were the last to appear. Da had a rule made that none of the vegetables was to be used until after the inspection day. I noticed a small gap in my scallion drill and vowed to catch the culprit. I would meet one of my brothers coming out of the garden gate and on getting a reply that he did not touch any of my scallions I would demand a breath test. If they refused it meant that they were guilty so I would tell them that I would have to take some of their vegetables. As a result of the threat they always consented. Standing still they had to take a deep breath into the lungs then breathing out the mouth slowly for my sharp nose to detect. On being found guilty I would be brought back into the garden, given a small portion of the culprit's vegetables and we both would agree "Quits" with an assurance of no repeat tresspass!

When "D" day arrived we were told by Da that all the plots were equally good so we all got 10 shillings each! With the Navan carnival time fast approaching we were all well satisfied. I think Da broke about even on that scheme, as there were potatoes and vegetables for about six weeks grown. My choice the following year was for peas. They grew very quickly and had to be held erect by netting wire, which they clung to as they grew. It was lovely eating them out of the growing pods when they were young and tender. Of course there were two drills of vegetables grown in the tillage field along side the potato crop. One of these drills was sown with carrot and parsnip seed and peas were sometimes grown as well. The other drill was sown with beetroot and cabbage plants. Cabbage plants were sown three times during the growing season. Planting the potato crop was a quickly done job as all we had to do was two drills each. The drills were about 180 yards long. The farmhand would plant two drills for himself and some of his family would help out with the picking of the entire crop. We disliked the picking which called for a lot of back bending and to add to the negative side of the job, a certain amount of potato pegging would be engaged in. Páraic was a devil at this and even though he was a coitóg he sent the spud with great speed and accuracy. Seán spent a lot of time trying to keep the peace amoung us and Da's roars could be heard a mile away. A half day's work on Saturday completed the job and the bags were emptied into there own special shed. After a few day's drying they were covered with a light coating of hay and then about two foot of straw to keep the frost out. In the month of February we were called upon again to turn the potatoes. This was done over two half days on Saturdays. All unsound potatoes were thrown out, seed potatoes were separated from the eating potatoes and the sprouts knocked off all of them. If February happened to be a very frosty month the job was postponed until the first two Saturdays of March.

In the month of March when land was at its driest and barest we had to pick the surface stones off the fields that were to be meadowed later on. The six of us would take a narrow scribe of land each - *no sex discrimination on our farm* - put the stones into a bucket and when filled emptied into the trailer for bringing home. Sometimes we put the stones directly into the trailer as Seán drove along. The time space from pram to tractor for Seán was a very short one. All trailer loads of stones were heaped in the haggart to be used in building or in drains later on. When our picking was completely finished a heavy concrete roller, that was home manufactured, was drawn over the same ground to bury the real small stones that we might have missed. It was the small stones that got wedged in between the sections and fingers of a mowing bar caused the breakage of one or other of them or sometimes both. Nowadays the rotary mower has solved all that labour and expense. The mowing bar of our old Fordson tractor was a midmounted one. Some farmers pulled the horse mower behind the tractor with success. At least the flies did not send the tractor in a gallop! Da had the drive of the mower fitted with a four inch wooden peg that would break if a stone became wedged between the sections and fingers. This also caused the mowing bar to move backwards and in doing so de-clutched the tractor. The mowing bar was then raised, the tractor reversed and the broken wedge piece replaced with a fresh peg. Da did a lot of mowing on hire and some farmers were careless about picking stones in their meadow lands or perhaps did not pick them at all. About one dozen of these pegs were brought in the tool box each morning.

Weeds were our greatest enemy as they had us on our knees for half of our Summer holidays. The only weed killer used then was Sodium Chloride, a greyish powder that killed all vegetation and was used in farmyards and driveways. This weed killer was very poisonous to animals and fowl and had to be used with great care.

About two weeks of our Easter holidays were spent pulling thistles in the corn fields. Da made a wooden thongs similar to the forge thongs to save us from stooping and getting prods in the hands. Presshog or sharlock was another enemy of ours that affected corn and tillage crops. It had a yellow flower and a unique wildish smell. Each bundle that we collected had to be brought to the nearest headland - that could be up to 150 yards away. Seán and Páraic would cut the tops of the sharlock with the reaping hook. We, the younger ones, would not be trusted with these sharp instruments. I had a desperate hate for the smell of sharlock in my younger years because of the labour it put us to, but strange to say I smelled a bunch of it this year, 1990, and it smelled lovely to me and brought back sad memories. I suppose the tulip pickers in Holland get a dislike for the smell of those lovely flowers, especially on a Monday morning after a booze week-end. Ma would spend half an hour at these weeding jobs to give us a bit of encouragement saying "Isn't it well for you out in the fresh air on this lovely day and not like me stuck in the hot kitchen". All the work we did was rewarded with money from Da who would encourage us to save it.

We got books to fill up with 6d saving stamps. When we had forty of these stamps in a book we exchanged the book for a £1.00 saving stamp book. Seán had a small red coloured pillar shaped saving box. He used get lots of silver from Da, tips for hire work and serving various masses. He served a wedding mass for a neighbour and collected four ten shilling notes or £2.00. This was equal to the weekly wage of a farm labourer at that time. This box had a small slit in the side of it for inserting coins. I helped myself to a few coins on a couple of occasions with the skillful use of a knife. I saw him open the box on a couple of occasions and pass the remark "I think there should be more in it!" Seán was a very generous young fellow and would share sweets and fruit freely. We all looked to him for knowledge and advice on fixing our bicycles and doing our home exercises. He was a gentle young daddy to us.

The months of January, February, and March in the early forties were very severe weather-wise. Hard frosts and heavy snow falls were a common Winter and Spring happening. I saw icicles one and a half foot long coming like huge carrots from the eve of the thatch. What was happening was that the sun was melting the snow on the thatch and as the water came down to the eve and onto the icicles already there, it immediately froze. The icicles increased half an inch a day in length and enlarged proportionally in width also. As one of these weighed three to five pounds, we were warned by Da not to walk underneath them. When the thaw came, now and then a miniature avalanche would tumble to the ground. We did our sliding in a quarry on the farm or down a hill on the road as traffic was virtually nill then. Horse nails were inserted in horse shoes to prevent slipping. The old people would put salt on our roadside if it were on their way to the pump. We thought them to be old cranks, but now fifty years later I understand their deed as I now dread a slippy road myself. Children came tumbling down several times with no broken bones exept a very odd one. The few lorries that delivered that time had to put chains on the wheels, to enable them to motor on. In 1940 a gale force wind blew ten inches of snow off the fields, into the hedgerows and formed huge snow drifts. A lot of birds and wild animals died from hunger and the low temperatures.

One of our domestic cocks, a huge red bird, used to get up on the outer kitchen window-sill and start crowing very vigorously during our dinner hour. Da said "I will put an end to that lad's crowing!" He fixed up a bit of wiring, electrified it at the press of a button switch. The following dinner hour he got us all to watch. The cock flew up, stuck out his chest, flapped his wings but half way through his crowing he gave a six foot backward leap into the air. Every hen, chicken, duck, turkey and even the guinea fowl came up to see what was wrong with the "King" of the fowl kingdom. We never saw that cock on that cill ever after!

During that bad spell Ma made double the amount of porridge which we would eat an hour before bedtime as well as in the morning. We all loved potato cakes and had them at least once a week. Some nights we would have "Bitties" as my Ma would call it. This was just white bread, sugar and a few raisins put into cold milk and brought almost to boiling point. It was very tasty and made a good nightcap. Some other nights we would have Ovaltine or Cocoa. Da would settle for a mug of bovril or a cup of coffee.

To get back to school again, I was in class two now. I loved arithmetic and learning poetry. I won a prize of the game of Ludo for my recitation of the poem *Old women of the road*. How true to life that poem was to the travellers of by-gone days and to some travellers to a less extent today. Two poems I learned in that same class two, two doggy poems. The first was *Poor Dog Tray* and went thus:

On the green banks of Shannon, when Sheila was nigh,
    No blithe Irish lad was so happy as I;
No harp, like my own, could so cheerfu;ly play;
    And whereever I went, was my poor dog Tray.

When at last I was forced from my Sheelah to part,
    She said, while the sorrow was big at her heart:
"Oh, remember your Sheelah, when far, far away!
    And be kind, my dear Pat, to our poor dog Tray."

Poor dog! he was faithful and kind, to be sure,
    And he constantly loved me, although I was poor;
When the sour-looking folks sent me, heartless, away,
    I had always a friend in my poor dog Tray.

When the road was so dark, and the night was so cold,
    And Pat and his dog were gone weary and old,
How snugly we slept, in my old coat of gray;
    And he licked me for kindness, my poor dog Tray.

Though my wallet wasscant, I remember'd his case,
    Nor refused my last crust to his pitiful face;
But he died at my feet, on a cold winter's day;
    And I played a lament for my poor dog Tray.

Where now shall I go? poor, forsaken and blind;
    Can I find one to guide me, so faithful and kind?

To my sweet native village, so far, far away,
    I can never retrun with my poor dog Tray.

The other poem had even nicer lyrics. It was the story of a poor traveller called Caoch O'Leary and his dog *Pinch*. It must be these two poems that gave me a great love for dogs, except greyhounds. The teacher explained to us in detail how faithful all dogs were to their master and that they really only took to one person. Many trained collie dogs are a treat to watch at work as we have seen many times on telly. I still remember the names of the dogs our two next door neighbours had in the late thirties. One was *Freddie* and the other *Ponto*. Dogs got fits that time that are unheard of to-day. It was supposed to be bad feeding. Distemper is a disease of the past as an injection gives life immunity against it now.

Lent was always a very cold and hungry period. The March wind was thrown in to increase the severity. We went to school with butterless bread and there was no fry allowed then, either in the morning or the evening as meat or its products were allowed only once a day in order to keep the fast. We were not obliged to fast as we were under 21 years of age but what our parents did we had to do also. Hard working men were exempt. Every Wednesday night at 8.00 p.m. we attended the Stations of the Cross. St. Patrick's day was a welcome guest, as fast and abstinence were not an obligation on that day. Dancing was forbidden during Lent but St. Patrick's night was a great ceile night from 8 p.m. to 12 midnight. We wore a large harp shaped badge, from whose base came three ribbons, green, white and yellow. All grown ups wore a sprig of shamrock in their button holes, cap or hat. Da used go to Dublin with a few of us to watch the Industrial Parade. The Railway Cup football and hurling finals were played in Croke Park in the afternoon. They drew about 40 thousand people from all over the country to see the best two provinces clash in each game. G.A.A. matches were better patronised then, as there were very few other attractions. Easter Saturday at 12 noon was the time that all the fasting ceased and the drinking, smoking and lots of other sacrifices made by most of the people came to an end. Ma always got a leg of spring lamb for the Easter Sunday dinner. We looked forward to it, for the easter eggs and lemonade. Da got a bottle of Powers Whiskey for the occasion. The only time in the year he drank was Christmas, Easter and on the visits of his cousins and other friends. For a bad cold or flu he would take punch made out of rum. Ma was a Pioneer. Our school was closed for a three week duration during the Easter time.

The toilets attached to our school were very poor. There was no running water or wash basin in them. A seven foot wall separated the boys' toilets from the girls'. Once we did our No. 1 over that wall and had girls screaming and running in all directions! The matter was reported to the head mistress who with a flushed face told us that if it happened again the C.C. would be informed. As he would use a horsewhip on us, we did that act no more. I have my doubts, if we were the first villains to do this.

We had no school bell, but the hand clapping of the head mistress sent us scurrying to the main door. The boys lined up against the main wall, the girls at a 45^0 angle between us and the porch. A pupil called David Butler would start whistling the *Boys of Wexford* while we la - la - laed it and kept time with our marching feet. We then followed the teacher in to the classroom and on to our desks keeping time all the while, till the teacher said "Stop a h-aon, a do, a tri". Prayers were recited before and after most classes and the angelus at 12 noon. We were told always to sleep with our arms crossed on our breast for fear we shold die during the night. All our religious knowledge up to the age of 7 was held in a $1^1/_2$d catechism. First Communion over, preparation for confirmation was started and a book of catechism notes was introduced. This book explained the 10 Commandments of God, the 6 Commandments of the Church and the 7 Sacraments. A Temperance Catechism had to be memorised also.

Once a year usually just before the summer holidays, a travelling show would do a *Punch and Judy* act, sing a few songs, play a few tunes on an accordian and a few tricks with rabbits and pidgeons. This cost us 6d for a one hour show. Some of the children would not have the money but when all that was possible to collect had been collected they were allowed admission. A show, probably the last one in that school, had been about 3 minutes in progress, when in came the parish priest, asked who had given permission for the show to be held, and literally roared for the show people to get out. Our monies that were scattered on the table were rushed into a sweet box and off they went! The priest followed them out and the two teachers were in almost a collapsed condition. The priest rushed back in, threw a brown letter on the teachers' desk and said "There is your salaries!" That was that, so back into our lessons we were put. About half a dozen times in the year the teachers had to encounter fighting parents as well, as they complained about what had been said to their son or daughter. After about ten minutes heated discussion the thing would fizzle out with a threat from the parent, if she had to call again. Nowadays the pupils are able to fight their own corner, as it should be.

The doctor and dentist called to see that we were sound in bone and body, once a year. The inspector was another visitor that brought a bit of a flush to the teachers' faces. Not being a native speaker, was a source of worry to the teacher, as the inspector did all his discourse in Irish. She had the fear of us missing some simple question as well. Mr. Watson was the inspector's name and he was the best groomed man I ever saw. A few extra prayers were said on the morning of his visit. If things went well the teacher would congratulate us and she would be in great form for the rest of the day!

Summer holidays to us on the farm was a working holiday except for the first and last week during which we were told to enjoy ourselves. Otherwise it was a 9 o'clock rise in the morning and a

6 o'clock finish in the evening. Weeding and thinning the turnips and mangolds, while on our knees, was our first introduction to six weeks' work. In later years an acre of beet was added to these root crops and we had to do the same for Séamus Boccán as well. The charlock and thistles had to be kept in check also. The churning was done twice a week, water brought in buckets for the house use, fuel for the fire, washing potatoes for the dinner and sometimes peeling them, making our beds, feeding calves, pigs and fowl. Each of us was assigned and responsible for our own jobs. On top of this we had to take out the back swarth during mowing, gibbing hay cocks, raking in around them with a hand rake, twisting the sugans, taking out the back swarth of corn and tying it in sheaves to leave it ready for the reaper-and-binder, and tramping the hay as it was brought into the haybarn. Seán did most of the tractor work. Both he and Páraic did the grubbing and landing of the potato crop. The other root crops had to be grubbed about three times. We, the younger ones, would have to carry weeds to the headlands, that were collected by the grubber. My sisters would bring the tea to the hay and corn fields. Máire, my eldest sister, went to Navan each morning for the newspaper and the required meat and groceries. Da said that working men were entitled to the best grub. The daily paper cost 2d at that time, so £1 would buy 120 papers. In this year 1990, £1 will buy only 2 papers!

The summer of 1940 was a very long, hot summer. I remember tramping the bays of hay in the haybarn along with Micheál and Páraic. You could not touch the galvanize as it was fit to fry rashers and eggs! Da would let an odd shout asking "Are you packing that hay at all?". Seán or the workman would answer, that we were making a good job of it. As we had no elevator, the hay was pitched from the trailer on to the first shess and from there to the top. We borrowed swap-help from our cousin, Séamus, for this work. When all the hay was pitched off the trailer, it was noticable how much insect life moved along the floor. We brushed them off with a wisp of hay. Ma once saw me brush off a hairy maggot and warned me not to kill it as it was "God's Horse". Seán replied "His ass must have been very small!" We enjoyed travelling out to collect another 8 cocks of hay. Two ropes were thrown off and the first cock loaded. We had to gather up the butt of the cock and make a small cock of it, to be left drying out. When the trailer was fully loaded the two ropes were thrown across the top and firmly tied to the draw-bar with the help of the harvester's knot. We all got up on top, by climbing the ropes. It was a lovely way to travel and it was very comfortable. We encountered a gentle jolt over and back as the trailer crossed each furrow.

That time, there were sounds to be heard on a summer's evening that alas are gone forever. As tractors were scarce more than $3/4$ of the work was done by horses. With flies and horse flies to annoy these animals, as much of the work as possible was done in the morning and the evening. A small leafy branch was secured to the horse's head- gear to ward off some of the flies. God provided the horse with a twitching movement to his hide, whenever he felt a horse fly. The noise of the horse mower carried a long distance on a summer's evening and the man's words of encouragement or disapproval likewise! It was a very homely noise and when put into reverse at each corner the ratchet gave a tell-tail of that movement. The tumbling rake was a sight to behold as it brought the wind-rows into the cocks under construction. It was an all wooden affair with seven teeth of varying lenghts. The four outer teeth were longer than the centre ones. When enough hay had been collected the operator gave a slight lift to the handles, the outer teeth stuck into the ground and the entire machine did a 360^0 turn into position, again leaving a large loose lot of hay behind. It was much easier to fork this lot of hay then the lot after the tractor and buck-rake. The reins had to be about 20 yards long as the machine had to be well away from the horse's rear!

The hay boggy had a unique sound also as it slowly pulled a cock of hay up its floor. A ratchet on one side of an axle was levered around by a long wooden handle. This coiled the rope that had been drawn round the cock when the boggy floor had been tilted to the ground at the butt of a cock. The cock slowly came up the floor and when $^3/_4$ ways up, the floor came down at the front to a level position again. A locking catch held it in position there. When the cargo arrived in the haybarn the catch was released, the rope round the cock was loosened and with the aid of the man's hand the floor tilted up. The horse was driven up a few yards and off came the cock. A farmer would draw in about 20 cocks from 7 p.m. - 10 p.m. and have them ready for the next morning. Another familiar sound was the sharpening of a scythe. This was an act that few farmers could boast about. A good scythe man was capable of mowing one statute acre of meadow a day.

Some men brought buttermilk, to the hay field, for a drink. Others preferred a $^{50}/_{50}$ mixture of water and milk. A great lot of coaxing and strong talk sometimes had to be given to the horses, to keep them up to their work, especially in the evening after a long day's work. We often hid behind a hedge listening to this with great enjoyment. Four letter words were in the vocabulary then as well, but a little less used! A man that used too much of them was a class of a marked man and parents would tell their children to keep away from him. I loved standing on the back of the tractor and mower and watch the grass heads give a little wriggle before they fell flat. Some of the riper heads would lose their seed in transit, noticably the meadow fescue. Da showed us the more popular grasses, e.g. timothy, cocksfoot, rye grass, wild oat grass and of course the two clovers. Corncrake, and less often hen phesants, would appear out of the meadow as it got smaller. If they had a nest they would walk off to a headland. If they had chicks they would stay fairly near and call them out. Most, or all farmers, tried to help the chicks to a safe headland as well as trying to avoid a nest. The magpie was these birds' greatest enemy, with the grey crow a good second. Da and Seán always went for the rifle when seeing one of these birds. An awful lot of them were shot from the kitchen window as they came to roost on a tree across the yard. They were that clever that they were in flight on hearing the rifle being loaded, unless done very quietly. I did see once a few pheasant chicks with the two legs mown off them. As mowing was done in July and August in the thirties and forties, young birds were well able to mind themselves. Now with May and June silage these birds don't stand a chance. The swallows never failed to come to our cowhouse, haybarn and a shed in a nearby field. Some years they built a nest right up against the eaves of the thatched cottage. There were two breeds of these birds, the ones with the white breast and a smaller bird with a red breast. Their nest is a highly engineered affair and a great deal of hard work went into its construction. The struts and ridge boards of a shed were used for starting the foundation. The bird spent a few days roughing the timber with its beak. It also roughened the whitewashed wall when building under the thatch. Then the little pieces of clay were inserted and joined together with small pieces of hay or straw. This work continued slowly at the start, but seemed to quicken from one quarter ways on. At this stage the birds worked from inside the nest as well as from the outer side. They started work at daybreak and took a rest on overhead wires or shed tops from about 10a.m. to 5p.m. They sang their song and groomed their feathers as well as feeding themselves. Work started again at about 5p.m. and went on till nightfall. These times varied slightly with the different types of weather.

The swallows kept a close eye on the cats and on the approach of one they took into a lot of low sweeping dives about five feet over the cat, while sending out a piercing sharp screech from their mouths. The neighbouring birds from the other sheds joined in this charitable act. Soon the cat ran off about other business. This exercise was more noticeable when the eggs were hatched out. The eggs were a blue colour with brown specks on them. Four to six eggs were hatched in each nest. When the young birds arrived the building time was replaced by feeding the young ones with flies and worms. An odd nest came to the ground in the haybarn and we lay the blame on vibrations from the wind-charger overhead. It was a delight to watch the parent birds getting the young birds to leave their nests and start flying. A feeding call got the fledgings out to the brink of the nest where they balanced themselves with their first wing flaps. This was repeated, for a day possibly. When all were perfect in this flapping art, the parent birds still with their feeding call kept flying around very close to the nest with a coaxing bait in their mouth. After some time the first youngster would lose its grip on the nest and off it flew with clumsy type of wing flapping. The parent birds kept it in view and close at hand until they got it to rest on a roof or back into the nest. They repeated this act till the entire clutch had left the nest. Soon the young ones were catching their own flies. The swallow was a good weather guide and when it flew low over the grass it was a sure sign of rain. My first school book had a poem called *Signs of Rain* and it went thus:

The hallow winds begin to blow,
The clouds look black, the glass is low,
The soothe fall down, the spaniels sleep,
The spider from his cobweb creeps.

Last night the sun went pale to bed,
The moon in hollows hid its head,
Puss on the hearth, with velvet paws
Sits wiping o'er his whiskers all.

Low o'er the grass the swallow wings,
The cricket, too, how sharp he sings!
The frog has changed his yellow vest
And in a russet coat is dressed.

The distant hills are looking nigh,
See, a rainbow spans the sky!
Red sky at night and morning grey
Sends the shepherd on his way!

These very hot summers of the late thirties and forties were responsible for some spectacular thunder storms. I remember one night when the lightning was almost a continuous flashing. With the head covered with the bed clothes it was still possible to see a restricted view of it. The thunder was very frightening with some very sharp piercing rumblings as if a bullet leaving a very powerful rifle. Mother was very much afraid of a thunderstorm and a premature family Rosary was said. This to our joy left us with a longer time for playing cards that same night! We were always reluctant starters especially when a game of cards was in progress. Other times we would be forced to wait till Da had finished a chapter of a book he would be dug into. The Rosary was always extended to cover special intentions. These were for the repose of the souls, the recovery of someone sick, a change in the weather to suit some farming need, success in examinations and finally our own special intention. We said our own night prayers after that. It was then off to bed for the younger ones of us. The ten o'clock news was never missed and this was followed by Irish Hospital Sweepstake, a sponsored request programme which was a great musical hour-and-half and produced by Bob Bastable. The late news brought Radio Eireann to a closedown for the day.

Coal imports were the first blow to Ireland as a result of the war. Turf and timber became very valuable as they substituted for the coal depleted stocks. The farmers, labourers and even people from the town took a bank of turf each in their nearest bog. About five weeks were spent in the months of April and May cutting, footing and reeking the turf bank. Country school boys were allowed two week's holidays from school to help out at this work. De Velera called on the army to save and stockpile turf in the Phoenix Park and other central points throughout the country. This turf was used for hospitals, GNR and CIE, to fuel the steam trains and to keep the important wheels of industry in motion.

A neighbour of ours, Seán Curry, brought me and my two older brothers, Micheál and Páraic, to help him reek the footings of turf that he had dried out. We were brought the five miles to and five miles back by horse and dray. As tea and sugar were rationed, we had to bring our own. Like the smell of the freshly turned soil of a ploughing field, the bog was a mighty place for a good appetite. It was grand to see all the smoke coming from the dining fires at about 1p.m. and again at 4p.m. The water was boiled in a "Tommy can" and it was imperative that a three quater match stick be left floating on the top of the water. This we were told took the smoky taste off the tea made from water boiled in this way. It worked in that respect and I saw two County Council men doing the same "match trick" thirty years later. I wonder do the boy scouts do this also? There was a bit of sod throwing by the younger folk but it was kept in check by a roar from the men that would see it happening. Anyone that came a distance brought a dray-load of turf on the journey home. There were professional bogmen who spent all Spring and Summer cutting and saving turf. This was their sole income and they sold the turf on Saturdays all the year round, as well as about three loads a week during the Autumn and Winter months. Bagfuls and even full dray-loads sold like hot buns in their nearest town or village. The army were the only men that lorried the turf.

Da did a lot of ploughing, discing and sowing on hire during the Spring months and we were too young for the bog work. He bought a new Aga cooker from a firm called A.H. Massers Ltd., from East Wall Road, Dublin. This was fuelled by anthracite and during the war years I think there was only Irish fuel to be had. This was supplied by a very efficient firm, M/S Cumiskeys of Balbriggan. Two ton was an entire year's supply and the price was £7.50 per ton. This cooker was a twenty-four hour working masterpiece and had a ten gallon hot water tank built into it. The hot water was a gift for clothes, washing, baths and heating animal feeds. Timber from the farm answered all other fuel requirements. Farmers gave the timber that came off a hedge they would be laying to the farm workers.

The Spring of 1940 brought in the rationing of tea, sugar, clothes, footwear and all grades of oil. A half-yearly book of coupons with different letterings for the various items was supplied to each household. This resulted in a lot of patched clothing and footwear being worn. Ma and Máire did a lot of extra knitting, patching and sewing. The foot-pedalled Singer sewing machine was well oiled, freshened up and put to full use. Da did the boot and shoe repairs as well as studing them. Studs were sold in a card that sufficed for one boot or shoe. There was a special, long, curving stud on each card for the toe and another, a wee bit different, for the heel. Seán was now a big help at this work although only eleven or twelve years of age. The rest of us supplied the raw material to be repaired. Da cut out rubber soles from used car tyres and tacked them on to the new footwear. This gave a great lease of life to the soles. Leather in the uppers was of an inferior quality as there was a scarcity of the proper tanning chemicles, so Da came to the rescue with hemp, wax, awl and needle. He must have spent a wet day or two chatting up a cobler at work because he could put on a perfect patch. Bicycle tyres were hard to come by as were new bicycles themselves. A new bicycle owner was talked about in the same way as a new car owner today. Tyres were patched and sometimes wire would be used to bring a bulge back to normality again. Blow-outs were common and meeting people walking to or from the town with a break-down was not unusual. Valve-rubber and chains were other scarce items. Trousers were a broad-legged affair and bicycle clips were used to tidy them up so they would not get caught in the pedal or chain. There were two types of clips to be had. One was a complete circular type that went round the entire lower leg with only a half inch break in it to allow expansion for entry. The other one was like a half inch wide hair-pin that slid up from the bottom of the leg and kept the folded trouser leg in position. Country lads simply folded the lower trouser legs and pulled their stocking tops over them.

Coffee and fruit became scarce and fruit went off the market altogether except for Irish fruit. Liquid coffee soon disappeared but coffee nuts were available and were ground down to a powder by the grocer's perculator. Da weighed out eight shares of sugar in one pound jam jars, one for each of us. There was a small tablet, much smaller than an aAspro tablet called, "satureen", that was used to sweeten tea. This it did but gave a new taste to the tea that was not at all nice. We missed oranges and bananas badly and the loaf of bread tasted just like its looks - very dull! Flour and wheaten meal were made from complete "Irish wheat", which gave an inferior quality. It was illegal to use white flour at that time. Da used keep a couple of barrels of the driest wheat threshed and give it a futher week's drying in half bagfuls beside the fire. He then had it put through the grinder, one of which we had. He then put that meal into a very fine meshed sieve and shook it to get pure flour out of it. This was done for pancakes and Christmas cake making and a few times during the year to make white flour bread for a welcome change. Silk stockings and later on nylon stockings were used by some men to get pure white flour.

It was compulsory for every farmer that he put a certain percentage of his land under wheat. A Department of Agriculture inspector examined our farm about the end of April to see that we had enough wheat grown. Da always erred on the right side and had no trouble with him as a result. He always had a drop of whiskey for important visitors. Mr Clancy was the name of our wartime inspector, and a grand gentleman from Cavan direction was he. He was killed in a car crash. That shocked people at the time as there were so few of them on the roads. Talking about percentages, Da taught us about them in an indirect way. He always tested his own wheat oats and barley for germination before using them for seed. He would get three dinner plates and level them off with fine soil. He sowed one hundred grains of wheat picked at random into one, one hundred of oats into the second and one hundred of barley into the last one. This test was carried out in mid January so the plates were kept in the bottom shelf of a press. They were watered and put out in the light on very mild days. In about three weeks, all the seed appeared and were allowed to grow about one and a half inches high. The blades of corn on each plate were pulled singly and counted. This gave the percentage germination count of each of the varieties sown. Da installed into us that *per cent* means *per hundred*. The count was always about ninty-five per cent. He always had the count high enough to sow his own seed.

Petrol was rationed except for priests, doctors, vets and government officials. Farmers with TVO tractors got a generous allowance of petrol for starting these tractors. As Da did a lot of hire work he had a great allowance. A coupon that bought one gallon of petrol worth one shilling and four pence, or sixteen pence out of the two hundred and forty pennied pound, was making one pound sterling on the black market. Da obliged several car owners with coupons and he had a couple of forty gallon drums full of petrol hidden in the garden. They were sunk three quarter ways into the ground and the rest of the barrels were covered with grass straws. This act was highly illegal and we got a strong warning to say nothing about them. This stock-piling was necessary as petrol coupons were valid for one month only.

It was the announcement by the then Minister of Agriculture, Mr James Dillon, that four stone of sugar would be given to farmers for every one acre of sugar beet grown that put hard work on us during the Summer holidays. All during that war the six counties of Northern Ireland had very little rationing and a great deal of smuggling took place. I think that it was the 1939 to 1945 war that started the first smuggling between the two States. I remember the large packet of twenty cigarettes that sold for twenty old pence, selling for twenty eight old pence black market price. Tea was making double its price on the black market. Clothes and food coupons were bartered among neighbours and relations to the advantage of both parties. There were one or two great advantages as a result of these hard years. Nobody had to worry about the next-door-neighbours, the "Joneses'" and it brought a great sense of hospitality among the communities.

With all the war talk that went on in our house we knew all about Spitfire bombers, torpedoes, tanks, parachutes, u-boats, trenches and air-raid shelters. We dug our own air-raid shelters into the bank of a quarry about two hundred yards from the house. The bank had a large layer of fox-sand about one and a half foot from the top surface of the adjoining field. This fox-sand was easily dug and we were able to do so with our seaside spades. We, the four boys, made one each and in doing so we excavated about one cubic yard of sand from each hole. Da spotted them on one of his evening "tour of inspections" and ordered us to fill them in immediately. As only eighteen inches of clay roofed these shelters, a twelve hundred-weight cow or bullock grazing on top was apt to come crashing down and perhaps on one of us inside the shelter!

This quarry was alive with all types of water loving flies, insects and very beautiful hedge finches, as one side of it had a row of blackthorn bushes. As the various breeds of crane flies were in abundance, including the three inch blue lad that turned to green depending on the angle he made with the sun and the viewer. Toads and frogs jumped about in the rushes and flaggers. We were afraid of the toads, or man-lepers as we called them, with their minature crocadile looks. Ducks and cranes or herons fed in that quarry during nightfall and rested there during the night.

I remember during these war years Ma coming into the house at nightfall and telling Da that she heard a plane. Da would get Seán to switch off the yard and shed lights and Ma to close the shutters of the kitchen window. Sign lights were forbidden during that period in the city and towns. We made toy boats and planes out of paper. The boat was a sailing type one and was made in this way. Get a single page (Fig.1) out of a copybook or writing pad. Fold in the centre, AB as in Figure 1, to form Figure 2. Still working from Figure 2, fold DC and DE back down towards middle base to form Figure 3. From Figure 3, fold one leaf up 180 degrees from line FG and other leaf back 180 degrees from same line to form Figure 4. Now at point 1 (Fig.4) open out fully to form Figure 5. Next, fold at JK (Fig.5) to bring top X up to Y, and bottom X the reverse way to form Figure 6. Now open out fully from M (Fig.6) to form Figure 7. Now repeat what you did in Figure 5 to form Figure 8. Next, repeat what you did with Figure 6 to form Figure 9. Now repeat the Figure 5 act again to form Figure 10. At point T (Fig.10) pull back the two 45 degree angles and you will have your boat. Please note that heavy black lines in each figure are the moves you make to get the next figure.

To make the plane, get a page of a copybook or writing pad and work on it as you did with the boat-making until you have Figure 4 formed. eg. ABCDEFG in Figure 1.

Fold the wing corners at lines CF and GE. You may pin them down or glue them or cut them off. Fold Figure ACE at line AV till point C meets E. While in that position, fold back from lines YZ and WX, Figure CYZ and EWX to a position at 90 degrees to plane body. That completes the half body and wings. Now cut out tall piece HIJKLM at least two and a half times the length of AV in Figure 1. Cut off the two triangles, HPA and IPB in Figure 2. Now cut off the two concave triangles, NJK and OLM in Figure 2. Now fold entire Figure 2 at line PQ. Next fold back AC and BD from lines RS and TU respectfully. (Figure 1 and Figure 2 are not drawn in proportion). Now common sense will put the plane together for you. You can use plain pins or glue to keep it well held intact. You may cut a narrow angle out of lower wings to the body to give it the streamline look.

THE BUZZER

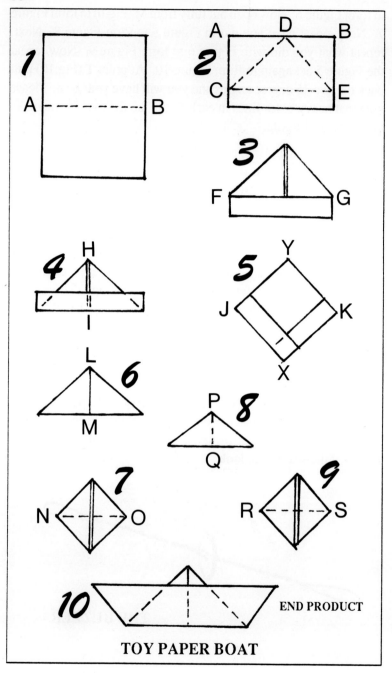

TOY PAPER BOAT

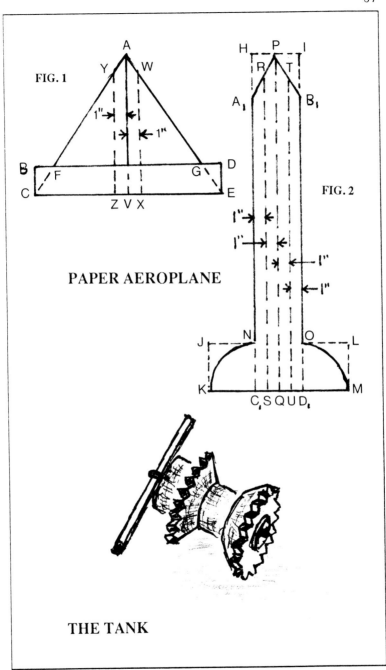

FIG. 1

FIG. 2

PAPER AEROPLANE

THE TANK

The tank was the best toy of the three and when wound up, went on its own power. It was made out of an empty thread spool, a narrow strip of bicycle tubing, two match sticks and a three-quarter inch of candle.

Firstly, cut V-shaped trianglular pieces out of the circumference of both ends of spool to make them look like cogwheels. Then cut a narrow V out of the full diameter of one spool-end to allow a half matchstick to sit into. Do likewise with one end of the three-quarter inch candle to allow the other match to sit into.

Now cut a six-inch strip of a bicycle tube the same width as the thickness of the tube. Next bore a hole in the centre of the three-quarter inch candle, the same bore as the hole in the spool. A hot six inch nail will do this. All is now ready for assembling. Double the rubber and push the two loose ends through from the side of the spool with the V-shaped cut. Put the half match on its grove so that it keeps the folded end of rubber from pulling through the spool hole. Now with a slight stretch on the two rubbers, shove them through the hole in the candle leaving the V cut end of candle on the outside. Next, put the long match in that V and tie the two rubber ends round it. Now start winding the long match and on leaving the whole object on the table it will start off moving.

One exercise we tried and failed at was parachuting. We had a piece of a reek cover and tied four ropes out of the corners. My two eldest brothers tried a jump from the top of a reek of straw to a lower bank of straw, three-quarter ways down. The fall was too short, which might have saved some broken bones. A toy we made that is very simple was called "Buzzer". Put the two loose ends of one yard of thread through the two diagonal holes of a large button. Join the loose ends. Now with the two thumbs in the two end loops of thread and the button in the centre of the thread twist so that the whole objcct goes round like a skipping rope. When three quarters of the threads are intertwined on each side, give a gentle pull and allow to twist freely. Play it in the same way as a yo-yo and with a bit of practice it will start buzzing.

Shortly after the war started, the Minister for Defence ordered a new military force to be organised. It was called the Local Defence Force and was to strengthen our defence power along with the Local Security Force that was already there. Both were voluntary organisations. The LDF were drilled in schools, parish halls and other public buildings that were available. Officers from the regular army and the LSD put these new raw recruits through the drilling exercises, two periods every week lasting two hours each. I don't think there was any money paid to these men but they were completely togged out with an army shirt, suit, topcoat and boots. The boots were heavily studded, leather soled and of much better quality than the ordinary man's boot. Our nearest drilling hall was in our own parish of Boyerstown and the hall belonged to a big robust gentleman called Tom Lawless. The hall always went by the name Lawless's Hall. We often listened to the drilling from the road. Between the thunder of the boots, the roaring of the army officer and the clapping of the hands on the rifle butts, it was a very noisy affair. The army coats were famous for their use on beds on a hard night's frost. Army manoeuvres took place on some Sundays on the farm of Ardbraccan House and we used to see army planes that flew very low on their way there. These planes were probably housed at Collinstown airport.

On our way home from school as many as twenty lorries laden down with turf would pass us as they went to the Phoenix Park to add another few yards to the turf reeks there. It was coming from school that we would meet a couple of empty drays being driven by men that delivered their loads of turf in the town of Navan. After some time we got to know the names of all these bogmen as they were called. They were strong hardy men and well tanned by the good wholesome bog air. I was called a bogman when I first started school in Navan and felt sore about it as I had no more sense then.

One man, Matthew Leech, always went home in high spirits and on a few occasions we saw the ass walking home while Matt slept in the dray. Matt, who was supposed to have the hens in his dwelling house, lived to be ninty-eight years of age.

I remember the night when the Germans bombed part of Dublin thinking it was Belfast. The windows of our house gave a slight shudder and we were thirty miles away from Dublin. A large family man got more cigarettes than a single man. Da was never stuck for a smoke as there were eight of us with rationing books. Our grocer always gave a Christmas box of a bottle of whiskey and a Christmas cake.

Da used to solder pots, pans and even buckets for neighbours as well as for himself. These items were very scarce and dear on account of the war. I loved looking at Da soldering with the blow-lamp, flux and soldering iron. Pot menders were also used for patching holes, in buckets mostly, as they were no use for pot ware that would have to boil water over a fire. Da was very informative when doing work and was anxious that we showed an interest in what he was doing. As well as teaching us the names of the various grasses he taught us the names of the different weeds, some of which we had four letter names for! Lambs quarter, chick weed, thistle, scutch and charlock were the main weeds we came across. He had taught us the various insects while walking us through the farm when we were very young. Beetles, ladybirds, snails, hairy maggots, wire-worm, leather jackets, slugs and the common maggot were the most usual ones we came across. He showed us the grasshopper, especially at the butt of the hay cocks. They made a lot of noise for their size, and had several different colours. The golden coloured lads were the most common, with the green fellow a close second. Fishermen love to get a lot of these grasshoppers into a jar when boat fishing for trout on a lake in the late Summer and Autumn. Weed killers and manures have diminished the numbers of grasshoppers to a very low level.

When walking us through the fields during late March and April, Da would set fire to any furze bushes that would be spreading their wings too far. In places where there was a large amount of them, a spectacular blaze would rise which would add to our exitement. At that time of year the furze are at their driest and the vegetation at the base of them was both dry and rotten, making it very easy to start them ablaze.

Da gave us a good knowledge of the more famous stars to be seen in the night sky. He would give us all a peep at the Moon, Mars, Venus, The Milky Way and the North Pole Star through the telescope as it was set on its tripod. He showed us how to find the North Pole Star by measuring seven times the distance of the points of The Plough from each other, away from the top point star and in line with the two points. He called us out one frosty night in the 1940's to show us a wonderful display of the "Northern Lights". I know the more fancy name for it but its spelling is another thing! The colours of the rainbow were all to be seen in it and the shifting car-like beams came right up to our sky zenith. That was the only worthwhile display I saw in my fifty-six years of life. We viewed a comet called "Arland Rowland" through the telescope also.

When thining and weeding the beet we were paid so much per drill. One of the fields was 365 yards long and we were paid six old pennies per drill. This was hard work for six to ten year old children when the sun was at its highest point in the heavens and the ground was rock hard. The clay got into the nail tops and became painful so we tried to keep them as short as possible. The skin at the butt of the nails would peel down in little narrow strips and cause some pain when working. A bandage would be put round the finger if it got too bad after giving it a rub of ointment.

The only time guide we had when working in the fields was a "sun dial" clock which Seán made with a fork stuck in the ground. It was pretty accurate but was not much use on a cloudy day. We also heard the twelve o'clock Angelus bell either from Navan or

Bohermeen churches depending on which way the wind blew. The Bohermeen bell was well known as "Paddy Monaghan". He was the man that paid for its installation. Another time guide we had was the whistle of the 4.50 steam train as it left Navan station on it's way to Kells. Sometimes we would be called from the tillage field to go gibbing cocks of hay and twisting ropes for them.

We used to ask Da why Séamus Boccán paid twice as much per drill for work than he paid. Da would explain to us that Séamus hadn't to feed and cloth us. At that time it made little sense to us but now we see the logic of it. Talking about cutting nails, Seán used to cut Da's toe nails with a sheep shears. We used have a good laugh as the clipped masonry went flying over the kitchen and Ma with the brush making sure none of them went astray! The last time I cut my toe nails I made a perfect job of them with my sister's pruning shears. A machine of interest, Séamus Boccán had, was a horse driven circular bench saw, the same as we had. The horse was out in the yard, going round in a large circle and Séamus was able to give commands from the shed to which the horse duly obeyed. He had a forge also as had three more of our neighbours. When horses were the only means of farm traction,the blacksmith went to farmers when called to do shoeing or the farmer did it himself.

Da taught us the card game "25" at a young age. We learned it quickly and started playing for one old penny. We would finish up with a 3d game and the first to get three games of "25" would be the winner. There would be an odd desperate argument over whether or not someone reneged. Da enjoyed this, but if things went too far, he would take in the deck of cards for that night. On a couple of occasions, he burned the cards. Ma seized this opportunity to start the Rosary. By the time the Rosary was said, tempers were restored back to normal.

Da could swim, and was very keen that all of us would know how to swim too. He admitted that the only stroke he had was the breast stroke, so that was the one he taught us, too. A cushion on a backless kitchen chair was our launching pad. With our belly on the cushion, our arms and legs were free to do air swimming. He taught us the hand stroke first, and having perfected that, the leg kicks and pullbacks were practised. The timing of both the hand and leg movements completed our course. It was not the easiest way to learn, but we were so keen that we did not complain. Now a place to swim was our only worry. The Boyne in Navan had a weir forty yards long and about fifteen yards wide. The people of the town went there in their hundreds during the forties and fifties, as the number of cars in the country was very low compared with now. The present people of Navan prefer to drive the twenty miles to Bettystown.

Farmers dipped their sheep in that swimming stretch on the Boyne in the month of May. As water entered and flowed out of it at a good fast rate, it had no trace of any of the grease washed out of the wool half an hour after the last sheep was dipped. That same swimming stretch was about 6' 6" deep, so it was no starting place for non-swimmers. We stayed nearer home and dammed a small river between our farm and a neighbour's, better than any beaver would! 1941 was a very dry spring and early summer, so we had to wait for about ten anxious days for the 4ft of water to build up. It was a Sunday evening after a holy hour, not the pub one, that we took the plunge in our football togs. It was in changing for a dip in this pool that Seán displayed his new crop of puberty hair with a shyish, teasing grin. Pointing to us in order of seniority he said, "You next year, you the year after, and you two years later". He had about half a dozen hairs on his chest, which gave him great delight. My impression of this, at that time, was that our blessed God-given procreation organs were ugly enough without putting them in the middle of a forest!

Having entered the water, our first approach was to close our eyes, take in a deep breath, go under and start our kitchen educated strokes. Even this exercise was very refreshing after a long day in the tillage field or hay field. After about a week, we were beginning to stay up for a few strokes. This gave us great encouragement to continue. Then disaster struck. As we arrived one evening, we found our dam completely demolished. Our dam had become the subject of a great chat in a pub after Navan fair. Our neighbouring farmer heard farmers who lived farther downstream complain about the little trickle of water that they had for cattle drinking. He let the cat out of the bag and decisive action was taken immediately. Seán knew another pool about two miles across the fields from our house. There was 5ft of water in this new pool, and it was much better than our first illegal one. Very soon we were all swimming and ready for the Boyne. With new bathing togs and a new towel each, off we went with a bit of pride to this grand new swimming pool. Seán and Páraic were first to try it. Soon they were able to swim the fifteen yards across. Now Micheál and I went in and managed to swim across under the careful eye of two good strong swimmers, that Seán happened to know well. Da was delighted when we told him that we were able to dive into the Boyne and swim across. Áine learned her swimming while on holidays in Skerries with Ma. Our eldest sister Máire never showed any liking for the water. When we were perfect swimmers, we would sometimes go to the real swimming pool in Dowdstown Park, which was about three miles the Dublin side of Navan and on the main road. All depths of water were to be found in this pool, and the depths were marked in feet and inches on one of the walls that ran lengthways, and in four equally spaced distances. There was a proper diving board in this pool also.

Apart from swimming, we had our field sports when the cooler weather came. High jumping, hop, step and leap sprints, a lap of a six acre field and of course, football and hurling. As well as work, swimming and sports, we had another obligation to fulfil. We had an hour's learning of the Latin Mass responses during the summer holidays of 1941. This took place from 9p.m. to 10p.m., except on a few occasions for some reason or other, and with Da's permission. He drummed it into us as we sat around a bare kitchen table with our one-and-a-half-pence catechism. Seán was already serving Mass for two years, so there were three of us to be togged out with surplice, soutanes and a dark pair of canvas shoes.

In the autumn of 1941 we served our first Mass. After that Mass, our head school mistress, Miss O'Donoghue, came over to Da outside the chapel gates. She asked him if he was the father of the four lovely boys and told him that he had made a great job in the teaching of our Latin responses. We loved serving, especially wedding, funeral and station Masses. We always got a reward of at least 2s6d from the parties involved. We had holy hours and the stations of the cross to serve as well. Our reward for these was the lovely smell of the insense that came out in little clouds from the tourable when shaken, and the carrying of the flickering candlelight from station to station in the chapel that left people's shadows bobbing up and down on the wall. The very first time I served the stations of the cross on my own, being a wee bit excited I made a very obvious blunder, leading out the priest after the altar prayers I opened up the altar railing gateway and made a left hand turn. I then noticed all the people in the front pew thumbing a lift the other direction! The priest, Fr. Michael O'Farrell, whom we called "Big Mick" was almost at the first station which was on the other corner of the church. In the vestry after the cermony he said to me, "Brady, you were in a great hurry to entomb our Lord tonight!" I had one very embarrassing fifteen minutes during a sermon while serving Mass. The parish priest, Fr. Thomas O' Keeffe, bellowed in the course of a sermon that there was never a saint called by the name of Natlu, Molly, Jack, Tom, Jim, etc. He wanted children to be named after Irish saints and martyrs and they to be given their full names. There was I facing a congregation of about 350, most of whom knew my name, and they after being told that I had a name that wasn't worth a button! Was I sorry when that Mass was over! As a point of interest, the same parish was rededicated to St. Natlu some forty six years later! An odd ceremony that occured during my serving Mass was the "Churching" of mothers on their first return to church after giving birth to a baby. There were about ten minutes prayer recited over the person, and a lot of holy water sprinkling on her, with a few Latin responses. The old people used to tell us that until this ceremony was performed that women in question were not worthy to be in church. At that time, or a few years before, they could not attend Mass or other church functions until that ceremony had been performed. How the husband had none of these restrictions put on him puzzles many people of today.

As the four of us boys had singing voices, we were called to attend choir practice after school a couple of days a week. Our teacher had a good singing voice, and could play the organ as well. Before a mission, which occurred every three years, long choir rehearsals took place four nights a week for a six week duration. It is sad to think that these choirs that sang at holy hours on Sundays between the hours of 3p.m.-4p.m. are now all redundant for that work. In these days Sunday Mass was for the duration of almost one hour. Prayers before Mass and the Acts of Faith, Hope and Charity took ten minutes to say. A sermon lasted for about twenty minutes. If offerings were read out after a short sermon, the two could last for thirty minutes. Prayer after Mass for the conversion of Russia and the De Profundis took another ten minutes to say.

In the spring of 1941, I had been promoted to the other three boys' bedroom. As this room had two double beds, I slept with Micheál. There was always a half hour's chat each night before sleep. We were a lively lot some mornings and sometimes a pillow fight would take place. These were as unpredictable and just as fierce as any of the cock fights that took place in Westmeath. Da caught us one morning with feathers flying in all directions, and put an end to this sport with a very strict warning.

As we were getting bigger and there was another child on the way Da decided to build an extension to the house. A local building contractor and his helper, along with our farm hand started work in March, 1941. The work was completed in the month of June and comprised a large bedroom, a bathroom and a badly needed separate toilet. A hallway from the kitchen to the back yard was also in the plan and it separated the bedroom from the bathroom and toilet. A concrete water tank, filled with water off the roof of the new building, was built for toilet flushing and cold water for the bath.

One morning on the 29th June, 1941, when we awoke, Mrs Devine was up in Ma's room. We asked Da if Ma was sick and he told us with a broad smile that she had a slight flu. Seán was sent to Navan that morning for the paper and groceries. Mrs Devine left at 2p.m., and a lady we often met on our way to school arrived on a bicycle with a parcel of goods in a brown bag attached to the handlebars of the bike. This lady was a Mrs Harte from Emmet's Terrace, Navan, and being a mid-wife, attended the birth of hundreds of babies. She had delivered all six of us before this extra child in that very same bedroom. We were outside playing when, at about 3p.m., Seán called us all in as Da wanted us. We were now all in the kitchen and not a word had been spoken, Da standing with his back to the towel rail of the aga cooker, and a huge smile on him, as on Seán and Máire. There was a low noise and movement in Ma's bedroom adjoining the kitchen. The next thing we heard the cry of a newborn baby to our great surprise, as not a word about it was ever told to us. Seán and Máire knew, but were bound to a very strict secrecy. I did recall the builder asking Ma if he would be finished in time and she, with a smile, replied "plenty of time". It was a baby girl and she was christened Maggie. She weighed only three and a half pounds at birth, and Nurse Harte did not think she would live. For the first three months after birth, every second drink from the bottle she had, would come up a short time later. After about six months, she started to thrive alright. I had the pleasure of seeing her breastfed in bed. I saw Ma hold Maggie in one hand as she bathed her in a small galvanised bath, and soap her with the other hand. We were all very fond of her and, of course, she became Da's pet. Ma asked Da about getting a pram for her, but Da replied firmly that there were six of us to carry her anywhere she would be going. Ma did not argue the point, and from what I saw after, Da was right as we often fought over who would carry her over the fields for a walk. In the coming years, she would tell Da everything. So we had to be very careful in her presence not to come out with any four letter words!

CHAPTER IV

In the early spring of our young years, Ma would bring a couple of us the two and a half miles to the garden of Ardbraccan House to get lettuce, scallions and rhubarb. Early potatoes were to be bought there before they would appear in the town's shops. These sales to nearby purchasers would pay the gardener and keep a constant supply of green vegetables to the mansion owners. It was a lovely building made of stone, as were all the spacious outhouses, set in lovely lawns surrounded by copper beeches among other lovely trees. We called into Ardbraccan graveyard to pray for all Da's relations that were buried there. It was in the same garden that the fruit for jam-making was bought in the autumn of the year. Our own vegetables in the tillage field were never ready until June.

Foot and mouth disease came to Ireland in the early summer of 1941. The nearest it got to our farm in Boyerstown was Dunboyne, a distance of about twenty miles. All fairs in counties Dublin and Meath were cancelled for a couple of months, as was the movement of cattle from one farm to another, unless a permit was procured. Department of Agriculture inspectors were very busy to see that all restrictions were being carried out.

For the pulling of the beet in October, Da employed an extra farmhand to help out. We would have to do one hour in the evening after school and all day on a Saturday. One year we had that great footballer of the late twenties and early thirties, Matthew Rogers, who wore the green and gold of Meath. He was number one at pulling and crowning the beet, and sometimes he would show us how to lift the ball while still running, if we happened to be playing just before he went home. He spent a lot of time trapping and snaring rabbits, which were plentiful then to supplement his weekly income. He ran a very successful hackney business as well. To rear at least ten children in the war years on one acre of land, and to feed and clothe them the way he did was a great credit to him. His sons, who served Mass and went to school with us, were all good footballers in later years, but none of them ever made the county grade. They were all good workers and made a great success in post school years. Matthew the father is still alive now, early 1990*, and he must be very close to if not over the ninety.

By now, Saturday was a very busy day for Ma. The house-maid got the day off. The eggs and the butter had to be readied for town. The churning was done in the early morning. The pounds of butter had to be weighed and clapped into shape on the butter plate. This was done with a hand clapper which was the same as a table tennis bat, but instead of the circular head it was a rectangular shape and corrugated for decorating purposes. The water had to be completely squeezed out of it also. About half the butter was kept for house use, and the rest sold, about eight pounds of it. The eggs had to be washed, and put into a basket type bag. About six dozen of these were sold. Some Saturdays she would bring out two young cockerels that weighed about five and a half pounds. Anytime Ma would see two hefty young cockerels fighting she would say "I will take the bucking of you two this weekend and if you are not in Peter McDermott's you will be giving us our soup and chicken meat, instead of roast beef!" These always fetched premium prices. The same load of eggs and butter was sold on Wednesday as well. The cleaver called every two weeks to buy eggs and fat chickens. He came in a horse-drawn cart with wire cages for the hens and chickens. The cleaver had the advantage in that he bought hens that had passed their laying days.

Ma's bicycle was carrying top weight coming from the town. A large bag came down from each of the two handlebars, a basket on the front of the handlebars was always filled, and a large cardboard box tied with a special light rope on to the back carrier, comprised the import freight. Ma was about fourteen stone weight, so the bicycle was well tested! I don't think Stephen Roche's sports

* Sadly died 1992. R.I.P.

model would compete! The goods that were sold nearly always bought the groceries. This meant that the products of five hand-milked cows and about fifty free range hens, fed on a little oats and the dinner remains, supplied the milk, eggs, bacon and groceries during the war years.

Rabbits always harboured on our land, and Da would shoot them with his .22 rifle whenever Ma needed a pair. He was now giving Seán an odd kill, much to his delight. The bullets came in a box of fifty in two distinct qualities. "Remington" were the manufacturers of the copper coloured "Superspeed" and the lead coloured "High Speed". Da preferred the Superspeed, and they did not dirty the barrell of the rifle as much as the lead-coloured High Speed.

At six o'clock or thereabouts on summer mornings, crows and pigeons were at their busiest eating potatoes and corn grains. It is not all they eat, but the large amounts of growing corn they pull down and trample on leaving it useless at harvest time. They were equally as destructive at potatoe crops. The young crows have an obligation to tear out the potatoes for the older birds. So good are they at this work, that they tear out as much as 100 times too much. Da made a "bird banger" in my very young days and it worked to perfection. A battery, gun powder and an old alarm clock were the main ingredients used. Our neighbours were astonished with it and one of them would joke with Da saying "You are sending all the birds of the country out to me!" That same man would be out bright and early looking after his own crops. He was one of the men that used Da's rifle to shoot crows for putting on stakes.

On Sundays in the thirties, forties and indeed the fifties, young country lads went hunting for badgers, foxes and rabbits. They went in groups of about six with a spade and crowbar, a 6ft. long gauge iron bar for following the direction of the burrow, set or den. A middle-aged man with a gun sometimes went with them, and of course, two or maybe three terriers. The nose of the dog that would enter the hole, and his barking action as a result, was the telltale as to whether the animal was at home or away. Some of the hunters would bring a ferret in a shoulder strapped-on box. A net would be set at the bolt hole and the ferret sent in at the front entrance. This drove the rabbit into the net. Some of these ferrets became useless, as they would kill the rabbit inside the hole and eat it. They would stay there until they were dug out. A small bell was attached to the ferret's neck for detecting his whereabouts should he go astray. The ferret handler wore a pair of gloves that were about half an inch in thickness to save the hands from the ferret's bite.

There were two coursing clubs near Navan, one in Ardbraccan and the other in Hanlonstown. About one hundred hares had to be got to enable the two-day's coursing to be held at each of the two places. About twenty men and young lads helped in the catching of these hares. A net some fifty yards long was placed mostly on the brow of a hill, as the hare with its shorter front legs preferred going up the hill. These nets were flanked on both sides and a beat of about twenty acres took place. A net-man took the hares out of the net. He had to be skilled at this work as a bite of a hare could take a finger off. One of these meetings took place in November, the other on St. Stephen's day. Hanlonstown was only six fields-from our house and we watched the coursing there twice. We did not take a liking to it, but had no objections to it. What does one do when he sees a cat playing with a mouse before the protracted kill, or a fly in a spider's cobweb? Why is there no protest to the fox hunter, the harriers that pursue the one hare with a pack of about thirty hungry dogs and the other hunters likewise?

As we grew up, we kept a close eye to our weight and height. These would be checked about every two months. Our height was measured in a barn wall, by means of a square and carpenters pencil under our names. A three-foot ruler of Da's gave the height in feet and inches. We engaged in weight lifting, and admired our neighbours who, in their twenties and thirties, were able to hoist the two four stone weights in a long arm stretched style, and hold for a count of ten. We had the 16-lb shot competition as well. A lot of these competitions took place on winter's nights, after the stations of the cross, in our neighbour's "Shanty" in which a fire was put lighting on the forge he had. The neighbours name was Seán Curraig, and he had a great sportsman of a son in Séamus. There was a ring board in the shanty as well. Shantys were common in rural Ireland up to thirty years ago, and were ceili houses for dancers as well as sport and chat houses. The name shanty came from the Irish words *sean tighe,* or "old house" in English. A hunting yarn I should have told a few pages back I will tell now. A man that went hunting with his gun every Sunday morning went over the first two fields before he branched out to hunt in earnest. This Sunday morning he was in the second field when he saw a fox sitting in a clump of rushes. His head was looking towards him and he was about thirty yards away, just a lovely distance for a gun. He pumped five shots into the fox when he decided to investigate. Over he went and found a fox with three turkey cock's feathers in his tail. There were ten men behind a hedge close by looking at the show!

We did some rope climbing from a rope attached to a cross beam in the hay barn. There was not a tall tree within a three mile radius of the house that we did not climb. I often had to climb trees to get turkeys or guinea fowl down from, as they often went to roost prematurely. I always got a few pence from Ma for doing that as she was scared of the foxes that we heard sounding for dogs that might be in the neighbourhood.

Apart from dancing, the picture house was the only other source of entertainment especially during the winter months and all Saturdays and Sundays throughout the year. Two cinemas in Navan got full houses for the above mentioned periods. From Monday to Thursday, during the period from April to October, only one cinema showed films, as the one man owned both cinemas. Young lovers used the cinema a lot, some of them up to three nights a week. There were young wage earners who did not drink or smoke that went to every change of film, which was almost every night. Da chose our films, and that would be only about six films in the year. I will always remember my first film which was named *Destroyer Man*. It was a war film, and I got much more enjoyment out of the cartoon film that preceeded it. A cartoon I was watching on the television by chance a few months ago, was as good as I ever saw. It showed a lovely young well-dressed rabbit walk up to a fierce-looking hulk that was about six times his size. The rabbit greeted him with a gentle "Hello there". The answer he got was "I'm Brutus, the greatest Vampire ever. "Shake hands", replied the rabbit, "we must be related because I am an Umpire". Other films I say in my young years were *The Song of Bernadette, Gone with the Wind, Great Expectations, Blood and Sand, Doctor in the House* and *How Green was my Valley*. Most of the boys in Boyerstown national school went to the matinee every Sunday. Monday during playtime, these lads with toy guns re-enacted the cowboy film they had seen the previous day. "Put up your hands, Bang-Bang", and the chap freezed up and fell on the stoney yard, sometimes cutting a hand or knee! Some of these young cowboys were as old as twelve. I thought it very silly of them, even though I was a few years younger. Another thing I remember was that when Indians did a war dance, a huge laugh came for the picture goers. Now I see dancing in the so called civilised world that would make Indians have a good laugh!

Bicycle parking on Saturday and Sunday nights paid a handsome reward for the eight hours' work, in the 40's and early 50's. Patsy Keenan, Railway St., Navan, carried on such a business with very little opposition. He once told me, he parked up to 800 bikes for both picture house goers and dancers on a Sunday night. At 6 old pennies per bike this came to £20. This was the equivalent of a county engineer's weekly pay at the time.

Young country lads that had finished school went to their nearest crossroads after work for a chat, a game of handball, pitch and toss, or perhaps a game of "25" with a pack of cards. The games that involved money were only played on Saturday night or Sunday after dinner. Wages were very small, £2 a week for farm labourers, and men with a small family could not afford to gamble. Most of them drank and smoked in moderation. Horse racing was restricted to a few racecourses during the war years, and Navan races were abandoned for that duration. Parts of bicycles were hard to get as well as the tyres and tubes, and I often saw men exchange these parts and even barter them for potatoes and vegetables. There were always a couple of men in each parish who were handy at cutting men's hair, which they did in their own house or the house of the recipient at half the price of the professionals. Da would hire one of these men on a Saturday night, once a month, to cut our five heads of hair before Seán took on to do it. That grand gentleman got a few shillings and a strong drink to help him on the job, which was performed during the course of a good chat. He got a good tea before he left on his way home.

By now, we were all growing at a very fast rate, as told to us by the markings on the barn wall. We ranged in ages from eight to fourteen except for Maggie, and we all had great appetites. Instead of killing one pig a year, Da would now rear two pigs for home consumption. A bonnam was bought in the month of May, for an August killing, and another in September for a December killing. The December killing supplied two Christmas hams for home use. These pigs were fed on small spuds called poreens (potatoes not just right for table use), boiled turnips with a few fistfulls of crushed oats on top, and the remains of scrapings left over from our dinners. A neighbour of ours did the pig killing. Da or Seán would knock down the pig with a bullet to the forehead. The pig was then hoisted, by pulling him up by pulley blocks. When he was at the right height for working on, the butcher's knife was inserted into the heart, and Ma collected the blood into a large enamel basin. Ma would not let anyone else do this job for fear some foreign bodies might get into the blood. I'm not sure, but I think something was added to the blood immediately, and it had to be stirred every now and then. When the last drops of blood had left the pig's body, the knife opened up the body from the tail, via the belly and up to the head, which was cut off immediately. The pig's entrails were collected in a barrow left under the pig and were buried in a nearby field. Buckets of boiling water were then thrown on the pig's skin, his inside and the feet were put into a bucket of boiling water, two at a time for five minutes. The hair was now ready for removing from the pig's skin, which was done by scraping down with a knife or a worn down tondish, which one man used with great results. The entire body was now washed down with buckets of cold water to complete the work until the following evening when the boning would be done. The pig's head was weighed, and for every pound it weighed, that was taken as the weight of the pig in stones. A neighbouring woman always got the pig's head, tail and liver which she valued for herself and her large family. Four stone of salt and some saltpetre was purchased for the curing of the two flitches of bacon. The boning was done on a large table that had been scalded with boiling water and then salted. The entire pig was cut in two by sawing down the full length of the back bone with a specially set and sharpened saw. The pork, liver, heart and kidney were then removed. Next, the two hams, two gammons and the four crubeens were cut out with the saw, and salted.

Our cousin Séamus Boccán and a few of our close neighbours got a helping of pork, as was the custom. The two flitches of bacon were now ready for curing. I think the saltpetre was used round the bones that were exposed when the hams and gammons were extracted. The salt got a fierce rubbing into the bacon. The bacon box that was freshly scalded and then rinsed with cold water, was put into position and rubbed with salt as well. The two flitches were then put in, one on top of the other. These flitches were reversed and freshly salted every week, until the bacon was ready for use after four weeks. This home-cured bacon became very firm, and had a nicer flavour than the factory bacon. Pigs were killed then when they were fourteen stone weight or over. Now twelve and a half stone is the ideal weight. Perhaps it was the home-mixed feed, that was sometimes mixed with a little skimmed milk or buttermilk that became too sour for bread use, that was responsible for the nice flavour. The black puddings were made the same evening the bacon was cured. Breadcrumbs, chopped onion and some spices were used in the pig's blood. The mixture was then funnelled into sheep gut, which was twisted every one foot length and tied with a light twine, to leave them in handy lengths when boiled in a pot for about twenty minutes. What a joy a deep freeze would have brought to the countryside in the years previous to the past forty years, before rural electrification came in use!

The feeding of the pigs, like that of different breeds of fowl, was left to Ma and Máire. All the fowl were free range and the pigs were likewise, for their first six weeks after buying them. They were housed for the remaining six to eight weeks when proper fattening began. Twenty turkeys were reared for the Christmas market. Thirty pullets and thirty two-year old hens supplied eggs for the house and the market. Thirty cockerels were reared for home use and the market as well. A dozen ducks and the same amount of guinea fowl completed the mixed variety of birds that were all reared from the chicken stage. These birds added to the sounds heard from the tractor and other working machinery around the farmyard and close-by fields.

The turkey chicks had to be fed on hard boiled eggs and chopped steamed nettles for the first four weeks of life. Talking about nettles, we came home from school one March evening, ate up our dinner and enjoyed it immensely, while Da was reading the daily newspaper with a great smile on his face throughout. I asked him what the smile was for, to which he replied, "Do you know that you are after eating a feed of nettles?" The older folk did not mind, but the three youngest, myself included, asked Ma how she could be so cruel to do such a thing. Ma was very vexed with Da for the information he had made known to us. The old people had great belief in nettles in the spring, as well as sulphur and treacle for purifying the blood.

We were amazed looking at the ducks letting down a full frog as it wound its way down its neck. They were the hardiest fowl of all. "Summer Wells" was the breed of hens Ma kept, and she won first prize for the best half dozen eggs at the Navan show any time she entered it. They were a large brown egg and were very uniform in size. In the springtime of the year, these eggs were sold as "birded" eggs, and fetched double the price of the ordinary eating eggs. I still remember how fiery a hatching hen got when a young chicken was taken up in a hand. It was lovely to see how all the young chickens took protection under their mother's wing when called by her on seeing a hawk, magpie, rat, cat or strange dog arrive in her vicinity.

Hens, turf and picture houses were the breeding grounds for fleas and lice during our young years. It was a sore-looking sight to see all the red pitted backs of the pupils, when the annual doctor came in to examine them. There were only two deterrents - an all out hunt, and the fine comb. The fine comb was made of bone or ivory, and had a double row of teeth, one coarse and the other fine. Ma did the hair of the younger ones while everyone did their own hunting in their bed and clothes. We didn't know how lucky we were, for I was reading where an American scientist discovered that a flea won't bite a person unless he is 100%, healthwise. Of course, every child's mother blamed another mothers child for the spread of these vermin to her darling child! "Who were you sitting beside at school?" was a commonly asked question. The fleas leap, for his size, must out-class that of all other creatures by leaps and bounds. Sitting out a three hour film in a picture house was an endurance test of great magnitude. The greatest sufferers in the flea war years were the ladies with fur coats, who would not be seen scratching at any cost, and who took the full severity of the feeding flea without a move!

Towards the end of the war, a chemical called DDT was invented by a German, that sounded the death knell for all fleas and lice. At that time, it was said to be the greatest invention since the wheel. It was a by-product of DDT that went into the making of insecticides in the following years. As well as having lice problems, some of the unfortunate children had an outbreak of scabs or sores as they were called. They were circular in shape, about 1" in diameter and were to be seen on all parts of the body, including the head, which caused some of the hair to fall out. After some weeks, the scabs cleared up, and all traces disappeared. Poor feeding that left the blood in a run-down state was supposed to be the cause. We never had any trouble with that menace, but I saw whole families plagued with them. It was in the years of the late thirties and forties that TB was at its highest. A few of my national school pals in Boyerstown died from this great scourge. There were other great friends of mine that had miraculous cures from TB before it was stamped out in the fifties.

By now, Seán was allowed to carry the rifle on his farm walks. I often went with him on these walks, and just like Da, he would swoop along the hedgerows, taking an odd look through any opening and go quietly out the gateway. I would be asked to lend my steady shoulder to act as a tripod should anything shootable be seen. This method was applied for a long distance shot, otherwise a standing shot was used. Seán would go off shooting at five o'clock on a summer's morning without wakening anybody. He would bring the bicycle and do his shooting from the road. I often saw him come home with from six to eight rabbits hanging from the handlebars. There was a way of knotting the back legs of two rabbits together with the aid of a penknife, which all good hunters brought with them. This done, they were easily hung from the handlebars without the use of twine. Two of these rabbits were kept for house use, the rest Seán sold for his own pocket money. Each rabbit fetched 2s6d, which was good money. A pair of rabbits would purchase forty cigarettes, and were almost a labourers daily wage. Some of the buyers were poor widow women rearing families, and payment would be postponed for a couple of weeks. He kept an account of these sales in his diary that Da gave him at Christmas. In doing these morning hunts, Seán had to be back at 8.30a.m. to get his breakfast and get ready for school. On a few of these early morning hunts, a fox was brought home as well as rabbits. There was a bounty of 7s6d for showing a fox's tongue in the Navan Garda barracks. Fox furs were a common sight then, as they were cured and worn across women's shoulders. These furs were often the cause of laughter during Mass among young boys and girls, as they saw on the foxes head his piercing still eyes, nose, mouth, and ears and of course, on the other end his bushy tail. Our rifle was never idle on a Saturday or Sunday. Da always carried the rifle on the tractor, and I saw him shoot rabbits on his way home after ploughing, with the aid of the tractor lights.

When my three older brothers and I ranged from eight to twelve years old, chess playing almost took the place of card playing. Da offered good money for anyone able to beat him, but this was almost impossible at the early stage. I know now, that at the beginning he would purposely loose an odd game, in order to keep our interest in the game. At the start, he played me with his queen on the sideline. When I improved so much that he could not beat me that way, he left in the queen and took off the castle. Seán and Páraic were quite good at it, and were able to hold their own against Da. Between the cards, chess, shooting and serving Mass, we always had a few shillings pocket money. Ma was always the poorest of us, except when the turkeys or other fowl were sold.

There were other occasions when I would receive money rewards. I would have to give Seán a hand to bring a cow or heifer to the bull of a neighbour about two miles away. The bull owner, on receiving the 7s6d for the service, would give me a tip of two shillings. These trips gave me an addition to my knowledge of the "facts of life". Before cattle were sold at Navan fair, they were driven a four mile journey to Robinstown to be weighed on a public scales. Local farmers would be very interested in the weights returned, as they would be a good guide as to the weight of their own cattle. Money would be wagered on weight guessing, and I saw good farmers that would be as much as half a cwt out in their guessing. Nowadays, young farmers can guess the weight to the nearest pound, from the knowledge they get from watching the cattle weights at the modern marts.

In the thirties and forties, there was no lorrying of cattle much at all. They were walked long distances to fairs, and then to the nearest railway station, to be railed to the nearest town of the buyer for more feeding or to the cattle boat at the north wall for transport to England. Seán once bought cattle at a fair in Delvin and walked them to Boyerstown, Navan, a distance of eighteen miles. I got three fair days off school to drive cattle with Seán to Navan fairs, which were held on a Monday. The starting time was 6 o'clock in the morning, so we had to bring a bicycle lamp and a torch to warn car drivers if there were any. This was a good healthy job on a frosty December morning, and I was well rigged out with a good heavy overcoat, scarf and gloves. Now and again, a beast would go down on his knees after slipping on the frosty road. Da sent Séamus Boccán to do the selling, as Seán was too young and a minimum selling price had been agreed. Sometimes, cattle dealers came out the approaching country roads to the town, and tried to clinch a deal before cattle got to the fair at all. Our cattle went the whole way to the fair, as Séamus Boccán did not arrive until 8 o'clock in his Baby Austin.

It was a lovely sight on the Fair Green, which was packed with cattle and sheep with an overflow to Railway St. and Corn market. These cattle were steaming from their bodies after the long journey and a certain amount of nervous fright after leaving their quiet green fields. Their pulse rate was slightly raised and this could be detected from the atomic-style clouds of breath that left their nostrils. Selling in earnest began at 8.30a.m. It was great to watch the handclapping of the buyer and seller, as both sought good value. There were middle men that were called tanglers, who had little wealth, but the gift of the gab. They acted as a go-between in a sale that would be taking place. They had the knack of winking at both the men in turn, with this act being visible to whom it was directed only. They were well known men, and even though they were a nuisance, they were accepted by both parties rather than insult them. They gave a hand to drive cattle and to hold them in their restricted territory, but with their good hearing, they were off like a bullet to a fresh commencing sale. Hygiene was not the essence at these fairs, what with all the spitting on hands, the hand clapping and then the final handshake. Occasionally the noisy selling act caused some of the cattle to break out of their confined ring and mix with another man's cattle, as did bulling heifers that upset the placidity of their male counterparts. Up to half the cattle at the fair would be making a train journey and a drive from the station to the north wall for export to England. Cows and calves were sold after the main fair was over, and Cornmarket was a popular place for these. Sheep sales took place there also. The sheep were tied together with hay-ropes and formed a class of a circle.

Poor people, unemployed or past their active working life, gave a hand on fair days for a pint and a few shillings reward. At 12 o'clock, when all the cattle at the fair were sold or brought home, a large bell would call the people to an auction of farm machinery, furniture, field gates, feeding troughs, and sometimes calves and pigs that were not already sold. A spacious square of ground in front of Herford Place was the site on which this auction took place, and it was conducted by the most highly rated man in Meath at that time, Brendan Smith of Patrick Smith & Sons, Academy St, Navan.

When this auction was over at about 2p.m., the farmers, who usually made a day of it, spent good money with the town's merchants before going home. God be with the good old days. Gone, but just not completely forgotten yet. I wish they were with us again.

There was one day in the year that Ma always waited for, and would never pass by unknown to her. This was St. John's day which occurred in the middle of June. The day before that day, the day itself, and the day after it were called the "Rogation" days. She would go around all the meadows and crops with a sprinkle of holy water and a silent prayer I suppose, as was the custom of people that time. This was the time of year when the countryside was looking its very best , and the weather was at its best also. After the Rosary each night, three Hail Marys were recited for good weather for the hay and harvest season, or for rain during a prolonged drought. It usually worked out all right and Ma would say, "You can't beat the power of praying".

In the month of April, 1940, Seán and Máire got their Confirmation. At that time the sacrament was given every three years in the country parishes so that left Páraic, I and Micheál, in slips for the 1943 ceremony. A huge big fat priest, Fr. Clavin, examined us for the big day. We got the result there and then and all three of us came through with flying colours. We all got a No. 1 which entitled us to a red certificate. We each had to select our Confirmation saint's name. I chose Patrick, Páraic chose Francis and Micheál settled for Joseph. We got a full new rig-out for the occasion, which meant our first new suits. Seán obliged us with our first hair-oil and he gave us a hand to get a "quiff" or "cow's lick" into our bobs, just like his own. When Ma saw this she said "I suppose you will be looking for girlfriends soon!" The ceremony was conducted in Bohermeen church and took the children from the two parishes-of-ease i.e. Boyerstown and Cortown as well. Dr. Dalton, who was to be elected cardinal in later years, gave us the sacrament with a gentle pat on the cheek. Ma made her way down on her bicycle. Seán carried Micheál on the carrier of his bicycle while Páraic carried me on the handle-bars of his bicycle. This wasn't the most comfortable journey I ever had and as the distance was a good five mile, I wasn't sorry to arrive at the chapel.

Our teacher who was there before us, marshalled us into our reserved seating. There were twelve of us from Boyerstown school all together. Photos were taken of us, before and after Confirmation. The chapel was packed for the Mass that opened the ceremony. It was when it was over that all the Das and some of their friends left to have a drink in Bob Reilly's pub, just opposite the chapel. The bishop gave us the sacrament before a very long sermon. He stressed on us how important it was for us to keep our Confirmation pledge, i.e. that we abstain from all intoxicating drink until we reached the age of 25. Benediction completed the ceremony which lasted two and a half hours. We were glad to get out and stretch our legs. We had a rendezvous with Ma for Bob Reilly's where we got lots of lemonade and buns. We collected a few shillings from the well oiled-up men folk. This was my first prolonged visit to a pub and first impressions were that it was a great place to be!

Seán and Páraic biked it home as Micheál and I got a lift in a very comfortable trap with a neighbour of ours. We had a good party at home that night and a free day from shcool the following day. It was about the time that I got my confirmation that I first learned to milk a cow. I had always envied the farm hand as he whistled a tune or sang *Little Sir Echo* while he sent froth rising a couple of inches over the top of the bucket. He had got me with a few squirts of milk when I was unaware and I was anxious to do the same with the cats or perhaps Micheál or Áine. After a few bad starts and a kick from an impatient cow, I managed to draw milk with one hand. It wasn't long until I managed the job with the two hands. It wasn't long either till the novelty of milking wore off me and I would keep away from the cow shed at milking time unless ordered by Da!

When Da was not working at the forge or lathe he spent his nights reading when chess or cards were over at about 9.00 p.m. Seán joined the Navan library so that there was always a fresh selection of books. Books that were picked up at auctions and bought, of which there were many, had all been read by Da. *Withering Heights, David Copperfield, The Tale of Two Cities, Gone With the Wind* and *Blood and Sand* were the names of a small portion of the books on the shelves. The only books I took any interest in were geographical books with their detailed illustrations. The daily *Irish Independent* was read every day to keep up with the latest war news and we all read *Curley Wee*. There was a weekly English farming magazine called *The Farmers Weekly* which was on special order and Da and Seán read it from cover to cover. Expert machinery men had their weekly columns in this book. The mighty A.G. Street of BBC radio note always came up with a first class article in it. Market trends overseas were given in detail. It was from the *Farmers Weekly* that Da learnt about the model farming brothers the *Hendersons*, and their two great farming books, *The Farming Ladder* and *Farming Progress*. The morning post was watched with great eargeness until they arrived and they were immediately read. It was a must, that all four of us boys read these two books. There is a lovely story told by one of the Hendersons in one of the two books mentioned. It related to an instance that happened to him when on an Irish holiday down in Killarney. One day he had a look at one of the mountains and decided to climb it. On his way down that mountain he was called over to a gateway by an elderly woman who looked in distress. On his nearing her the woman told him to come quickly as she had a cow in labour for a couple of hours and she was unable to pull the calf. He hurried to a shed a field away with her and had the calf safely delivered after rectifying some complication. The old lady was very pleased and brought him to have a very tasty meal. There was a delicate lassie in the kitchen, a daughter of the old lady whom Mr. Henderson was quite sure had T.B. which was at its peak that same time. The man was very impressed by the old lady's faith in prayer. She told him she had prayed to St. Brendan, the patron saint of travellers, to send some animal knowledgable man to help out with the calving of the cow. She got exactly what she had prayed for, a man who had calved hundreds of cows for themselves and neighbours, with all sorts of complications presented to him as well. A lovely story with a lovely ending. It was from that same *Farmers Weekly* he learnt about ear tagging for identification purposes. He purchased an ear-tagger and five hundred ear tags which were sent on by post from England. He used these tags on heifer calves and recorded the dam and bull of each animal. This was long before AI or TB testing came into existence. The same weekly was responsible for his purchase of a soil testing outfit, which tested soil for acidity. There were two fields that were starved for lime, which were duely looked after, with amazing results, and it was from this example that a few of our neighbours did likewise.

The liming of the acid lands brought up the P.H. to a level that the full benefits of the phosphate, pot-ash and nitrogen dressings showed their full value. A mole drainer was once hired from the Committee of Agriculture, Meath County Council, to drain the only field of rushes we had. This field was high at the centre and gradually sloped down to stone-made shores about ten yards from the two opposite sides that mattered. This field had furrows every five yards that had been put there possibly a couple of hundred years before. The mole drainer was used in each of these furrows so that each line of mole drain had only two and a half yards of earth each side of it to drain. It was a pleasure to see the flow of water that left the stone shores and flowed into the ditches after the first heavy fall of rain. With liming, manuring, and a topping at the end of May the field was transfigured. The rushes we went through on our way to school, and that were almost as high as ourselves, completely disappeared. The grazing output of that field at least doubled to the delight of all. Our old Fordson tractor was unable to pull the mole drainer without wheel-spin so our neighbour, Seán Devine, with his newer Fordson Major on spadelugs answered the call.

A grass seed barrow was bought at an auction about the same time. This saved the job of hand-shaking the seed and it achived a much more even distribution. This machine was used by all our near neighbours who did a machinery hire business with us. There was one snag with this grass seed barrow. Even though people were told never to reverse the machine, as it distroyed the brushes that put out the seed, it happened occassionally. Da had an answer to this problem. He built in a free wheel gear of a bicycle into the main drive of the barrow. Now when the machine was reversed to take another scribe at a headland, the free wheel came into operation and the driveshaft of the barrow stood still. This was the old fashioned seed barrow, about twelve feet wide, which sat on a wooden spoked wheel and pushed by hand. It was used on the tractor buckrake in later years to simplify things. This way allowed the tractor tracks to mark the ground, instead of shifting three marking stakes.

It was about that time too that the bearings of the disc-harrow were gone beyond their working life. With the old bearings to guide him, Da turned out the eight half bearings on the lathe. He used a very good type of timber and he wondered how long these wooden bearings would last. They happened to out-live the discs and were in use sixteen years after! It was I who bought an almost new second-hand Pierce disc-harrow for £42 in 1956 and to my surprise, it, too, had wooden bearings installed. On inquiring I learned that they were the original bearings of that machine!

All these years a sharp eye was kept on our weight and heights. Much to Seán's disappointment, Páraic was growing at a fast rate and was level height with him. As we turned out fully grown, Seán was five foot ten and a half and I, Páraic and Micheál topped the five foot eleven and a half. If his height disappointed him, Seán's strength did not. He was the only one of us that could lift the back wheel of the Fordson tractor clean off the ground and hold there for a count of five seconds. He was the only one of us that could bend a six inch nail with his bare hands and it was he alone that could catch two loft rafters and pull himself off the ground and hold for a count of five seconds. The only help he had doing the last feat was his thumbs and index fingers. Seán now had a full man's work to do which was mostly tractor work as a lot of hire work was done. The farm hand looked after six cows, calves, cattle and fencing. He did the hedge clipping, whitewashing, and other jobs round the farmyard as well. Of course, he gave a hand at the hay, corn and the weeding, thining and pulling of the beet, turnip and mangold crops.

Maire was now fifteen and had two years secondary education completed at Mercy Convent, Navan. Seán was fourteen and finished his school days to help on the farm. Páraic was thirteen and started his secondary education in St Patrick's Classical School, Navan. Micheál was twelve and he started his secondary schooling in the Navan Technical School. I was ten and sent to the De La Salle schools, Navan. Áine remained on in Boyerstown national school for another three years.

The Christian Brothers, as we called our teachers, were a very strict bunch of lads. A cane was used by half of them while the rest got their relief out of a heavy leather strap. It was a huge change for me as all subjects except English and religion were done through the medium of Irish. There were forty six pupils in class five, my first class in the Brothers. This was a big difference from the three in my class four in Boyerstown National. Having got a good start in Irish in Boyerstown, I soon was able to manage the maths, history and geography in our native tongue. The flush toilets and wash basin were a gift. They were kept in a very clean condition and it was one of the good Brothers that got the Oscar for this deed.

During dinner break we kicked an old tennis ball in the very rough play yard. One old handball alley was always in use as there were about four hundred on the roll book. One class that paid into a fund bought a new football and that class alone were allowed to play with it, supervised by their class teacher, Brother Norbert. Anyone outside that class that stole a kick at that football got three of the best from the strap. That class supplied Navan O'Mahony's with great footballers in later years. Looking back on photos of the classes taken in 1946, about twelve who have died in their young years were all good footballers. Meath's two greatest men, Joe Loughran and Tony Donnelly, Cavan's two great players, John Joe Reilly and Phil Duke, and Kerry too had some of their "greats" die young men.

Lunch and milk was supplied to the poorer children in the Brothers' school. Two nice crusty buns and a tin of milk was relished by about forty pupils while the rest of the town's children went home to dinner. The country boys brought their own lunch, except for about six that got the two buns and milk.

The classrooms were heated by water filled radiators and the boiler pipes that connected them. A mighty big furnace fuelled by timber and turf heated the big supply boiler. There were two vegetable gardens, right in the centre of the huge stoney yard. A Brother Gerard looked after that business and should any pupil be seen coming out of it, he got six of the best from the heavy strap. Brother Gerard often hired a couple of country lads after school to do thinning and weeding. He always paid two shillings for this and never had any trouble getting volunteers. It was this same Brother who shot pheasants and wild duck in the fall of the year. He had two lovely dogs, a red setter and a pointer. He had a lovely, well looked-after kennel for them and never failed to give them their daily exercise, no pun intended!

There was always a couple of bare fisted fights after school which were paired off by the bully boys. A certain amount of hatred was spurred into these fights by propaganda. I had to do my fair share of these fights and always had a dread of them. The fight ended with a bleeding nose, a black eye or a fit of crying. The Brothers turned a blind eye to these fights as they probably thought it would make better men out of us.

My first bicycle was got for cycling to the Brothers' school. It was purchased at an auction and was a full "crock". I had endless trouble with the chain, centre axle and wheels. Seán gave me a good training for a while and then let me do my own repairs. Of course, tyres and bad tubes were very common as they just could not be got when required, due to the war. Seán, who had a new Raleigh with a hub dynamo, three speed, etc, often helped me out with the loan of it. I got an awful land one evening when it was missing from the school grounds. I reported it to the Gardai and they asked me if I had the frame number. Seán had it in his diary which was a great help to find it. There was a boy missing from his home in Navan and he was found in a back street in Dublin city. He had a fair idea where he left the bicycle but was unable to pin-point it. I got word the next morning that the bicycle had been found and was in the Navan barracks. The Gardai told me that if they had no number to go on, they might as well be looking for a needle in a hay stack!

After one year in the Brothers' school, I was selected to sit for a Meath County Council scholarship, on my second Easter. This scholarship covered all expenses to St Finian's College, Mullingar. It was also transferable to any other secondary school in Meath. Studying for this examination entailed going back to study from 5p.m. to 7p.m. from September to April which was examination time. We also had to do the first half day on Saturday studying. Three Brothers took on the task of teaching these extra hours and I'm fairly sure there was no extra pay for their hard work, after a day's teaching. Irish, history and the geography of the world were done in great detail. Arithmetic, geometry and algebra were also learned. They were the five subjects we were tutored in, as well as what we learned during the day.

My memories of these night school days are of frosty starry skys with the smoke running at right angles to the town's chimneys and the flashing lights of the Lyric cinema which were very visible from the school gates. I had to admire the town boys that went to the stations of the cross every night after that night school during lent. I hurried home to my dinner as all I had after day school was my lunch and two cups of tea that I got in the Tara Restaurant at the price of 3d per cup.

Brother Bernard was the principal teacher and taught class seven. He was over seventy years of age and never failed to bring his two wire haired terriers for a walk every evening, first thing after school. Whenever I met him with the Irish terriers, his walking stick and slow styled leisurely way of walking. I always thought of the poem *Caoch O'Leary,* which went thus:-

One winter's day, long long ago,
    When I was a little fellow,
A piper wandered to the door,
    Grey-headed, blind, and yellow;
And oh! how glad was my young heart,
    Though earth and sky looked dreary,
To see the stranger and his dog -
    Poor "Pinch" and Caoch O'Leary.

And when he stowed away his "bag",
    Cross-barred with green and yellow,
I thought and said, "In Ireland's ground
    There's not so fine a fellow".
And then he stroked my flaxen hair,
    And cried, "God mark my deary!"
And how I wept when he said "Farwell,"
    And thought of Caoch O'Leary!

Oh! God be with those happy times!
    Oh! God be with my childhood!
When I, bareheaded, roamed all day -
    Bird-nesting in wild-wood.
I'll not forget those sunny hours,
    However years may vary;
I'll not forget my early friends,
    Nor honest Caoch O'Leary.

The seasons came and went and still
    Old Caoch was not forgotten,
Although we thought him dead and gone,
    And in the cold grave rotten;

And often, when I walked and talked,
    With Eily, Kate, and Mary,
We thought of childhood's rosy hours,
    And prayed for Caoch O'Leary.

Well - twenty summers had gone past,
    And June's red sun was sinking,
When I, a man, sat by my door,
    Of twenty sad things thinking.
A little dog came up the way,
    His gait was slow and weary,
And at his tail a lame man limped -
    'Twas "Pinch" and Caoch O'Leary.

Old Caoch, but, oh! how woe-begone,
    His form is bowed and bending,
His fleshless hands are stiff and wan,
    Ay - Time is even blending
The colours on his thread-bare "bag" -
    And "Pinch" is twice as hairy
And "thin-spare," as when first I saw
    Himself and Caoch O'Leary.

"God's blessing here!" the wanderer cried,
    "Far, far be hell's black viper;
Does anybody hereabouts
    Remember Caoch the Piper?"
With swelling heart I grasped his hand;
    The old man murmured, "Deary,
Are you the silky-headed child
    That loved poor Caoch O'Leary?"

"Yes, yes," I said - the wanderer wept
    As if his heart was breaking.
"And where, *avic machree*," he sobbed,
    "Is all the merrymaking
I found here twenty years ago?"
    "My tale," I sighed, "might weary;
Enough to say - there's none but me
    To welcome Caoch O'Leary."

"Vo, vo, vo!" the old man cried,
    And wrung his hands in sorrow,
"Pray, let me in, *asthore machree*,
    And I'll go *home* to-morrow.
My 'peace is made'; I'll calmly leave
    This world so cold and dreary;
And you shall keep my pipes and dog,
    And pray for Caoch O'Leary."

With "Pinch" I watched his bed that night;
    Next day his wish was granted:
He died, and Father James was brought,
    And the Requiem Mass was chanted,

The neighbours came; we dug his grave
    Near Eily, Kate, and Mary,
And there he sleeps his last sweet sleep -
    God rest you! Caoch O'Leary!

Every year from 1943 to 1947 we had a few weeks of snow covered ground. This never stoped us from school. One Spring, of those mentioned years, however, the school was closed for two weeks, as a dirty bad flu brought the country to a crawl. This unexpected holiday resulted in the Easter and Summer holidays being shortened by one week each.

Páraic did his Intermediate on his second year at college. He was a very dedicated boy at his evening studies and also managed to attend morning study for half an hour before school, proper. There was a boxing club in St Patrick's and a few of the boys managed to reach the Leinster championships. Páraic had a vicious straight left, he being a ciotóg, and managed to win all his college fights. He picked up a few nice medals and money also that the President had won by backing St Pat's and which he divided between the boxers. The club came to an end for lack of space, as the number or pupils was increasing by 30% each year. Seventy was roughly the number of pupils from Navan and the adjoining countryside, in the mid forties. Six, or thereabouts, went to St Finian's college from the town as boarders.

I found myself with a commissionable job before school during the last two years of the war. Páraic was now a marksman as well as Seán, so I had to bring pigeons and rabbits into Peter McDermot's egg and poultry shop, Bakery Lane in Navan. Peter was later called "The Man In The Cap" by Micheál O'Hehir and was on the Meath team that won the 1949 All Ireland senior football final. Pigeons were fetching 4s0d each and rabbits 3s0d each. This was great money for school boys when you realise that ten pigeons would be as much as a farm labourer got for a five-and-a-half day week. Firearms were a rarity then and about two rifles and maybe a shotgun were all the contents of a parish in that respect.

CHAPTER V

On my first year in the Brother's school I had the pleasure of attending Duffys' Circus for the first time. It was a great occasion in those years and they did four shows in two days. The five o'clock show was a matinee and school children got in for half price which was one shilling. Before the first show, at about 3.30pm, a full pipers band paraded through the main street of the town, Trimgate Street. I once saw fifteen elephants march head to tail down that same street marshalled by a skinny little Indian man, as he brought them down to the Boyne for a drink. As many as thirty horses participated in that circus. The tent was a huge affair that housed up to one and a half thousand people. Should the wind be too strong the circus would have to be abandoned. They say when you see one circus that you have seen them all. This I found to be true enough as my first one was by far the most enjoyable.

It was at my first circus that I got my first real "Eirigh an Phenis". A lovely young lady, clad in a short skirt, lovely shaped legs and thighs, performed on a small piebald pony, jumping on his back and even dancing to the band on his back while the pony trotted around the ring. This was far removed from what I ever saw in the chaste fields of Boyerstown. From the chat of my more informed school mates, I knew I was not some unique creature but a perfect healthy young man as some of them loosened up their shirt collars. There was a story told about a farmer who had only one son and was very keen on him not being sent astray with girls thinking it would upset his working capabilities. He kept him away from all functions including school so that he would not see any girls. Hoping that he had suceeded, he decided to bring the boy for a drive through the town when he was fourteen years of age. The boy made no remarks about girls until he was nearing home, to the great joy of his father.

Just then out of the blue he said "Da what were them yokes we saw walking with boys in the town. "They were mummies," replied the father. The boy being up to date in all other respects to the father's amazement and disappointment replied "Daddy I want lots of mummies and I want them now!"

It was the bicycle riding, the trapeze and the lion tamer that I enjoyed most. I was delighted with the music that went with each act which was performed by a small numbered brass band. At that time there were roughly one hundred people employed as actors and labourers and about fifty animals to be cared for. Three pennies was the fee charged to see the zoo after the circus and it was well worth it. Following the circus which all at home had gone to, we tried our hand at the bicycle stunts, the tight rope walking, walking on stilts or spades which we used, walking on our hands and doing cartwheel turns. I'm afraid none of us would qualify as a circus actor. Da would watch our efforts at these acts with delight.

Seán was now more than a boy and had to take on a man's work. Although only fifteen years of age, he had to do the shopping for machinery parts in Dublin. He used the early morning bus and was always back for evening milktime. He went to auctions of machinery and sometimes made a purchase under Da's strick instructions. He went to night school to learn carpentry and iron work. For his enjoyment he joined the Young Farmer's Club, went to ploughing championships and field days. On his return home from these outings Da would ask for a detailed report of the goings-on he had seen, which were duly given.

Cars and lorries were now becomming more plentiful and lorrying cattle forty miles to the Dublin cattle market became a regular feature. This had the effect of greatly lowering the numbers of cattle at fairs, within a forty mile radius of Dublin. Similarly, round the country some town's fair would grow greatly in numbers which resulted in the closing down of five or six smaller fairs. In the coming years these towns would have their cattle salesyards just like "Ganleys'" at Prussia Street, Dublin. Store cattle, cows, calves and sheep were all auctioned in the same way. Fat cattle were sold in the same way but the bigger number of them were sent to the factories by the farmers themselves. These cattle sales seem to be the best chance of getting the top price but if I had the running of a cattle mart, I would send the buyers that congregate around the entry gate of the ring, into the seating area provided for sellers and buyers alike.

As the Navan fair became less and less attractive Da decided to lorry his cattle to the Dublin mart. Seán would go up with the lorry man, Tony Newman, who lived only a couple of miles from our house. There was no charge for this lift but there was a reasonable fee of 7s6d for each cattle head and 4s0d for each ewe or lamb head. Our fat cattle and sheep were put into "John Connell's" stand and store cattle to "Ganleys'" sale ring. A few tanglers survived this big change but about 90% became redundant. My first visit to the Dublin Market was a few years later. Seán brought up a few barren fat ewes and as it was during the Easter holidays I went with him. We had tea and sandwiches in the bar of the City Arms Hotel, Prussia Street. I was amazed at the good working of the drover's collie dogs and the great control they had over them. About one quarter of these dogs were crossbreeds of every discription, that worked just as well as the pure-bred cattle and sheep dogs. An Irish coffee was a great favourite of the cattle men in that same hotel. A shoe-shine boy stood at the ready beside the hotel and got plenty of customers. He was the first and only one I ever saw.

That day Seán was surprised to get £14 for each ewe. This price was equal to quarter the butcher's price of a fat heifer at that time. A farmer today would want to get £250 for a similar ewe to equal that price. I think that market was around the year 1948. That price was only to last for a couple of months that year and was on a par with the eggs that sold at ten shillings near Christmas about the same time, or the wool that fetched £1 per lb. during one of the war years.

As we were now getting bigger and stronger our work on the farm became more robust-like. During our holidays we had to cock hay and head them on our own steam. No longer could I lie down on my back on the wind-rows and for a long time watch the sea-gulls gliding in the blue skies ever so high above me and squeaking out of them at the same time. We had to fork the hay brought into the hay barn. At harvest time we stacked the stucks after a week's drying. We gave a hand at beet pulling and crowning the tops off them. We pulled the turnips and mangolds as well, mostly on Saturdays. At threshing at home and with the neighbours we had to cut the sheaves and keep the chaff pulled from the bottom of the mill.

Christmasses were very happy occasions for all of us then. I have very happy memories of our carol singing in the cow shed during milking before Christmas. As we were all in the choir this was a good practice for us. Seán would start the hymn in question and I and Micheál would join in. Ma would call in to bring in the house milk and had no hesitation in joining in the singing as she would attempt a little bit of conducting as well. The *Adeste Fidelas, Angels we Have Heard on High,* and *Silent Night* were the hymns in question. We performed in firsts, seconds and thirds at the *Venitaes* and the *Glorias.*

An open doorway to the north of the shed would expose a starry, frosty sky and an odd robin would light on the cow's manger to pick up any grains of crushed corn the cows might have left behind. Once our neighbour, Seán Curry, came into the cow shed and said "Is this where all the beautiful noise is coming from? I heard it a full field away," as he caught us barefaced! There was no shame shown by us that time as it was probably a common act then. These memories of almost fifty years ago are as clear as crystal in my head today. I wish they were with us again!

We all watched Maggie's growing up with great interest. We received a good education in child rearing. Nappies were a simple two foot square of linen cloth that were folded diagonally to form a right angled triangle. The child was put sitting on it, the right angled corner was brought between the legs, the two forty five degree angled corners were brought round the back and all three corners were joined together at the front by a large four-inch safety pin, close to the belly button. These nappies might not be as streamlined as the more modern spongy ones but the signal for change came much sooner and the child hadn't to carry the full 12-7 for any time longer than necessary. Modern day nappies make all babies look like the babies of spacemen's wives.

I have memories of our farmhand bringing Maggie for a short walk after his dinner and he humming a little tune to her. We watched her first creeping, her first standing and her first few steps. Her first standing was in a field as she pulled herself up with the help of a bunch of timothy grasses. Walking was soon followed and all the falls that go along with it. She had a great love for cats and I once saw her walking in a field with five cats after her. Unlike the rest of us, she had no other child to play with. I have recollections of her making necklaces out of daisies and making a small shop in which she had delf, dolls, flowers, potatoes, etc. She started school in 1945 and had Áine to accompany her for her first year. That same year Máire started school in St. Martha's Agricultural College, Sion, Navan. Ma had to collect Maggie at two o'clock from her school for the entire second year. Our old Morris Cowley car had engine trouble and Da thought it was not now worth repairing.

During our young Summer days we were aware of the dangers of bee and wasp stings. I would say it is true that we all got a jab or two in our time. Finding a bee's nest in a meadow was quite common but extracting the honeycombs from it called for great skill. I now think that we could have smoked them out because during my hardware years after, I sold bee smokers. Our way at that time was to thwart the bees with the grain of a fork and then a swift run was executed. Two or three bees might try to attack you so you had to ward them off with fierce hand swinging. When the nest seemed quiet again a repeat performance was enacted and so on till all the bees had deserted the nest. The honey that was extracted fresh from the nest seemed to be better flavoured than the jarred honey we got in the supermarkets. The wasp came much later in the year and it was in the month of October that one had to be careful of them. Ma used jam jars with nail-holed caps in the kitchen window, both inside and outside, to catch wasps. It was a very effective way of keeping them at bay.

Da had an aunt, Séamus Boccán's mother, a school teacher and I think there was a good bit of it in Da as well. He showed us, that side of him, in our young years and I saw him teach Maggie her sums before her school days. He was anxious that I do well in my scholarship exam so he took to teaching me Irish history which was my weakest subject. All I remember in dates now is 1014 and 1690, the year of the battle of the river I did my swimming in! In the other subjects I was a wee bit ahead of Da's knowledge. History should be read as a novel in post school years. The *Tuatha Dé Danann* and *Fir Bolgs* are not much to the young men at Dublin and Shannon airports on their way to the USA and continental Europe!

It is the history of borders and man's greed to increase his boundries that are the cause of all wars. The bully countries that expanded their boundries are all finding a backfire reaction. Thus we have the troubles in Northern Ireland. How much money did the Falklands war cost England a few years back? Hitler tried to rule all Europe but met his waterloo. Russia swallowed up a lot of weak countries and see the trouble they are in today at the start of 1990! South Africa, who now own four fifths of the wealth of that country, although only one fifth of the population, will some day soon be sorry for their bullying attitude. God divided up the land of the earth by oceans, seas, rivers, lakes, deserts and mountain ranges. These God-made boundaries had a big purpose in making life easier and more pleasant to man. Not alone is man fighting over land boundaries but now they are fighting over imaginary boundaries! No matter what bullying and wars go on we are all umbrellaed by the same sky, energised by the same sun and have a common burial ground - mother earth.

The only good I learned out of Irish history was taught to me by head teacher, Brother Bernard. He told us that a people called the *Fianna* who were a type of *Tarzan* in the stone age, had three great commandments that they never broke. These were in Irish: *Glaine ar gcroí, neart ar ngeag, is beart de réir ar mbriatha*r. In English they read: *A clean heart, strength in our muscles and action according to our word.* He instilled this in us and told us that if we followed these three commands we were destined to be very successful in life. Looking back on the world as I see it today his words of wisdom were 100% correct. That same Brother Bernard was a great violin player. He made some very fancy faces when tucking the machine under his chin. This brought fits of laughter from a few lads at the back of the class. He must have understood his compulsory clownish act, as he never punished anyone over the laughter. All he would say is "Leave them alone Brother, don't look up Brother!" in a very low, deep tone of voice. That poor man was approaching eighty years of age. It is no wonder that the boys could cod him as they read their *Beanos, Hot Spurs, Dandys* and *Supermans* to their heart's content. Da had warned us never to buy that "thrash" as it was a waste of money and also encouraged bad spelling. We took his advice and never bought any of them. We did read *Curley Wee and Goosey Goose, Mutt and Jeff* and *Little Sport.*

I liked the Irish language and had no trouble getting the silver fáinne when examined by a huge big man by the name of Peadar

O'Ceallaigh. I did well at the comhrá during the Feis Na Midhe competitions held in Park Tailteann, Navan. It was under Brother Bernard's conducting that we won the competition for the two best Irish songs in County Meath, three years in a row.

Three or four times a year Da would pay a visit to the attic. Our only means of ascent was up a loft ladder brought in from the barn. Two or three of us would follow him as we enjoyed this expedition into the unknown. Important war news, like D-day, Hitler's march into Russia, the battle of the River Plate, the bombings of Belfast and Dublin, etc, etc, were rolled into a tidy bundle and tied with twine. A large number of newspapers concerning World War I were also neatly left aside in the attic. Three brides' trunks all lined in beautiful silk cloth found their rest there also. One was Ma's, another was Da's mother's and the third was Da's grandmother's. All the bride's clothing and other valuables were carried in these lovely boxes with their very elaborate lid fasteners, to their final resting place. They were now used for housing the rolls of antique newspapers, receipts for new machinery bought, receipts for the groceries, spirits, porter, snuff, tobacco and clay pipes bought for my grandmother's and great-grandmothers wakes. There were about half a dozen very old cameras there also.

There were about ten pairs of assorted leather laced leggings that were worn with boots up to about forty-five years ago. I just about remember two gentlemen cattle dealers that wore that "foot outfit". The older generation than the one that I grew up with only wore wellingtons when going through wet fields or cleaning passways and mucky farmyards. They maintained that they were unhealthy and also bad for the eyesight. The wellingtons were also dear and scarce in my young days. They were called "Russian boots" and "top boots" also.

Odd bits of the car and tractor that needed to be kept dry were stored in the attic also. Dynamos, magnetos, old car wipers and horns comprised most of these. The old gramophone found its way to the attic also. Receipts for farm buildings and other capital expenditure were carefully left one side. Among old letters of interest there was one sent to Ma from a Rev. Mother in India sympathising with her on the death of her sister, Margaret, who succumbed to malaria in her late twenties. An old type of weighing scales and a set of pewter drinking measures added to the variety that was stored in the attic.

One day in my life that I forgot to mention was a day everyone faces sooner or later and that day is the day I saw the first corpse. I was about seven years old when Mr William Reilly, the man that the parish priest used send us with the message that he would be attending him the following morning, had died. An old lady had crossed a good few fields and came in to Da to get directions to the dead man's house. Da had no hesitation in sending me to show her the way. This lady was a sister-in-law and would be close on eighty years of age. She was delighted to get such a guidance and rewarded me with 2s6d or what we called a half-crown.

I had no intention of going into the house but was invited to see the corpse and say a little prayer for him, by the dead man's aging wife. There was a lot of men and women in the kitchen and plenty of drink being passed around. I got a large bottle of lemonade and a couple of lovely currant buns. I was then brought up to the room and on seeing the corpse I got a bit of a fright but tried not to show it. My first thoughts were would Ma, Da, all my brothers and sisters come to this state? I gave the man a kiss on the forehead and got another shock as I did not expect it to be so cold. He had a crucifix and rosary beeds entwined in his joined fingers as I kneeled down to pray for him. I think I said an Act of Contrition for myself first! I remember that day just as plain as the day the Pope came to Ireland, the day John F. Kennedy was assassinated or the day De Valera was buried.

I heard a good yarn once about two men that had a lot of drink taken and took a shortcut home with a graveyard crossing. The night was dark and the man carrying the flash-lamp was so slow that the other man went on ahead of him. After a little while the lamp-man heard a lot of shouting and headed in that direction. On coming to the spot he shone the lamp on a man in a grave and he shouting "Pull me up quickly, I'm famished with the cold!" "Why wouldn't you be cold", was the reply, "lie down again and I will cover you up and stay quiet this time and you will be all right," as he got hold of one of the shovels that was there!

Da played the game of Stocks and Shares. He studied the goings on in the financial news on each day's paper. Cement, Carrolls and national loans were his main interests. Long distance car drivers were a rarity in the 1940's. Da's furthest drive was to Ard na Crusha. He went there to see the start of the Shannon electricity scheme. He brought us all to see the Drogheda cement factory. He took a great deal of interest in the overhead container wagons as they went their lazy way to the factory from the quarries and vice versa. All Stocks and Shares documents, Bank deposit receipts, drivers' licences, taxes, insurances, other business documents, our annually taken photos, all our examination reports, Confirmation and exam certificates, our birth certs, valuable brooches, a gold watch, a few sovereigns and half sovereigns, and the camera and writing pad were kept in a Victorian writing desk that was locked by a brass key that Da kept in a special pocket in his waistcoat.

When this writing desk was opened we knew there was some important business to be transacted. Usually I would be sent to the bank the following day to do some business for him. Many is the half crown I got off the bank manager who was a grand old man, who had a chat with all his customers and was always carrying a smile. Bringing in a deposit receipt and bringing back cash or cashing a cheque for farm produce were mostly the transactions I performed.

Da had no belief in using a cheque book but he always kept a ledger and kept it up to date. All farm transactions, hire work, our school fees, etc, etc were recorded the day they happened. The lower part of that writing desk had a large area for holding books. There were about one hundred motorbicycle journals there with all up to date news on the various models, and news of the racing results throughout the world. Stanley Woods was Da's favourite man of the motorbike. He had seen him in action in the "Skerries 100" a few times. He loved the motorbike but never told us so, knowing the danger of it if not properly handled. Seán had read the books on motorbikes and later took to them like a duck to water. He helped out a couple of neighbours when they had a major repair to do.

From 1945 on a lot of our spare time was spent at the local crossroads. We took part in the pitch and toss school and played road handball while the older folk sat on a bank and had a good chat. The handball was played in a rectangle, forty yards by six yards. A centre line left twenty by six yards for each team to defend. The ideal number per square was four. One man played near the back line, another in the centre and two guarded the front line area. A penny was tossed and the winning captain had the choice of hands or square. Just like the handball played in an alley, a winning stroke counted to the server of the ball. A losing stroke to the serving team was a hand out. Each team had four hands in a row until they lost four rallies. A front line man tossed up the ball to the back line man in the opposing square. The ball had then to be struck into the other square by the back line man. This hitting of the ball from square to square had to be done after one ball hop or on the volley. The rally finished when the ball went out of bounds or one of the team due to return the ball failed to do so.

Handball games finished when one side reached twenty-one and the teams changed at half time. It was for all purposes the same as tennis played within the perimeter lines only, without a net, four per square instead of two and of course the hands instead of a racket. Four per square was the ideal number but it was still enjoyed with two or three per square. Traffic did not bother us much in the forties but I can't see that game being played at many crossroads in the nineties. There were six crossroads at which this handball was played and they were all in or centred around the parish of Boyerstown.

The teams were named thus, Clarkes' Cross, Lawlesses' Cross, Bohermeen Cross, Greetiagh Cross, Ardbraccan Cross and Knockumber Cross. The Catholic Curate of Bohermeen parish put up a lovely cup that he won at a coursing, for the best team out of the six. This was an annual event and each team had to play the other five teams, with two points for each win. A win was the best of three games, each game to the first team to reach twenty-one rallies. The two teams with the highest points after their five games, played in the final for the best of five games. For the final there would be about one hundred and fifty spectators. That night the cup would be filled several times and a good bit of music played in the chosen pub. The cup won was surrendered every year to be played for the following year. I don't know if this game was played apart from these six teams, nor do I know when this game started.

The pitch and toss was a much less energy-sapping game than the handball. Any number from four to twelve pitched two pennies to a fixed marker usually a stone. Their nearest penny was left, the other being picked up. The person first to toss was he who was nearest the stone. At that time in the 1940's he would put down 2s6d on the road and all others subscribed until they had another 2s6d down on the road also. All the pennies that were pitched, were tossed two at a time from a pocket comb. They had to be faced two harps up on the comb before the toss. The tosser won all the pennies that he "headed" plus the 5s0d on the road if he headed more pennies, than he harped. Otherwise he had to give the 5s0d to be divided among the subscribers to his first 2s6d bet. Then all the harped pennies went to the next tosser, i.e. he who was second nearest the stone. This was repeated until all the tossed pennies were won. That was that, so another bout of pitching started.

The handball was a gambling game also, but it was played for small money. The young lads that left school at fourteen years of age had plenty of money for these games and were the envy of the boys that stayed on at school to do their Leaving. We were always under strict orders from Da to be home from the cross before 11p.m. unless we got permission for a tournament or a challenge with a team from another crossroads.

CHAPTER VI

A great sigh of relief was breathed by all when World War II ended with the horific bombings of Hiroshima and Nagasaki. It took a few months for things to reach pre-war status again. For us school goers it was grand to see oranges, bananas, dates and figs in the fruit shops again. The best change of all was probaby the lovely white loaf in the bakeries. Everyone was fed up with the greyish loaf that was in no way appetitising. Our old pre-war friend Barney Kane came again on the horse and cart with a bag of white flour and another of wheatenmeal. He worked for Lawlor's Bakery, Trimgate Street, Navan from the time he left school and was now approaching the eightith year of his life. He got 1s1d which would buy him two bottles of stout from Da and a drop of tea from Ma to help him on his journey.

The first four loaves Ma brought home did not last long in our house as there were nine of us to be fed. Tea and sugar gradually increased in supply, doing away with the coarse tasting ground coffee and saccharine tablets. Tobacco and cigarettes were once again put on the displaying shelves and extra cars began to trickle onto the roads. New bicycles and all their spare parts were put into the shop windows again, and the drapery and hardware shops had a much better variety of goods to display. Dry and wet batteries for radios and lighting lamps were now in full supply and the humble match that often had to be split up the middle, likewise.

Our maternal granny who was eighty-four years of age had suffered a couple of mild heart attacks during the war years. She lived with my Aunt Rose and Uncle Jack. We as youngsters had visited them on several occasions especially when granny was sick. They were comfortable farmers and took life in a very relaxed style. There was always a good supply of eating and cooking apples there in the Autumn and granny never failed to open up her purse as we bid goodbye to her. In the Spring of 1946, I met Uncle Jack in Navan and he told me that he was on his way out to tell Ma that granny got a severe heart attack. On my telling of this news to Ma, she rushed over on her bicycle to see her and was told by the doctor that she would never recover from that stroke. She lived for five weeks as her heart got weaker and weaker.

Well I remember Da, Seán and Séamus Boccán going to the 2p.m. funeral on Séamus's pony and trap. Da had a new suit and hat for the occasion and I never saw him looking better. Even though we were three miles from Navan, we heard the funeral bell toll on St. Mary's lovely church. Ma with watery eyes told us, "That is the last of your poor old granny!" Aunt Rose took the death very bad so Ma took her in for a few weeks. Da then suggested that she would be better off in her own place looking after Uncle Jack as it would divert her mind from the death. Ma agreed and in a short time Rose was over on a Sunday to visit us and she in the best of form. The diversion of her mind from the "natural happening" cured her.

That same Spring I was busy studying for the County Council scholarship. It was held the second week after Easter so I had to study during the holidays right up to exam time. Our learning knowledge for this exam was sufficent to get Intermediate honours in geography, English, Irish, arithmetic, algebra and geometry. The exam being completed, I got three weeks belated holidays. Da was delighted with this, as the sowing season was just started. All I had to do was sit on the top of the sower and tip a hand gear lever in and out of gear at each of the headlands while Seán drove the tractor. I was well rewarded for my three week's work which just suficed to finish the sowing. It never rained a drop and up to one hundred acres were sown.

Summer holidays were not far away and Páraic was busy getting ready for his first cut at the Inter Cert exam. The results of my exam came in June and as I came twelfth out of forty-six, no scholarship was awarded to me. There were six scholarships awarded, three for town boys and three for country boys. The first three places were always lads from the town so the first three country boys after third place got the remaining three scholarships irrespective of how many town lads come before them, i.e. a country lad in fortieth place could qualify. My greatest achievement in any exam was to come first in Algebra out of the forty-six runners in that County Council scholarship. I was still young enough to do a repeat of that exam in the Spring of 1947.

The late Spring and Summer of 1946 was the wetest that Da had ever seen. I remember all the trouble we had with weeds in the alleys of the tillage drills. It was impossible to get them dry enough to grub them. Weeds that we had pulled and left down in the alleys were starting to grow again after a week's time. The hay making was another nightmare. Most of the meadows had to be rushed into small cocks or "lap-cocks" as they call them in the west, as oncoming rains did not allow enough time to cure the hay for large cocks. These small cocks had to be shaken out and turned with a watchful eye kept on the sky all the time. After about six weeks hard work all the hay was made in fair condition.

With the modern machinery of the 1990's and good weather five days would do the same amount of hay making. The old peoples' saying about corn crops, "Easy to get in, hard to get out" was very true in 1946. The harvest was that hard to save that the Government had to call on the army and volunteers from factories and business premises. I saw the entire staff of Arnotts of Dublin, the famous drapers, working on a neighbour's farm. They were very good workers when shown what to do and how to do it. Sandwiches were prepared in the County Council offices and collected by the voluntary workers who were dispatched to the various farms from there. The ladies came out in force to add a bit of spice to the job. There were some good jokes told about that 1946 harvest. The tractors and binders were able to do about three

which we knew as Lawlesses' Hall with three of these Aladdin yard lamps hanging from the ceiling of the hall. The Aladdin table lamps were on the same working principle but were very well got up and very decorative. These lamps are all antiques now, as are the lovely brass wick lamps. Tilly and Aladin had lovely style heaters that for all purposes looked like the gas heaters of the present time.

The Spring of 1947 was one of great severity with both snow and frost. From the middle of January to St Patrick's day there was no let up. There was frozen snow on the roads of the county for the whole of that eight weeks. Just as the roads were about to clear up, a fresh fall of snow would come and then more hard frost. I got it hard riding the bicycle home from night school. The wind was all the time coming from the north-east. That reminds me of a film I saw, *When the north wind blows*. There was a lovely scene in that film of a tired hungry man brushing back a pack of hungrier wolves with a coat as the north wind blew. There was another scene in that same film of that man trying to catch some mouse-like animal in a trap to fill a hole in his tummy.

St Patrick's day in that Spring of 1947 was cold and it snowed for most of the day. The most deafening silence I ever experienced was in the middle of our biggest field during a heavy snowfall. There was no sound of tractor, car, lorry or animal and no wind either. The large flakes came down in their millions, each one having a certain amount of weight as well as its own unique shape. Contrary to all expectations, there was not the one-thousanth of a decibel of noise to be heard. This experience even outclassed the stopping of a tractor engine after a long day's ploughing and it on full throttle. The weather then took a complete change and all frost and snow disappeared overnight.

That Easter I repeated my scholarship exam but again finished down the field as regards winning one. The Spring work ran very late and I remember sowing oats in the first week of May. A great addition to our old Fordson tractor that year was the putting on of a pair of new back wheels with pneumatic tyres and tubes. The tyres were *Goodyear* and measured eleven by twenty-eight. The front ones remained solid rubber. Seán brought me on my first bus trip to an auction in Kells to look at a second-hand binder, as our *Woods* machine was suffering from fatigue, and breakages were becoming all too common. The binder in question was also a *Woods* model and was in worse condition than our old one. We had lemonade and sandwiches made from cream crackers and cheese. I think that was the nicest snack I had in my whole lifetime.

Da was left with no option but to buy a new machine. A six foot *Deering* was his choice. He and Seán went to the railway station to bring home that lovely new machine that was made in Canada. At the station, alongside our machine was another new binder with the trade name of *McCormack*. On inquiring who owned that machine it transpired that our next door neighbour Páraic Devine bought it. Da and Seán had a couple of drinks in McArdles, Railway Street, Navan to celebrate the purchase. The following Sunday after dinner, Da and I walked to the head of our laneway and into Mr Devine's yard to have a good look at his binder and to compare the two machines.

That grand old lady, Mrs Devine, came out with an orange and two apples to me. The only differance in the two machines was the reel drive. Ours was a bevelled cogs and shaft drive while the *McCormack* was a chain drive. That Autumn we reaped one hundred and eighty-five Irish acres at two pounds per acre and had a trouble-free harvest. The knotter was almost perfect and about three loose sheafs per acre was its biggest mistake provided the twine did not run out. There were over eighty grease nipples on the binder and greasing these was a must, first thing every morning or last thing at night if fog happened to come down early. Da would not cut the corn unless it was perfectly dry as it would delay hand stacking and drawing home to the hay barn.

Mission time in these days took place every three years in each parish for a duration of two weeks. Every man, woman and child over the age of six attended this great function, which the old people maintained brought great luck to a parish. Soul searching sermons, the rosary and benediction at eight o'clock each evening and Mass followed by a quiet sermon at seven o'clock in the morning were the order of the day. Anyone who did not attend was regarded as a castaway, for even the toughest of men humbled themselves to attend the ceremonies. In these days the men had their own side of a church and the women likewise with the middle row for the married couples and children.

There was always a sermon on hell given early-on at these missions that left people ridged with fear and drove them to confessions with the shame of their sins dampened down. After the mission the people of that parish showed more respect for each other and they were as happy as the people walking the footpaths of a town on a good Summer's day. People from outside parishes attended missions in their neighbouring parish. The mission wheel has done a full circle, for instead of the vast majority of the parish criticizing the absentees, it is the absentees that are in the majority and it is they that criticize those people that attend a mission!

Seán always attended Navan mission as well as his own in Boyerstown. Coming home from an evening mission he collided with an elderly man on a bicycle and as a result that man broke his leg. Da was in very bad form for a few days but as the injured man only wanted his hospital fees and a few hundred pounds compensation, he soon got over the mishap. That same man had worked on our farm before I was born and his wife had worked for Ma in the house so there were no ill feelings over the whole affair. That couple had worked very hard to rear a big family and they were always in good humour.

Máire finished her education in St Martha's Agricultural College in the Summer of 1947. Eggs in the Spring of that year as well as for four weeks at the end of 1946, were fetching 10/- per dozen. That money would buy eight pints of stout or one hundred-and-twenty cigarettes at the time. That was the equivalent of a dozen of eggs making £11.50 in 1990. Da decided to build a new henhouse with a capacity big enough for one hundred laying hens. This shed was built by Seán under the supervision of Da. It took three months to complete the job as the routine farm work had to be kept up-to-date. When it was completed, a wooden frame with fifty nesting pigeon holes was secured to one of the inner walls. Roosts were nailed to the roof rafters and the two large windows were fitted in to complete the work. Ma went to an auction and purchased a hoover and incubator both in excellent condition. One hundred birded eggs were set in the incubator. Máire looked after this end of the farming, sprinkling water on the eggs and turning them every twenty-four hours. After twenty-one days, ninty-six good healty chickens burst forth from their shells. The females were kept for egg production and the cockerels fattened for table use. The project paid well for about five years until mass production raised its greedy head, so the business was toned down as the bottem fell out of the egg prices.

CHAPTER VII

On the 3rd of September 1947, my fourteenth birthday, I started my secondary education in St Patrick's Classical School, Navan. That same day the Inter Cert results were given and Páraic had passed his exam with honours. My class, i.e. first year, were arranged in their seats in alphabetical order and the textbooks were given out to complete the first half day. We were allowed home then with the second half day to ourselves. During the first few weeks each member of my class had to be ducked under a tap of cold running water by older students. That was an old custom and it was strictly adhered to. Some pupils rebelled fiercely against it only to be given a more thorough ducking!

As there were only about eighty students on the roll, forty from the town and the other forty from the country, everyone knew everyone else enough to form a big happy family. A rope, a leather strap, a swing of an open hand on the face and the pulling of the locks of hair directly upwards which made the eyes run watery, were the main forms of punishment. If you were unlucky enough, or lucky enough depending on the attitude of your parents, to bump into the President when any time one minute or more late, you were sent home. The punishment we got was taken in good heart and the devil a bit of harm it did us. All five priests that taught us were gearing us up for the world and had their full hearts thrown into this end. My thinking about education is that there is no substitute for fifty years of life even though when we were young we could not see eye to eye with our parents.

I never liked English and found learning poetry off by heart a great waste of time. It is grand to read a book of poetry in after-school life. I had no o'clock for Shakespeare and if he 'eard half the curses bestowed on him by students trying to learn some of his more notable lines off by heart, he would not be too prayed!

146

All I know of four of his plays that I learned is that McDuff was a capital mugger! Touchstone would have got a good job with Duffys' circus if born in the early twentieth century and that Rosalind and Cecelia were two good things!

A tennis court and a handball alley were our chief source of sport in St Pats. If we were not involved in these sports or smoking a cigarette in the toilets we walked round the perimeter walls of the school chatting to each other. We had no green field to engage in some of the more robust games but some of the rugby enthusiasts played a crude game with a tennis shoe in the open grounds that was surfaced with chippings. The numbers being enrolled each year now were increasing by fifty per cent. In the Spring of 1948 a new science hall and large classroom were built to relieve pressure for space. I joined the first science class there in the Autumn of '48. I had to stay back in the evenings and do my home exercises from 3.30p.m. to 5.00p.m. when my science class started. That class finished at 7.30p.m. when I headed home straight after to get my dinner and finish my home study. That science class took place two nights a week, Tuesday and Friday. We had school for a half day on Saturdays in those years.

1948 was the 150th anniversary of the 1798 uprising and St Pats put on a drill display to the music of the Number One Army Band. That pagent was held in Park Tailteann every night for a week. The parallel bars, horse and spring board, the treble bicycle wheels and the clubs had to be pushed each night from the school to Park Tailteann in a car trailer and back again after the drill display was finished. The only other time we gave a drill display was at the annual prize-giving day.

In connection with that anniversary of '98 a big day was fixed for the hill of Tara in the month of June. Seán got his directions from Da so we, the four boys, set off on bicycles on a lovely sunny Sunday after an early dinner, as three o'clock was the arrival time of Eamonn De Valera. We went by Robinstown and Bective, returning home by the main Dublin/Navan road. The day being ideal for this outing, a crowd of twenty five thousand people went through the turn stiles. De Valera made a half-hour speech and got a standing ovation from all present. He was a class of a hero that time, after steering us safely through World War Number Two.

There were guide men there to explain the mounds and hollows of that famous hill. The only thing we were interested in was the lovely view of the countryside around us. On a clear day, as it was, it is possible to see eleven different counties from the peak of the hill. We noted the statue of St Patrick with it's broken arm. We had been told that two men who were responsible for that breakage came to a tragic end. One of them was torn asunder on his return home by his own dogs. The other man is said to have jumped off Nelson's Pillar the following day. Later on, the fingers of the second hand were broken off and it is alleged that as a result a treble drowning tragedy resulted. The Tormeys who own that hill should know all about these allegations. St Patrick's other hill, the Hill of Slane, is quite visible from Tara. The only ruin that impressed me on Tara was the size of the Banqueting Hall. It would be great if we could buy a video of one of the outings that was held there fifteen hundred years ago!

One morning I was ten minutes late for school and ran into the President. One word came from his mouth - "Home". I was afraid to go home and tell Da so I went on a trip to see the caves of Newgrange as I had the whole day to get there and back, a total distance of about twenty-six miles. The huge stones around the entrance with their motifs, that I know nothing about, impressed me. These huge stones are supposed to come from Wicklow, by what means I don't know. I have been assured that the ruins date back at least two thousand years before Christ! The real mystery of Newgrange is the little beam of daylight that shows up in the main chamber on the 21st day of December and on that day only. The beam has to travel about thirty yards with projecting stones all along the passageway into that chamber. The engineers, how they managed that great feat - and remember that the shrinking of the soil and stones had to be allowed for as well.

Of all the monuments I saw, Bective Abbey is the one that most impressed me. The stone work of the arched hallways and the design of one of its rooms' ceiling are well worth seeing. I was never too fond of history so my lack of real interest in these monuments. The stone work of church steeples and round towers impresses me greatly. In County Meath the round tower in Donaghmore, just a few miles outside Navan, and the steeple of St Patrick's Church, Trim, are a perfect example of these. It is the perfect tappering of these buildings as they go up that brought out the best in their builders.

I and Micheál spent one lovely, fine day on a tour of Trim. Having got directions from Da and £1 each, off we went on our bicycles. Da had told us the places of note to visit. St John's Castle that dates back to the twelfth century, the Wellington monument that must feel a little wobbly at the knees in present day history, the Echo Gate, St Patrick's Church and Brogans' Hotel were the places pin-pointed to us. There is as you see plenty of history attached to this very ancient town. The Echo Gate is directly across the Boyne River from St John's Castle. Standing at that gate your voice throws back a perfect echo from the castle ruins. The meal of mixed grill we got in Brogans' Hotel cost 3s6d each. That day was one of the most enjoyable in my life and although its over forty years ago, it is as fresh in my mind as the day it happened.

Some bicycles that time had a fixed wheel drive which meant that you had to keep pedalling when the bicycle was in motion. I had one of these for a while and never liked it. On my way to school one morning while carrying an empty two-gallon can on the handlebar and going down a steep hill, my knee came up to the bottom of the can. Not having the free-wheel, the handlebars gave a sudden turn to the right as it was the left hand handlebar that the can was on, and I was thrown clear over the handlebars and down in the middle of the road. I had to leave the battered bike into a neighbouring house, the woman of which gave me a few plasters to cover my wounds. I got a lift and went to school a sore man. I got another fall, similar to that one, going down the very same hill. The loose stay of the back mudguard came in contact with the tyre. This caused the tyre and tube to burst and it brought the circumferance of the wheel into the centre axle. Again I was thrown forward across the handlebars.

Most evenings after school, I had the job of bringing home the meat and daily newspaper. My reward was 2d which used to get me two cigarettes in Josie Kinsella's shop which was very near the school. She sold minerals, ice cream, sweets and buns and the boys from St Pat's were her main support. A teacher once barred us from going into that shop because of our smoking there. A visit by Josie to the college Presideent soon reversed that decision. I think most schools in the country have there own shebeens to have a smoke, drink and a chat about the strange happenings of that day.

On one evening every three weeks as the windcharger was out of commission, I had the tedious job of bringing home the charged-up wet battery of the radio. As this battery contained acid, I had to be very careful that it did not fall or come in contact with my clothes. One bad habit Da got us into was backing horses. He would do bookie and take any bet from half a shilling up. I got interested in looking up the runners and the results the following day. I noticed that the two Smiths, Doug and Elf, were getting a lot of good priced winners and placed horses. In the 1940's the stay-at-home bookies paid quarter the starting price for a placed horse. You could also do a five pence bet and credit bets of that five pence win if you so desired. There were shrewd backers that time who played this credit game and from a £1 start they often brought their winnings to three figures. Gordan Richards was the champion flat jockey that time. Other jockeys I took a fancy to were W. H. Carr, Rickeby, Elliot and Y. St. Martin, the French jockey.

Navan races returned shortly after the war and as it was only five miles from home, Da would give us a few shillings and let us go if it was a Saturday meeting. His advice to us was to back each way on the tote as it paid much better than the bookies. I always managed to get free entry through a hole in the galvanize along the road. The best Irish jockeys at that time were Martin Maloney, Frankie Carroll, R .B. Brabazon, Jimmy Eddery the father of Pat and Paul, H. Holmes, Kinnane, Pat Taaffee and Toss Taaffee. One horse I remember well was *Bright Cherry* and I won money by backing her a few times. She was a greyish animal and ran in long distance races. Being a front runner all her wins were from trap to winning post. After four furlongs she would be up to twenty lengths ahead of her nearest rival. I backed her about eight times and I think she won all but two races. This mare being the mother of the mighty *Arkle* was probably more famous after her racing period than during it. It was at Navan races that *Arkle* won his first race at a price of 20/1.

I loved the day out at a race meeting and always went to the Grand National meeting at Fairyhouse. I biked it there one year, a return distance of forty miles. That was the year that *Fortria* won the Grand National. It was at Fairyhouse I saw the three-card man and his co-partners at work. I saw there too the thimble riggers and the tricksters selling winning horse numbers for the six races. Da had us strictly warned to avoid all these gimmicks and how some men had been beaten up fighting for their rights from these men.

I suppose 99% of the people of Ireland have at least a few bets during there lifetime, 50% will have a few bets in the year, about 20% will have a few bets every week and about 5% bet every day. There is no teaching in schools as regards betting and the tote which every punter should know. I always check my winners and have been underpaid and overpaid on several occasions. The use of a calculator does not mean that the office clerk can't make an error. The tote pays out all the money taken in after deducting tax and the wage that goes to pay the tote operators. The least number of tickets put on a horse the higher the winnings on that horse. Example, if there are two thousand winning tickets taken out on all the horses in one race except for one ticket on no. 6 horse and that horse won, the lucky winner would draw two thousand pounds if all the tickets were one pound shares, less the tax money and the one sixth of the wage payout for a day of six races.

The place bets are calculated in a like manner. A bookie can leave a meeting with ten thousand pounds taken in and not one penny taken out of that. Lads often came to me with say nine horses written down from nine different races and ask me how many cross doubles in nine horses. Others will want to know how many x trebles in nine horses and yet others, how many accumulators in nine horses. There is a simple formula for calculating the answer. I will work out the three different answers for nine horses but the same method is used no matter what number of horses is used.

The number of doubles in $9 = \dfrac{9 \times 8}{1 \times 2} = 36$

The number of trebles in $9 = \dfrac{9 \times 8 \times 7}{1 \times 2 \times 3} = 84$

The number of four horse accumulators
$= \dfrac{9 \times 8 \times 7 \times 6}{1 \times 2 \times 3 \times 4} = 126$

The number of five horse accumulators
$= \dfrac{9 \times 8 \times 7 \times 6 \times 5}{1 \times 2 \times 3 \times 4 \times 5} = 126$

A YANKEE = doubles + trebles + accumulators in four horses which $= 6 + 4 + 1 = 11$. Thus a £1 yankee will cost you £11 plus the tax. The lotto can be worked out in a similar way. To get all six numbers right, the number of different possible ways it can be done is:

$$\dfrac{36 \times 35 \times 34 \times 33 \times 32 \times 31}{1 \times 2 \times 3 \times 4 \times 5 \times 6}$$

Answer = 7 x 34 x 33 x 8 x 31 = 1,947,792. (6 right nos.)

It has to be done almost two million ways to be certain of the right six numbers.

Five numbers right = $\dfrac{36 \times 35 \times 34 \times 33 \times 32}{1 \times 2 \times 3 \times 4 \times 5}$ = 376,992.

Four numbers right = $\dfrac{36 \times 35 \times 34 \times 33}{1 \times 2 \times 3 \times 4}$ = 58,905.

While I am on Maths, I might as well finish with the last one that might be of interest to you. In years gone by the gypsies had their own way of multiplying two numbers together. They could multiply by two and divide by two with their fingers to help them. Say a dealer bought seventeen horses at £37 each. They put their own way at working it out called "Gypsy Multiplication".

Divide one line by two	*First Way*	17	37
all the way down until		8	74
you reach number one.		4	148 = 629.
Ignore any 1 that is		2	296
left after dividing		1	592
an odd number.			
Multiply other number	*Second Way*	37	17
by two all the way		18	34
down until you are		9	68 = 629.
in line with number one.		4	136
		2	272
		1	544

Now cross off the numbers from the even numbers on the divisor line. Tot up the remaining numbers of the multiplication lines to give you your answer. You will get the same result irrespective of which number you choose to divide and multiply. A Fr Healy of Bohermeen parish showed me how to do that after a station in the house one morning twenty-six years ago. He told me that the computer is based on that principle.

To get back to the horses which I have trotted away from, I was always fond of a small bet on horses. Backing horses for small money is a pleasant hobby provided it does not interfere with your work or keep the food off the table. I backed two Aintree Grand National winners in my life, *Nickel Coin* in the late forties and

Nicholas Silver in the late fifties. I actually dreamed about *Nicholas Silver* passing the winning post the night before the race. I only got one genuine tip for a horse in my life. It was for a horse called *Gay Challenger* that won a flat race at an evening meeting in Navan. It came from the breeder of that horse, Patrick Clarke, who himself was born and reared in the famous Dunderry Stud, a few miles from Navan. His blacksmith, Thomas Markey, called "the Red" was at the races along with me and Mr Clarke told us straight to put all we had on that horse, that he would not be beaten. What we had left, which was not much, we did as told. The horse was one of the last with half a mile to go but to our delight he ran up a good eight lengths winner!

Dunderry had another couple of famous horses. Paul Larkin of Stonestown, Dunderry, bred *Right Track* that won great races in England. *The Maverick*, a great show jumper was bred by a Richard Healy, from Dunderry parish also. Mr Joseph Clarke, Dunderry Stud, bred the top price for a yearling at Goffs' Autumn Sales in the late fifties and his yearlings are always respected and fetch great prizes at that yearling sales.

My parish, Boyerstown, had an industry for a few months back in the early thirties. It employed two and the product shares were gilt edged in that it manufactured half-crowns! Eight of these made up £1 in the old money. One half-crown would buy at least two pints of stout or one glass of whiskey or thirty cigarettes. One of the two men was a blacksmith that engineered the project, the other was a farmer that financed it. Things were booming for a few months but they came to an abrupt end when, after a race meeting in Navan, they were arrested in the most posh hotel that evening, The Russell Arms Hotel. I don't know the end of that story but our parish priest at that time said that the Gardai put an end to the only little industry that was ever in the parish! That priest had a few of them that were put on the offering table during funerals, as the half-crown at that time was a very respectable offering. The half-crowns were a perfect duplicate of the true one but as the basic raw material was white metal, the jingle was not in them.

I heard a true story about that word "posh" that I have mentioned a few lines above. It was a word that had it's origin in the Panama canal. A much higher rate than the standard got a more privatised seat coming and going through the canal. These more wealthy passengers were allowed to sit "portside out" and "starboard home" which eliminated extreme heat from the sun. Thus the abbreviated word POSH was formed.

In the month of April, 1949, our cousin Séamus Boccán got married to a lady from Carberry, County Kildare, the place where the Boyne River rises. Ma, Seán and Máire were at the wedding. It was Seán and Máire's first appearance at a wedding which they looked forward to, and enjoyed very much. The couple stayed in the wedding reception hotel until the following morning, when they went on a tour of the south of Ireland. Late in the evening of the wedding day, the best man and my brother Seán went up to the honeymoon bedroom to make arrangements for a "Home Coming". Lads were telling them to make sure to give a good knock at the door, as you wouldn't know what might be going on! Séamus opened the door and asked them in to finish the rosary, which had only started! The reluctant starters knelt down on the floor without a whimper out of them. I was invited to the "Home Coming" which was my first big public entertainment. We had a great dance in the big barn, which was lit up with a tilley lantern. Some lad threw down oats from the loft to make the yellow clay floor danceable, saying the hens would eat it in the morning. Séamus Boccán, who never danced in his life, made an appearance, and gave his bride a dance as was customary. After the "Jolly Good Fellow" act, he bolted back to the parlour where there was a big game of "25" going on. The music for the dance was two accordions, one played by Matthew Rogers, the ex-Meath Senior Football player, whom I have already mentioned earlier on in this book. I had a few dances, the first with my Ma, who tried her best to get a bit of flexibility into me! There were lashings of drink, and a running buffet of tea and sandwiches. The outing finished at five in the morning, but the card game went on until 7a.m. Looking at the group of fifty-two that were there that night in 1949, there were thirty one of them dead in the spring of 1990. One pleasant memory of that night is of George Donoghue of Navan, singing Al Jolson's song *Mammy*, while standing on an anvil with a large bottle of stout in one hand! Séamus Boccán's wife was a fine woman, and he being not too robust a man, some of the lads said he could have got a handier bundle than that as he carried her across the threshhold! The card game went down so well with the people that played it that night, that it started a series of exchange card house parties that went on for a couple of years until the novelty of television took over.

Whist drives were all the go in the thirties, forties and up to the mid fifties. Prizes were good, so that drew a large crowd. There were always private games played before the whist, which always started up to one hour late. The same parties played immediately the whist was over, as the counting of the score cards took about one hour to sort out the winners. In country halls that had no caretaker, these games often went on till six o'clock in the morning, when the lads went home to change their clothes, get their breakfast and hop off to work. Winter was the time for these card games, and many is the time I went home on a crisp, frosty morning coming up to Christmas, as all the cocks of the parish started crowing at about 6a.m., as they always do coming up to that great feast.

In the month of May, 1949, Seán purchased a new Wolsley electric fencing unit. As it was the first one in the parish, neighbours came to see it working. It was powered by three small wet batteries joined together in such a way to give a combined strength of six volts. A charge lasted for about six weeks, and it could be substituted with a six volt dry battery in an emergency. On the first day of its construction for work, Seán lead us all one by one into a

The author's home and farm buildings.

Maggie's First Communion photo, taken in field at front of Brady house.

Seán and Máire, taken in 1931.

Áine and Maggie.

The author's mother and sister, Maggie.

The author's mother.

Padraic, Seán, Ultan and Áine.   The author's sister, Áine.

Seán on his way to herd cattle.

Snapshot of the author.

Áine. A snapshot taken on a beautiful summer day.

Seán's girlfriend, Mary Buchannan.

The author, Ultan, Maggie and Micheál.

The author's father, Patrick Brady on the Ford Minor tractor.

A snapshot of the author, Ultan Brady, at four years of age.

Old Fordson tractor showing the engine with the magneto in the centre.

A Sunday afternoon common scene in the pre-1950's.
Dogs - Rabbits - Guns!

A snapshot of the author's aunt, Mrs. Mary Hilliard,
admiring the greenery in front of her dwellinghouse.

The 1947 freeze-up was the worst snowfall in the author's lifetime.

First Communion snapshot of the author, 6 years old. Ascension Thursday, 1940.

Seán behind the Morris Cowley.

An old snapshot showing the bleakness and beauty of Bohermeen bog.

Seán and Máire in the "Johnny Walker"
pram that carried the first six of the
family from A to B and B to A!
It was as well sprung as any of to-day's
best cars!

Máire and Seán.

trap and gave us all a shock. He had his rubber boots on, and asked for a piece of tying wire to be handed to him while his spare hand was in contact with the fence. He was used to stronger shocks of magnates and spark plugs. He showed no mercy, for he walked Ma into the trap also! It was controlled by two points coming in contact every two seconds to give an A.C. shock. The fence shocked, dead on the contact of the two points at which moment a click sound came from the fencing unit. By listening to the clicks, it was possible to hold the fence wire between every two and get no shock.

There was one grand auld gentleman who used to play tricks on us by asking us catch-questions, puzzles and other sums. Sometimes we came home from school through his yard, which was not far from Boyerstown school. Once as he was ploughing with the horses, he got me to hold the handles of the plough. I thought myself wonderful to be turning a piece of the globe upside-down. I was about eight at that time, and admired the two strong horses, one a bay and the other a piebald. Seán Curraig was that man's name. It was he who gave us the puzzle of the laying hen.

"If a hen and a half, lays an egg and a half, in a day and a half. How many will she lay in a week?"

I answered seven. He told me I was very near right, only that I was not allowing for something. "Allowing for what?" said I. The reply he gave me was "For wear and tear on her backside". I felt some idiot, and the man having one of his hearty laughs at me! I knew well what wear and tear meant from the time of the beet growing. In later years, he had a good puzzle for me.

"Three men went into a hotel for a good feed. One of them went to the office to pay and was told it would be £10 per head. He paid up and got five single pounds back. He gave £2 to the office girl, kept £1 for himself and gave the other two lads £1 each. Now, the feed cost each man £9 which comes to £27, and the £2 that the office girl got leaves the total coming to £29. Where is the other £1?"

Another puzzle he had was to measure the width of a river without crossing it or throwing a length of rope or tape across it. His answer was not a joke this time, but sound logic. First you picked out some mark of the opposite bank. It could be a stone, a rush or a tuft of grass, and is indicated by "A" in the sketch. Stand on the bank directly opposite that mark, and put down a marker "B". From point "B" measure fifteen yards and put down a marker at point "C". Walk another fifteen yards along the bank, and put down another marker at point "D". Now walk at right angles to the river and away from it, until "A" and "C" are in line with your standing point. Note that the standing point is "E" in diagram. Measure the length of DE to give you the width of the river as it is the same length as AB. I think theorem eight proves AB=DE.

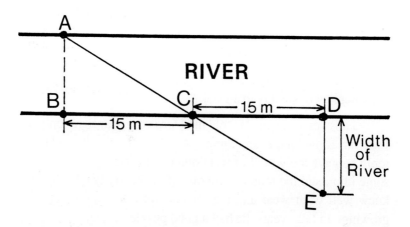

From the time I got my first shock from the electric fence, straight away I had my mind made up to shock Seán Curraig with it to make up for the great laugh he had at me. I knew he would be coming to look for the reaper and binder, as his barley was almost ripe. In a few day's time, I saw him on his way and went out to meet him, as the fence was working between where the two of us were. He showed great interest in the fence, and dared me to tip it. I listened to the clicks of the fencing unit, and tipped it between the clicks. He enquired how I was getting no shock. I told him you would want to touch it for ten seconds to get a shock. Low and behold, my trap worked, and this poor man got the shock of his life. He was raging with me for a little while, as I said to him "There's a bit of wear and tear for you and you're late in allowing for it now!" The premeditiated trap had worked to perfection. Da was undecided when I told him about the incident. He felt sorry for the man, but still laughed when I demonstrated what he did and said after getting the shock.

Another incident happened one morning, as Páraic and I went to school. Páraic opened the middle gateway on the boreen, and walked on a bit with his bicycle. I was closing the gate but got a profile glance of a desperate jump by Páraic, and the bicycle falling. What happened was that Paraic had H20'ed on the electric fence and paid the consequences! It did him no harm, as he reared five good healthy children in later life. Is it by accident or design that his only two sons are electrical engineers? Kevin, the older of the two, is on his second years work in Germany. James had his final examinations in the summer of 1991.

The spring of 1949 saw the last days of our old Fordson tractor working. A new Ford Minor tractor was bought, and was as different to the old Fordson as chalk is to cheese. It had all pneumatic tyres and a hydraulic lift and power drive the very same as the Ferguson tractor. It was over this similarity that there was a big law case between the two giants, Ford and Ferguson, the outcome of which I don't know. But I know that they got good advertising. It was a TVO fuelled machine that needed a petrol start. It being a lightweight and speedy machine, Seán used it a lot for bringing goods from Navan. They were got when wanted, and there was no waiting for a delivery lorry. The steering was as light as that of a car, and it was just as easy to drive.

It was in the spring of 1949 the acreage of our land possession was increased by almost 50%. Seán bought twenty six acres at an auction for £1500. This was a high, dry bank of land, halfway between the home farm and the town of Navan. It was well known for its fattening qualities and ability to grow first class crops of corn. It proved that in the coming years, and it was not long until that farm had paid for itself. Da visited it every weekend and found the Ford Minor very useful for that purpose. It was set for the first year after purchasing it, at a price of £14 per Irish acre. That brought in £224 for sixteen acres. Land, at that time, was bought and sold by the statute acre, and set on an eleven months system by the Irish acre.

The spring of 1949 was one of a lot of strange happenings for the O'Bradaigh family. It was the first year that we had any sickness of note in the family. Áine had a slight pain in her tummy and stayed away from school. That evening she was feeling much better, so no doctor was called. At about 6a.m. the next morning Máire came up to our bedroom to tell us that Áine was very ill. We got up to find her rolling in bed with pain. Seán went for the priest, and I went for the family doctor, Dr. Dargan of Bedford Place, Navan, as fast as I could ride the bicycle. The doctor's house was the middle of three lovely stone buildings, each having a basement. The first storey was approached by about twelve steps up from the footpath. I banged the knocker, which was a very heavy old-type one. It was a calm morning, with no noise to be heard, as it was only 6.30 in the morning. The knocking was so loud, that I thought it could wake up half the town! I sure woke up the doctor, who showed me an unlit night bell when he arrived down. I told him the story, and he told me to go home and keep Áine as quiet in the bed as possible until his arrival. On my arrival home, the priest and Seán were in the room with Áine, and Seán followed my instructions. The doctor was out in about ten minutes. He told us that she had peritonitis or a burst appendix, and that he would arrange for an immediate operation. He told us to bring her to the

County Infirmary as soon as possible. A neighbour obliged us with his car, and Seán carried her out into the back seat. On arrival at the hospital, she was readied for an operation in great haste. She was two hours on the operating table, and the doctor was satisfied with the way it had gone. That type of operation was considered a very major one at the time, as they had no penicillin. She was very sick for the first week, and visits were restricted to one a day. In the middle of that long week, Ma banged her head off the axle of a trap that was in dry dock, and hanging from the roof of a shed while she was looking for eggs in it. She was a very worried woman over Áine. The next morning at about 4a.m., Máire came up to our bedroom and told us that Ma was dead. That was the message Máire had been told by Da. Seán went for the priest and doctor, and I went over the three fields to tell Séamus Boccán. He told me that he would be over in about an hour. We were all very upset, with Áine pretty bad in hospital and now this to mother.

On the arrival of Séamus, I brought him up to the bedroom, the two of us still thinking that Ma was dead. I was delighted to see a slight movement in her body, as was Séamus. She had been anointed, and a bed was being readied in the same hospital as Áine. She was unconscious, and from her looks, she was in great pain. The problem was diagnosed as meningitis. Áine was not told about Ma's illness until things got better. For twenty days Ma remained unconscious, with tubes attached to her nostrils for medical purposes. We all prayed hard during this crisis. Áine was much improved after nine days, and was told about Ma. It was a Sunday morning on the 21st day of Ma's illness, that my Aunt Mary, Ma's sister, was in to see her. She called her by her name, and there was a definite slight response. From that day on, a very slow but sure improvement took place. Her first words were "How is Áine?". Áine was well enough to spend a few hours each day with her. They both came out of hospital within days of each other. Áine had missed two months at school, and it upset her whole year. She had to drink one bottle of stout per day to help increase her appetite, and give her strength.

Da, who was unable to move around freely, went through a very bad patch during that bout of illness. It was he who sent out a false alarm that Ma was dead, as after hearing a strange noise from Ma, he called her a few times and got no reply. He sent Máire up to our bedroom before he had got a light to look at Ma. God was very good to us, as both could have lost their lives. This would have been a shattering blow to us. Dr. Dargan said that it was the dose of salts that Áine had taken that caused the appendix to burst.

CHAPTER VIII

The summer of 1949 was a very good one, and the hay crop was saved early and was of first class quality. The barley crops were in very early, and one of our neighbours got Da to reap his crop on the 3rd of August, the earliest that Da had ever reaped. There was no winter barley or winter oat crops out then. I remember a crop of winter wheat on our land, the breed of which was called "Square Head Master". It was a great yielder, but was very susceptible to lying. Attle was nearly the only spring wheat then, and though it was a great millable wheat, it broke no records in its yielding capabilities.

On our return to school in early September, 1949, Páraic got the full result of his Leaving Certificate, and had won himself a scholarship to university. As the scholarship was a three year one, he chose engineering. He started his third level eduction in October, and had full board in some house in Muckross. He remained there during the weekends and only came home during the three holiday breaks in the year. He found that this arrangment gave him a better chance to study. I remember his first day going away to university, and Ma's eyes filled with tears although he was only going thirty miles away. He brought one large case and his bicycle with him. Those were the days when the bus conductor would put a large case or bicycle up on the roof top, and it was a common sight to see up to half a dozen bicycles on the roof of a bus.

The last Sunday of September, 1949, was a great one for all Meath people. We got our first grip on the "Sam Maguire" cup after beating Cavan by 1-10 to 1-6. Every square inch of space available was taken up by spectators for the great occasion. These were the days when the people on Hill 16 and in front of the Cusack, Hogan and Long Stands did the "Mexican Wave" not from side to side but up and down the steps. How no one got killed was a bit of a miracle.

164

The night we watched the slaughter of a lot of people in some continental arena, on the telly reminded me of Croke Park in the late forties and early fifties. These were the days when football games wera more robust, as the handpassing act was much more difficult to perform, and there was no place for ballet dancers or basketball players. The first handpass that I used was the overhand pass with the two hands. The present pass is more in tone with basketball, and it is so hard to dispossess a player in possession, that when the foul comes, it can't be anything else but a bookable one. The best game of football in my forty years watching Senior Finals and Semi-Finals was the 1949 All Ireland Semi-Final between Meath and Mayo. For good, sound, clean shouldering, kick and high fielding, it would be very hard to surpass. We now have five All Irelands at Senior football level. One in the forties, one in the fifties, one in the sixties and two in the eighties, to make up for our failure in the seventies. One every ten years is not bad going. I have a hunch that our win in the ninties will come early. As a matter of fact, it could be this year 1991 after that historic four-time battle with Dublin in the first round of the belated Leinster championship. I give my heartiest congratulations to a young Dublin man, Paul Griffin, who brought the first European gold boxing medal to Ireland since the Mullingar man, Maxi Mc Cullagh, in 1949. Another young Westmeath man missed a gold boxing medal by inches. Ken Doherty is another Irish man to note in the professional snooker world after a good showing against the top men in the spring of 1991.

The Young Farmer's Club in Navan was a great source of past time for Seán. It brought him to field day outings, a few dinner dances in the winter months, farming instructions and farming films. Máire and Páraic were allowed to go to farming club dances. Da, who according to Ma was a hopeless dancer, considered three or four dances a year enough for anyone. The show dance, the local hospital dance and the County Council dance were other dances they were allowed to go to. Other dances they attended were managed without Da's knowledge, by going to bed a bit early and moving out very quietly! Ma knew about this and actually approved of it. In the coming years, we all got in on this act and Ma must have been praying hard that none of us would get caught. I went to lots of whist drives and dances in Lawlesses' Hall, which was in Boyerstown parish. I dread to think what would have happened if Da found us out.

It was in Lawlesses' Hall that I learnt my dancing. It was mostly ceili and old-time dancing, with a few local lads playing music. One man on accordion, one man on drums and a fiddler made up the band. All the local boys and girls, men and women, even fathers and mothers, within a four mile radius came to this hall every Sunday night. The admission fee was one shilling. *The Walls of Limerick, The Siege of Ennis, Paul Jones, The Hokey Pokey* and *Hands, Knees and a Bumps-a-daisy* were the dances that were very popular then. The hall lighting was three Aladdin lanterns, and the heating system was one you generated yourself by dancing around the floor.

If Da had been more mobile, he would have been more "with it" as regards dancing. Seán was a lovely dancer, and got great enjoyment out of it. Ma taught us the old-time waltz on the kitchen floor to music on the radio, while Da would tell her that she had a lovely leg! Micheál, like his Da, had no desire to dance. Páraic did most of his learning to dance in The Crystal and The National during his college days in Dublin. We were all fond of football, but Da did not like us playing except among ourselves. He feared that we might get broken bones, as he told us often to mind our bones as "we only have them once!" What he was experiencing with his slight handicap, he did not want us to go through the same.

My only two trips on the old steam trains were to football matches when I was a substitute on the De La Salle, Navan, under-fourteen team. Both these trips were to Kells, a distance of

10 miles, which I enjoyed greatly. I loved the smell of the steam as it passed by the windows.

In the spring of 1950 I got pleurisy. Instead of going to my science class at 5 o'clock, I went to Dr. Dargan. He gave me an injection and a prescription, and told me to stay in a warm bed for at least a week. I tore up the prescription and said nothing about it, as I did not want annoying them so soon after the other two bouts of illness. I was lucky enough, as the bill came incorporated with the other two accounts and was not noticed! Da made sure that I studied in bed, as my Intermediate Certificate exam was coming up in June. I scraped through that exam with a pass. Páraic had got first class honours, which made my results look very disappointing. On my return to school, as well as getting a bad result, the principle made the entire class repeat the same exam again. As I did not start my secondary education until I was 14, I would be almost 18 by the time I had my second Intermediate Certificate finished, and almost 20 if I stayed on to do the Leaving Certificate. This, I was not prepared to do, if at all possible. I asked Da if I should look for work, but he said it was better for me to do another year. So that was that.

Seán, who was 21 in 1950, was anxious to start a dairy to send milk to Merville Dairies in Finglas. Three of our neighbours were selling milk there and were highly delighted with their financial returns from the milk sales. He had asked Da before, and was shot down, as Da mentioned that it was too much trouble bringing cows and heifers in heat to a bull two miles away. Worse still was the dread of contacting contagious abortion, which was capable of putting any farmer on the road. Seán now had A.I. on his side, and a phone call to Athboy brought a premium Hereford, Shorthorn, or Frisian bull's capabilities, breeding-wise, in a test-tube to the required female at a very reasonable price. My first phone call was to Athboy A.I. station, and I was very surprised to hear a female take all the required details from me. Da reluctantly agreed with

Seán, but told him that it was a class of slavish way of farming. Seán told him that the rearing of home-bred calves instead of paying up to £20 each, when a bullock fetched about £60, would save buying both calves and store cattle. Mick, who was eighteen, and just finished school, was kept at home to help out on the farm.

Our old cow byre was built of yellow clay and cobblestone floored. All the wall had to be scraped down, to take off several layers of whitewash, picked with a little hand pick, scudded, and smoothly plastered. The floors had to be concreted to very strict specifications, concrete dividing walls erected, so that two cows shared the same space and concrete mangers at the head of the cows. Dual purpose drinking bowls were fitted in the middle of each stall to service two cows. They were gravity supplied, as there was no electricity in our area until late 1952. Ten cows was the starting number of milkers, with about three heifers in the pipeline to fill the place of dried-off cows. They were hand milked for the first year, and the twelve-gallon milk churns were cooled in a fifty gallon tub of spring water. A new strainer that resembled the Sam Maguire cup was on a smaller stand. At the base of that strainer, there were two perforated circular discs, between which was a slightly bigger and circular cotton pad, that collected any foreign bodies that may have got into the milk. The cotton pads were disposable after each milking, and could be bought in various sizes. As we always had about five cows, the purchase of five freshly-calved cows in the Dublin cow market got the dairy in full production. Seán bought these new cows, and as well as being good yielders, they turned out to be very lucky. Da got a new ledger book, and a 50-lb hand dial "Salter" weighing scales, to record the cows' yields of milk individually. Two days per week were recorded, and each cow's annual yield was noted. If any cow's yield did not come up to a satisfactory tally, she was sold after calving and replaced by a better one. An acre of oats, an acre of barley, and an acre of kale were grown with the feeding of the cows, sheep and dry stock in mind. Half the kale was marrow stem, and was used for feeding from

October to January. The rest was "hungry gap" or "thousand head" and was fed from January up to grass time.

Our daily newspaper came with the milk-collecting lorry every morning. Milk cheques were good, extra calves were fed, and a prize for clean, good quality milk supplied the first year, all enticed Da to extend the dairy by five more milkers. This suited well, as there were four good heifers due to calf in September, when the good winter price per gallon came into force. A shed joining the existing cow byre came in useful for the extra five cows. The only snag about this plan was that a corn loft had to be dismantled, and rebuilt in an adjoining part of the barn. Tubular steel divisions between each pair of cows and one long manger with a feeding passage in front of the cows, simplified the construction work. As things were pretty busy in the spring of 1951, a local handyman was hired to help at the building. Da was now very keen on the dairy, and decided to get a new milking machine, "Alfa Lavel" that was widely advertised in the *Farmer's Weekly* and *The Farmer's Journal* (which had just come into publication). It was a Swedish make, and Da had great respect for Swedish steel. It was somewhat dearer than its rivals, but had a better pulsator system and the teat claws were a better finished job.

A Dublin man, of the typical humorous type that was very common in Dublin city in those years, came down to erect the machine. He called the hammer "The Persuader" and the sun in the sky "Mc Cormack", and argued over Dublin's football capabilities over Meath. There was even a big debate as to whether Matthew Talbot or Oliver Plunkett would be canonised first. A "Petter" petrol engine was got for driving the vacuum pump of the milking machine. It took two days to erect the machine, but that man came down for another couple of days, until Seán was satisfied he could manage it on his own. That man was well fed, got a drop of whiskey and a hand out at the finish. Da said to us when he had gone that he can't go back to Dublin and say that he was dry or hungry down in County Meath! The machine cut the milking time in half.

It was now 1951, and both Seán and Páraic had broken their confirmation pledge. I thought this a great sin, but on enquiring, I was told that it was only breaking a resolution, and only a very small sin. Their drinking was a very restricted one, for fear that Da might find out. I once went on a bus to Dublin to shop for some drapery in McBirneys, they had advertised a great summer sale. I had a splitting headache, and went into a pub for some aspirins. I, being in bad form, envied the lads there, who were chatting and laughing. I wondered if the pub attendant would give me a bottle of stout, if I asked. On an impulse, I ordered one and up it came. I thought one would be of no use, so I bought another. I was feeling better now, and decided to move on, in case I might get drunk. I did my shopping, after which I got a mixed grill in The Palace restaurant near O' Connell Street.

On the bus home, there were a party of about eight young people singing, and I gave them a willing helping. On my arrival in Navan, I went to Campbell's pub, which was opposite the old Garda barracks. I had another bottle of stout there. That pub had a snug, so no- one could see me drinking, most of all, any of my brothers or sisters. Two grand old chatty ladies ran that pub, and I enjoyed their good humour and slow lifestyle which was very pronounced. On my later visits there, they would treat me to a mug of soup or coffee, and a couple of sandwiches to soak things up, as they put it. That drinking, which I had just started, was to continue for the next thirtythree years and just like my smoking, which I started in my very early years, with a gradual worsening all the time.

About that time an incident happened to me, and I had a narrow escape from fatality. Seán was driving the Ford Minor, which was drawing a trailer on which I was sitting. We were on a strange road, and I wanted to ask him about some large farmer's place we had just passed. I went to get up on the back of the tractor, which was going at full speed. I put one foot on an iron stabilizing bar that ran from the trailer shaft to the front of the trailer. There were two of these stabilizing bars that ran at an angle of forty-five degrees to the shaft and were joined by one strange bolt at the shaft. When I put my foot on one of the bars, it collapsed, and I fell down. I caught the drawbar of the tractor with my right hand. I was able to pull myself into position to grip it with my second hand also. I was going to shout to Seán to pull up, but I decided not to. The toes of my boots were dangling on the road under the front of the trailer. Gradually, I pulled myself forward, and managed to get one knee up on the drawbar. I then put my hands forward to climb up the back of the tractor. I was now safe and able to stand up. I must have been ghost white but never told Seán or anyone else in the family about that mishap. It was a miracle how my right hand had caught the drawbar as I fell down.

All my dreams in after life, apart from my love ones, stem from things that happened in my youthful years. I often dream of falling from the top of the hay barn. This is probably due to my fall from a shed when I was about three years old. I also dream of being chased by a tiger, and that my feet are stuck to the ground. Da once told me when I was very young, that a tiger would rip a person asunder with one stroke of his paw. I often dream of being at school without my trousers or sometimes Mass in a similar plight. I blame that from the time I went about the farmyard in good weather with nothing on but a petticoat. I sometimes dream that a war is on and I see the enemy coming to our house. I slip out the back door and hide in a ditch. Just as they find me, I wake up as in the other dreams, thanking God that it was only a dream. That dream is a result of the war talk I heard in the kitchen during the war years. Is it during one such dream that a man with a bad heart dies?

A football team was formed in Bohermeen parish, and Seán and I were asked to play for them. We had to play all our games unknown to Da, saying that we were playing handball at Clarkes'

Crossroads. We were a very crude team, made no progress, but enjoyed ourselves very much. These were the days when we had to change into our football drapery at the back of a ditch, or in a car, if we were lucky enough to have one, as they were a scarce luxury then. The team managers did their best to keep clothes dry on wet days, there being no plastic covers. Dressing rooms were to be enjoyed in the towns, and showers were for the football gods that made it to Croke Park. Páraic gave that team of Bohermeen a hand when he was home on holidays from college. Micheál got his place on the team when superstars were scarce. Our training was done with the Dunderry team, who practised in a field that was called Lug an Eannaig, two nights a week. The crude playing field was only half the distance that Bohermeen training grounds were from our house. The Dunderry lads were a grand bunch of lads, and had no objection to us training with them. Two teams were drawn up, one played as backs and the other as forwards. Two coats were put down for goal posts. The ball was centred into the two opposing sides by a couple of strong boys who were always available. When the forwards had scored three goals, the two teams played vice versa. When the evenings got too dark, a smoke and a chat followed.

Dunderry and Bohermeen men comprised 90% of the labour force on the Bohermeen and Jamestown bogs in the years before and after the war years. I suppose they were still a good 50% during the war years. They had a language culture of their own, which sounded a bit coarse to others, especially townspeople. To me their talk was a grand soft drawl, and they had their own grammar. This culture was very noticeable in the public houses that surrounded the bogs e.g. the two pubs in Dunderry, one in Bohermeen and one in Greetiagh. This hardy race of people kept to these country pubs and had their own dancehall, known as Lawlesses' Hall. Men met their lifelong wives there, so they were a close knitted race, with their relations only a few doors away from any one household. They sometimes danced in the White Quarry Hall which was not as central as Lawlesses' Hall. They were all great ceili dancers, and when sixty to eighty of these people got up for the *Walls of Limerick* the strength of the hall floor was tested to the full! They were a very hard-working race, very honest and a great pay for hire work done, as Da found out. A more modern couple of halls were built in Dunderry and Cortown in the late forties, with toilets and supper rooms, causing Lawlesses' Hall to shut down. Good bands, especially during Dunderry carnival, brought town and country people together, and marriage contracts were drawn up from a much wider area of the country.

Once there was a local football match between Dunderry and Bohermeen. As usual, there was a kick-around before the game started. As this was in progress, a big Dunderry chap they called the "Major" drew a kick at the ball, and injured a Bohermeen man's leg. On being told that evening, that the chap's leg was broken and in plaster, the "Major" answered by casually saying "It must have been rotten!"

I have been in the pubs where these lads used to frequent in the late eighties and find that all the older lads are dead, and most of the younger lads are either in England or working in town factories in Navan. They are married to town girls and vice versa, so that the old language culture has almost disappeared. The bog has been unused for over thirty years except for five or six old stagers that cut turf for their own use. There is a comeback to the bog again in the past six years, since machinery for cutting the turf started, and the price of coal and briquettes jumped in price. The farmers, building and factory workers spend a few evenings footing and clamping, and with modern tractors and trailers to draw it home, the job is very much simplified. A few of the old names I remember are Mallons, Cregans, McCormacks, Reillys and Garrys. There are a few of the younger generation of these still in the locality. The thatched cottages are all replaced with bungalows, the fire on the hearth with cookers, and the stone boreens with tarmacadam. Time and tide will wait for no man, and so old customs die hard and fast. Would they were with us again!

Emigration took an awful lot of the young lads all down through the years, and unlike now they seldom returned to settle down here or return home on holidays. In my national school in Boyerstown, there was a picture of an ass with two large baskets or cleeves of turf stradling his back, being led by a man on his way from the bog. While I was on holiday with Páraic in the west of Ireland in 1955, I saw that picture become a reality. It was a sight to behold, and must stretch back to almost the time of Adam and Eve. Páraic took out his camera to take a photo. That reminds me that since I never saw the picture I must look it up, as it would bring me back that thirty five years which was a lovely summer's afternoon. There was another bog picture in our parlour that was made of Beleek china. It was a picture of an elderly man with a hat in his hands, an elderly woman with hands clasping each other, and a barrow full of turf between them. The Angelus was the subject of that picture, and it was engraved into the picture. We had another couple of Beleek china ornaments. There was a lovely hand basket, three greyhounds on a stand and a tub with some shamrock stems on the outer side. Ma used the tub for lump sugar the morning of the station or for visiting relatives.

In the summer of 1951, I repeated my Intermediate Certificate exam, with an examination number of 999 in St. Michael's convent. There was only one other boy from St. Patrick's college with me as the rest of my class were sent to the Mercy Convent. Four other boys from Preston school made up the half dozen males doing the exam, and we were among about forty lovely girls from St. Michael's. On opening my desk each morning, I collected about six love letters and put them into my inside coat pocket as fast as possible, to look at them after the exam that evening! I kept up correspondence with a girl from Cootehill, Co. Cavan, for about one year following the examination. The result of my exam was a pass with honours, and I decided, if at all possible, that I had enough education. Páraic had his second year at university completed and got first-class honours. As things turned out Da was resigned to me, having completed my fourteen years at school, looking for work.

CHAPTER IX

During that summer of 1951, I was on the look-out for work. I tried a few chemist shops for a job as an assistant, but my knowledge of chemistry at Intermediate Cert. would not suffice. However, Ma was trying for me as well, and she got me a job in the hardware shop of one of the biggest merchants in Navan. My starting pay was 7s6d per week, and I had to pay the union 4s0d per month out of the thirty shillings per month I worked hard for. Being a farmer's son, with all the hardware equipment Da had at home in the barn, this job was ideal for me. Da was pleased to see me there and took a keen interest in my progress. My working hours were from 9a.m. - 7p.m. four days a week, 9a.m. - 1p.m. on Thursday, our half-day, and from 9a.m. - 9p.m. on Saturday. I had to ride the bicycle three miles home for my dinner, and three miles back in one hour. This was great exercise, and I was as fit as a fiddle. There was a separate grocery and bar owned by the same firm, adjoining the hardware shop. Between the three, there were thirteen employed altogether. We were one big happy family and the crack was good at times. There was a fully qualified hardware assistant over me. He was a gentleman to the toes, who had to work in the grocery on Fridays and part-time on some Saturdays also. He even gave a help out in the bar when the barman was on holidays. The cash office was situated between the grocery, hardware and bar and was serviced by an overhead cable that took in the cup sized and shaped cash boxes, that were spring ejected to the cash office. The office girl sent the boxes back in the same manner. A ticket with the amount of money to be taken was sent in, and the right change sent back.

I enjoyed opening the well packed boxes that came off the delivery railway lorry, checking the goods with the invoices and arranging the goods on their proper shelf. The cost price had to be marked on every item in code, so that when stocktaking came around it simplified the job. Our code lettering was "May God help us". In the old money twelve letters were used as there were twelve pennies in one shilling. I loved dressing the two display windows which was done on Tuesday, the quietest day of the week. Monday, being market day was fairly busy. Most of the goods coming in would be in a dusty state, so a good rub of a soft cloth put them shining again. Our main suppliers were Henshaws and T. & C. Martins; Blaxindales, Dunnes, Healys for sports wear, and gardening and farming hand tools were supplied from local suppliers with the brand name "Boyne Valley Tools Ltd." We did good business in second-hand furniture. The boss Mr. Markey went up to Dublin city on Thursday afternoons, and got great value from dealers along the docks. He purchased most of the goods from Lawlor Briscoes. The furniture bought was collected by the railway lorry the following day, so we had it on Friday afternoon.

I often had to take grocery, hardware and bar orders from phone calls. A medium sized van, which was all the time on the road, delivered these orders. We had some great customers within a ten mile radius from Navan. Captain Eccles, Dunderry; Mr Boles, Churchtown, Dunderry; Major Burke, Stackallen; Captain Collins, Durhamstown; Mrs Foster, Ardbraccan House; Mercy Convent, Navan; Loretto Convent, Navan; Preston College, Navan; St Martha's Agricultural College, Sion, Navan; Major Medge, Dublin Rd., Navan; Slane Castle, Riddle Martins, Blackcastle Estate; Bective Estate; Balreask Stud, and Williamsons of Randlestown were the pick of these. Dr. McCann, Protestant Bishop of Meath, who had his Palace at Bishopcourt, Ardbraccan, was a lovely warm-hearted man whom all that knew him loved. He lived just a few fields away from our home place in Boyerstown. Accounts were settled every month, with a 2.5% deduction to the prompt customer. The firm was called James Sheridan & Co. Ltd. and was situated in Trimgate St., about the centre of Navan. Many is the frosty morning I watched and pitied the two men from O'Hagan's greengrocery washing herrings and other fish in a 40-gallon barrel of cold water. They had to gut a lot of them as well. The only other greengrocery in the entire town and only two doors away from O'Hagan's had the same hard work come frost, hail, rain or snow. Joseph Keapock was the owner of the shop and he had a lovely character of a sister in Eileen who never failed to decorate the shop with fresh flowers every morning. She was a great whist player and always played poker before and after each whist-drive. All shop owners swept the street's shop front each morning.

That time, publicans bottled all their own beers. Many a time I watched the yardman fill the clean bottles, label them, cork them and shelve them for a three week maturing period before sale time. There was a snug attached to the bar, and four private compact rooms with electric heaters and bell buzzer, where the gentry had their drink and chat. These people usually got personal attention from Mr. Markey himself. They left their grocery and hardware requirements with him. These orders got immediate attention, and were put in the gentleman's car, while he enjoyed his restful drink.

We were agents for Pierce of Wexford. We sold ploughs, mowing machines, swath-turners, hay collectors and turnip sowers. All the spare parts for these machines were stocked also. After about six months, I had all the more common parts numbers off by heart. As there were eight different styled horse mowers, learning all the part numbers for these was quite difficult. My senior assistant, who was over thirty years at the trade, had all these numbers on the tip of his fingers.

We were holders of a firearms certificate to sell new and second- hand guns and rifles, and the cartridges and bullets for them also. A box of twenty-five cartridges was 10s6d in 1951. I think a box of fifty .22 bullets was six shillings. A book with detailed accounts of all these sales and purchases had to be kept up to date, and ready for inspection, at any time, by a member of the Garda force.

There was a scheme for Council house gardens, whereby the owners got four stone of seed potatoes, and .5oz of the main vegetable seed, free of charge. I loved getting up a lot of these orders during a slack period, and leaving them to one side, ready for any customer with the qualifying certificate. We sold primus stoves, which people brought on picnics, the old-style farm lanterns, table and wall lamps, and the globes, wicks, and burners for them. Tilley and Aladdin lamps and heaters were all the go at that time. The spart parts for these had to be kept in plentiful stock. The days for all these lights and heaters were numbered, as rural electrification was about to get into full swing. Vacuum cleaners also sold well. The principal buyers were for large estate houses, colleges, convents, parish houses, and the more well-to-do town houses. Nowadays, almost every house in the country has a vacuum cleaner.

One very valuable customer of ours was the last blacksmith in the town of Navan, as Percy Muldoon had just gone to his reward. That man was Gussy Curtis, who was a small man but was power-packed with energy. His father was the administrator of the town's new cemetery, and there was a saying round the town of Navan "You are next for Curtis!" This was said to a person with a bad cough or a man looking bad after a bout of flu. Gussy shoed horses, turned scythe blades, renewed cutting knives of mowing and reaping machines and put the shoeing on cart and trap wheels. He got all the raw material from my firm and his monthly account came to a big amount. He had one very good-looking daughter, that was the envy of many of the Navan girls from the number of boys that were mad about her. The only other blacksmiths around Navan were the Markeys of Kilcarn, who shoed most of the racehorses of the county. Michael was the head man in Kilcarn and he was a full brother to Thomas, who lived in Boyerstown, and known locally as the "Red". The blacksmith family of Markeys originated in Ardbraccan, Navan, where their father Michael ran a very successful blacksmith business. He was well known for his feats of strength.

Da, in all his love of shooting seldom used a shotgun, but relied on the rifle for all his sport. Seán was always on the lookout for a good second-hand shotgun, with pheasants and wild duck in mind. He had told me to tell him if any good second-hand guns came into our hardware shop for sale. It was the Saturday night before the 1st of November, 1951, that he came in to examine a double-barrelled gun. He was very pleased with it and was satisfied with the price of £7. He was a very proud and happy man as he walked out of the shop that night with the gun and twenty-five cartidges. Pheasants were fairly plentiful, and Seán got his fair share of them, especially around Christmas time.

Mr. Markey, my boss was a good golf player, and took it very seriously. At that time, there was a daily article in the *Irish Independent* with a heading *Play better golf with Harry Bradshaw*. I am almost sure it was Bradshaw, but if it wasn't, it was either Bobby Locke or Christy O'Connor. Mr. Markey put the paper on the counter, got a golf club out of a golf bag which we sold. He would read a sentence out, no-one listening but myself, as I went about my work. He would get the right grip from a detailed sketch on the paper, and start swinging as the paper had ordered him. I was more than afraid he would hit a customer that might step quickly inside the shop door, or let the club fly as it swished through the air and hit me. I was not sorry when that golfing article ended!

About the end of May, 1952, Da got a stroke that was to be fatal. It was about 2a.m. in the morning when Seán and I had returned from a card game. Máire told us that Da had a desperate headache. Seán went up to his bedroom, and decided to get the priest and doctor. The priest arrived very promptly, heard his Confessions, gave Holy Communion and annointed him. He was only out the door when Da fell into unconsciousness. The doctor attended him daily for about ten days, and then arranged to send him to hospital. After about two weeks there, he fell into a coma and died within a few days. It was procession day in Navan, and a lovely June day when we got the news. He had enjoyed the best of health, apart from a few backaches, and the gradual slowing of his mobility from the first time I remembered him. We never knew his age until then, and at the age of sixty he had a full head of hair with a few grey ribs. I had the honour of giving him his last hair-cut, the first one I did and the last. I had my fair share of the whiskey that was bought for the occasion. I had just enough to be in good form for the week, or thereabouts, it lasted. He had a huge funeral for a man that travelled little in the last twenty years of his life. Páraic and Áine were unable to attend the funeral, as they were both in the middle of important exams, especially Páraic, who was at the end of his term in U.C.D.. Ma did not attend the funeral, as was the custom at that time. Da's first cousin Tomás Fagan had died some five years previously, and his death, which was very sudden, had given Da a shock. Tomás was about sixty years of age also. Da was a heavy smoker, and went through at least forty Sweet Afton per day. He would give us an odd half of a cigarette, and also get us to light one for him as he read his book. He never inhaled the cigarettes, but still he had an odd cigarette cough in the morning. A man starting to smoke twenty cigarettes a day for forty years went through 292,000 during his life span! At three inches per cigarette, he smoked fourteen miles during his life! I am a heavy smoker and at fifty-eight years of age my mileage is almost twenty one miles, which is the distance of Drogheda from Dublin! It took a great pair of lungs to churn all that smoke, and a good set of jaws to bring it all into them! Well, as the Yank would say "I guess my life's length of cigarette must be at the butt stage now!"

To show respect for the dead up to the fifties, a man had to abstain from dancing and picture house films for a six month period. He also had to wear a black diamond piece of cloth on the right arm of a coat for one year, as well as a black tie. We obeyed the rule for three months, but then danced and went to films further afield.

The late summer brought good news, with Páraic getting his B.E. degree, and Áine getting her Intermediate Certificate with honours. The rural electrifiction was started in our area also. The wiring of houses, outhouses, and yards was a private affair when doing the job so long as the ESB passed it. Seán with his knowledge of electricity from the days of the windcharger, wired our place and about half a dozen neighbours' houses and outoffices as well. He did this work after his day's work on the farm, and it was often midnight before he returned home for a good night's sleep. Da had looked forward to the ESB connection line, as he said it would bring untold cheap power to the place. He failed by a few months to see his ambitions realised.

How right he was, as when switch-on came, a three-quarter horse power motor brought water to the kitchen, bathroom and toilet, cow house and dairy. Another one-and-a-half horse power motor drove the milking machine, a small crusher and the lathe, with a big saving in petrol bills. There was less danger of farmhouse or shed fires, as the new lighting system did away with naked flame lanterns and wall lamps. The new radio did away with wet and dry batteries, the clock which kept almost perfect time without winding, and the iron was much easier readied for use and much cleaner than the red irons that were heated in the fire. All in all, it was a transformation to much greater comfort. The radio, iron and clock were all presents given to the household. Páraic gave the radio, Seán bought the iron after backing Martin Maloney's five winning mounts at Navan races and I gave a present of the clock after backing Lester Piggot's first Derby winner, Never Say Die, in 1954.

Páraic started his first employment in August 1952. He was working with that great construction contractor, Cormack Murray, from Ardsallagh House, Navan, and the man that was responsible for a lot of new schools, extensions and a couple of new churches in Co. Meath. He built the new stand in Pairc Tailteann, and it was he who drained the football pitch which must now be one of the driest in the country. A car was supplied to Páraic, and as the summer of 1952 was very warm, he brought us all to Bettystown many an evening for a good swim. The car was the old style Ford Anglia, two door, and its registration number was ZN 701. The centre of gravity was fairly high on the car, and it was easy enough to put it on two wheels when rounding a sharp corner. He always brought a couple of neighbouring lads to Bettystown with us, and we usually had a couple of drinks in a pub in Slane to finish up a pleasant cheap entertaining evening. Slane is a lovely clean little village, and how it never figured in the Bord Failte prize-winning villages beats me. There are four lovely stone-built, old-style houses, at the crossroads in the Drogheda side of the village, that are unique in that each pair face each other, diagonally to the two crossing roads. Francis Ledwidge was born and reared near Slane and my favourite poem is *A Lament for Thomas Mc Donagh* which was written by him.

He shall not hear the bitten cry
    In the wild sky, where he is lain,
Nor voices of the sweeter birds
    Above the wailing of the rain.

Nor shall he know when loud March blows
    Thro' slanting snows here fanfare shrill,
Blowing to flame the golden cup
    Of many an upset daffodil.

But when the Dark Cow leaves the moor,
    And pastures poor with greedy weeds,
Perhaps he'll hear her low at morn
    Lifting her horn in pleasant meads.

What a lovely simple picture these three stanzas of poetry paint in the imagination! The dark cow was probably a Kerry cow, they were highly valued for their high butter-fat quality milk. That great Irish-born man, John Boyle O'Reilly who became so famous throughout North America, had a great love for the River Boyne and basin, just like Francis Ledwidge.

September, 1952, I took my first two week's holidays from my work in the hardware. I decided to do a tour of Co. Wicklow on the bicycle. I brought a primus stove, a kettle and frying pan to cook my meals during the day, and paid for bed and breakfast as well. The weather was the very best and I swam a lot. I bought the best of food, enjoyed cooking out in the open, and enjoyed the night life in a hotel where a sing-song would be going on. I climbed Bray Head, the Sugar Loaf Mountain, and toured all around Enniskerry. The lovely woods and waterfall on the Powerscourt domain are well worth seeing. My holiday came to a premature ending, when I spent too much time playing the slot machines in Bray one night! I was stony-broke at midnight, had to get on my bicycle and ride the forty five miles home, as I did not have the price of bed and breakfast! It was 5a.m. when I got to bed that morning. I swore I would never play with the "one arm bandit" again, and I kept that promise to the present day.

In October, 1952, I answered an advertisment that was in the *Situations Vacant* in the *Irish Independent,* for a hardware improver position. I sent my qualifications and references as requested. In a few day's time, I got a reply, requesting me to come as soon as possible to start work. I gave my boss in Navan two week's notice, which was union requirement. Páraic drove me down to Enniscorthy, my new place of employment, on a Saturday afternoon. It was a part of the country he had never seen. The scenery was lovely all the way through Wicklow, especially through the Vale of Avoca. I was very lonesome leaving home for the first time. We arrived down at 7p.m., and I had my interview straight away. My new boss was Michael R. Moran, whose hardware business was in the town square, that proudly displayed a statue of Father Murphy. My boss was a man of about thirty-five years of age. He had spent fifteen years as a radio operator on ships that travelled all around the world. It was no wonder that he had a radio business, including repairs to radios, attached to the hardware business. He sold gramophones, and kept a huge selection of records as well. The rest of the business was the same as I learned in Navan. Having gone through all the business, we were treated to a lovely tea. After saying goodbye to Páraic, my boss brought me to my digs, a place he had selected for me a few days previously. There were four other lads in this "Full Board" house in Court Street, from various other parts of the country. The landlady had four school-going children to care for, so she was a pretty busy woman who never complained. My rent per week was £2, and my wages were £5 10s. I had a comfortable living without any great luxuries. My hours of work were the same as Navan, but my half day was on Wednesday instead of Thursday. I had plenty to do in my spare time. I fished on the River Slaney with two red-headed twin brothers, Padge and Séamus Kiernan. They worked in shops adjacent to where I worked. I played football with the Enniscorthy Emmets. I tried hard at the hurling, but could make no fist of it. I did a line with a girl that worked at the same business as myself. She lived near to me and I met her on my way to work. We went for a walk most evenings, a dance once a month and the picture house every Sunday night. The seats in the picture house were all numbered and for the Sunday night show, they were booked at 11am on a Sunday morning. I didn't have to worry about the booking, as my girlfriend got the tickets. She would never let me pay for them, as she was getting a better wage than I was. We went to the greyhound track occasionally, and it was here I saw my first hurdle race. A story hard to believe is that on my first visit to that track I backed seven winners out of the seven races run there! I have gone to the dog races hundreds of times since, and it is a great night that I come out with four winners out of eight races.

We were at a staff dance for the North Light razor blade factory workers and friends. This factory was about three miles from Enniscorthy, and was managed by my girlfriend's brother. It was he who gave out the spot prizes. My girlfriend had it arranged with her brother to give out a spot prize for the first up with a 1929 Irish penny, which I had. He waited until we were near the stage to make the announcement, so I had no bother jumping up on the stage with my penny which I had ready in my hand. She got a lovely box of chocolates and I got five hundred cigarettes, which were the best prizes given out that night. Now, lads, you know where the spot prizes go!

The Wexford people are a very warm-hearted lot. They are like the western people in that respect, and they are more or less isolated from the rest of the country, being bound on two sides by the sea and the Black Stair Mountains. They had the old-type fires on the hearth, that were blown up to give more heat by a hand spinning wheel that fanned an underground bellows. This drive needed a fan- belt. On my first day in my new job, I was asked by a lady for a fan-belt, and I directed her to the nearest garage. She looked at me in surprise, and after a bit of explaining she got the required belt. She asked me was I from the north, as she detected a slight northern accent in my speech. I didn't think Meath people sounded like that. But they must, as many more Wexford people made the same observation. There was a traveller for Dunnes of Dublin who wholesaled light hardware, and he happened to be a neighbour of mine at home in Boyerstown. Another traveller from Navan that I had known well was Wilfred Elliot, and he sold farming and gardening tools, and the handles for them also. I was kept up to date with goings on around Navan by the two men. I got the *Meath Chronicle* every week on a special order with an Enniscorthy newsagent. Going home for Christmas, 1952, brought me right through the Vale of Avoca. The river itself is peculiar in that it has a brownish colour which it gets from mineral deposits there. The railway runs parallel to the sea coast for miles, and only about twenty yards from the water's edge. It was my first trip by rail, in which there was a dining and wining service. It was doing a lively trade, as it was an afternoon Christmas Eve journey.

The spring of 1953 I did a lot of cycling around the countryside of Co. Wexford in my spare time. It was near

Enniscorthy that I saw the first field that had been cleared by a forage-harvester. It was on the lands of Warrens, an auctioneering firm well known in Co. Wexford. I thought at the time that it was a field that had been lawnmowed for some big game that might be coming off in the near future. The Co. Wexford farmers planted their potato crop before corn crops. Well, this was the Model County, and the sunny south-east, so they were making use of the early market for the higher prices. As well as that, if the field was cleared in time, they followed with a crop of barley, kale or turnips. A noticeable sight in the hay, corn or tillage fields was to see the women of the house out helping the men and children to get the work done, just as you would see in the west.

It is a great county for ceili music and dancing, and many is the Sunday afternoon I went out to O'Neill's of the Still, a pub just one mile from Enniscorthy. I drank little at that time, and three bottles of stout at 9d per bottle was my limit. I rode the bike in the summer of 1953 to Curracloe one Sunday, and Courtown Harbour the following Sunday. They were both lovely seaside resorts at that time, and you could say that they were grossly underdeveloped for two such beautiful seaside resorts. Vinegar Hill is only one mile from Enniscorthy, and many is the time I climbed it. There is a lovely view of the countryside all around. It was from the top of it, I first saw Mt. Leinster that tops the Black Stair mountains. I decided there and then, to cycle to that countryside on my half day the following Wednesday. This I did, and was glad to have seen the Rackard homestead either in Rathnure or Killane, where the three mighty Senior Wexford Hurlers were born and reared. I noticed when going through the countryside, that every second garden, be it a farmer's garden or a council cottage garden, had about one dozen bee hives. Wexford is noted for its honey markets as well as its strawberry ones in the summer months.

It was good to be in Co. Wexford in the early and mid fifties, when hurling was on a very high keel. I saw that great team in training for two weeks in Belfield, Enniscorthy, before their meeting with Kilkenny in the Leinster final of 1953. I am almost sure Kilkenny beat them by one point. It was good too, to see Rathnure and St. Aidans, Enniscorthy, fight out the Wexford Senior Hurling final. Here, there was a great clash between Nicky Rackard and Nick O'Donnell, all in a great sporting manner. Belfield was always packed for these occasions. August of 1953, I got my holidays which coincided with Páraic's. I went with him on a tour of the west. We spent our first day and night in Salthill, did a lot of swimming in very fine weather, and enjoyed a few drinks and a sing-song that night. Our second day was spent travelling through the heart of Connemara at a nice leisurely pace. We got out now and again to do a bit of mountain climbing and see some of the magnificent views. The silence around Maam Cross is good to behold, and to a city dweller must be something wonderful on a fine summer's day. The best things in life are free, and silence is definitely one of them. Any man that does a long day's ploughing with a high powered diesel tractor, at full acceleration, will tell you so when he switches off the key that evening. We then went on to Co. Sligo, and paid a visit to Yeats' graveyard. We had a lovely swim some place right beside that burial ground. Ben Bulben, which can be seen from far off on all sides, is a mountain one could never forget from its unique shape. We had our second night's stay in beautiful Bundoran. Its lovely beach and swimming facilities are as good as anywhere in Ireland, and the volume of visitors there proves that. The afternoon of the second day, we headed northwards through Barnsby Gap, and from there we went to Killybegs. There, we saw fishermen in action mending their nets, others emptying their boats of their valued catches and others in the far off distance reaping their harvest. Going through the kind hills of Donegal, it was quite noticeable how every man, woman and child gave a friendly salute. It had the same effect as the handshake with your nearest friends at the present day Masses. We stayed the third night in Bundoran also. In the afternoon, on the fourth day, we headed for home via Sligo, Mayo, Longford and Westmeath, after a short but very sweet holiday. We were blessed with good weather, good food and the whatwiths to wash it down.

I had a good rest after that holiday, before returning to Enniscorthy, for another year's work. The spring of 1954 was a fairly mild one, with no severe frost and very little snow. Áine went down to Cork to work in the hotel business. Magie started her secondary school in St. Michael's, Navan, in 1954 also. The late spring and summer brought one of the wettest seasons on record. It rained every second day, and on a few occasions it rained three or four days in a row. The townspeople blamed the bad weather as a punishment from God on farmers, for bringing myxomatosis into the country. The rabbit was the poor man's meat, and what lovely meat a roasted rabbit was! It made lovely soup, and a rabbit stew was beautiful. In the hardware shop, I sold hundreds of rabbit traps, thousands of snares and loads of ferret bells before that shocking rabbit disease broke out. One pipe-smoking woman, who bought lots of rabbit traps and snares from me, was a great rabbit trapess from what her neighbours told me about her.

Tuesday was the fair day in Enniscorthy, and this brought great business to the hardware shops especially. Trade in horses was buoyant at that time, and I saw two men on horseback in typical cowboy style bring at least fifty horses to the Enniscorthy fair. The numbers that were exported for their meat in the forties and fifties, left very few to continue farm work, and to breed showjumpers. This was the end fate that was meted out to the big, quiet and most willing animals, that ploughed, mowed, reaped and sowed the land of Ireland during the busy, large tillage years of the war. Tractors almost completely took over, except for the very extreme horse lover, who would not budge one inch. Diesel fuel powered engines came in the early fifties, giving much greater horse power, much less fuel consumption and at almost half the price of TVO fuels. With the exception of the starting, charging and lighting system, the diesel tractor was free of all the electrical faults that were all too common in the TVO and petrol tractors. Dampness, dirty plugs, faulty distributors and wiring faults did not trouble the diesel engine. It was a great comfort to know that you could hose down your diesel tractor with water for half a day, press your starting button and have your tractor ticking over again. Seán was quick to note all these advantages, and bought a new David Brown 30D in the spring of 1954. It was bought off Mackey Burns, Leinster St., Dublin, who were main David Brown dealers in Ireland. It was a machine that Seán was proud of, and with a new 3-furrow Ransome plough and 8-foot combined seed and manure corndrill, he was able to cover the spring work in half the time. The tractor had one fault, in that the crankshaft was too light for the power of the engine. After a couple of months heavy work, it broke. The tractor, being on guarantee, was fitted with a new shaft free gratis. I got this news by letter from Seán, as I was not home since Christmas. I had the pleasure of driving it when home on holidays in the month of August, 1954, as I gave a hand at drawing in the hay. As a reward for my help, Seán gave me a ticket for a day excursion to the Isle of Man. Micheál had another ticket so the two of us journeyed with the rest of the Navan Young Farmers' Club members. This was our first time in a sea crossing, which was a very pleasant one on a lovely August day. It was a bank holiday, and most of the crowd aboard were Dublin city day trippers. They had musical instruments, and their best singing voices that added to our enjoyment. Our drink got cheaper when the boat was so many miles away from the Irish coast. My only glimpse of the English mainland was the Welsh mountains on that day. We had a swim in Douglas, and I got a scratch of a rock in the tummy on a beach much cruder than Bettystown. We had a good meal that looked very cheap. One of the lads with us said "Why wouldn't it be cheap, with sliced roast horse or ass for meat!" I think it was mountain mutton, and it was lovely. The horse trams in Douglas, on which we took a short ride, were a fine sight. We took a journey up a mountain on an electric train, to view some huge water-driven wheel that was used for factory power. Coming back to Dublin, it was a lovely sight to see the lights along the Dublin-Bray coast line, and I am sure it lifted the heart of many an Irish exile coming home to stay or on a holiday. There was a great sing-song, dancing, and music on the return journey, and there are no people like Dublin people to see to that. All in all, it was a day in my life I often look back on with pleasant memories.

Meath played great football, and reached the All Ireland Final, as did Wexford in the Senior Hurling, in 1954. I went by train from Enniscorthy to the hurling final, and it was very disappointing to see Wexford go down to Cork in a great final. Three weeks later, I went by train to Dublin again for the Meath v. Kerry All-Ireland Senior Football Final. I had an appointment with my brothers and a few of our friends at Nelson's Pillar, which was doomed for disaster twelve years later. I had the pleasure to climb to the top of it once, on paying 6d to the caretaker at the base. I counted the steps on the way up and there were 123. Nelson's Pillar was a long established rendezvous for friends down through the years, especially before Store St. was built.

Not in keeping with the rest of the 1954 summer, this last September Sunday was a lovely day for football. All the papers and 99% of Irish people opted for a Kerry win, but Meath people had other thoughts. We were positioned in front of the then Long Stand. Seán told me to look back and have a good look at poor Séamus Duff with his leg in plaster. He had been a kingpin in Meath's victories, until he met with an accident. Séamus, by the way, was father of the present day singer, Mary Duff. Meath played to perfection and won quite comfortably in the end. They had beaten a mighty good Cavan team in 1949, but one Kerry defeat in an All-Ireland Final is as good as two All-Irelands to any county. We had a few pints in the Flowing Tide, Marlborough St., after the match, and the crack was good with the Dublin boys. They wittingly attributed Meath's victory to the the lessons they learned from Dublin on the way up!

I hadn't a lot of money left, and Seán gave me £2 for my tea and a few bottles of stout on the train journey back to Enniscorthy. I had a very enjoyable day, and a few pounds to collect as a result of Meath's win on my return to the hardware shop on Monday morning. Seán told me that day that he had taken a few acres of land for corn crops, and bought a new combine harvester as well. It cost £1,500 and was the largest Massey Ferguson at that time. He bought it from a firm called Porter Sons & Co Ltd from Oldcastle, Co. Meath. Seán drove it the twenty odd miles home to Boyerstown. He told me he had a few big contracts of harvesting on his book, and at £5 per acre it looked a good investment. I wished him the best of luck with it, and the hope that a big improvement in the weather might come about. That was the last Sunday of September, and little did I know what was in store for me on the last day of October.

I was lying in my bed on Friday 29th October, at 8 o'clock, as the news was being read on the radio in the kitchen underneath my bedroom. I had a slight hearing of an O'Bradaigh been mentioned and hoped there was no accident at home. I got up, had my breadfast and went to work, thinking nothing more about it, as there are an awful lot of O' Bradaigh's in Ireland. During my dinner in my lodgings my landlady showed me the bad news that Seán had been accidentally shot in the right upper arm, while on the combine harvester and that he was in a critical condition. I went back to work, told the boss, and while still talking about it, his sister called me to answer a phonecall. It was my sister Áine, who had phoned to tell me the bad news about the accident, but that Seán was not too bad and the doctor thought he would not lose the arm. I decided to work on and keep in touch with the hospital. About one hour later I was again called to the phone and went prepared for the worst. It was from my next-door neighbour, Seán McGlew, from

Boyerstown, who told me the worst possible news, and it hit me like a blow of a sledge. I thought of the Saturday evening that he had bought the gun from me. I broke down and the boss took over the phone and arranged a Nelson Pillar meeting for me at 8 o'clock with some of my neighbours. I had to get a taxi to Dublin as I was late for either a train or bus journey. I met Páraic and a couple of friends at the appointed time. We had a couple of half ones before going the thirty-three miles home. There were a few neighbours there, and I was surprised how well Ma was taking the tragedy. I presumed she had some sedation tablets taken to help take the sting away or subdue it. Half the family cried a lot, the other half did not cry at all. Micheál and Máire took it without a tear, but seemed to be the worse of that later on. He was buried on Sunday, the 31st October, at 2p.m., and the rain came down in torrents until about 5.30p.m. The coffin was carried from Boyerstown to Ardbraccan by members of the Boyerstown football team, all of whom got a desperate drenching. It was a large funeral, and many of Seán's dancing partners were in tears as the grave was filled in. Our friends and neighbours were most sympathetic, and a great source of comfort during that time and in the following weeks. Seán was to our family as a rudder is to a boat. He was a great man to talk and make good sound suggestions, and always looked for approval before acting. He knew as much about engines and machinery at the age of twelve as did his Da know, and between the two of them there wasn't much left for them not to know. Seán used to keep a good eye on Páraic, Micheál and me so that we did not do something Da would give us a good slogging for. If there were tools used and not left back in place, Da would ask Seán who was using them. Seán often blamed himself to save us a beating. His sudden death was such a blow that it affected half the family in a small way. He, being the kingpin of the family after Da's death, it was never the same again. He was full of life and talk and enjoyed his work. His main pastimes were football and shooting. He took a few drinks on a Saturday night, and before a dance, but he never overdid it.

How the accident happened, I did not ever look into. I was having a drink in a pub in Navan some weeks after the death, and was told by a man that was in the same hospital ward as Seán, that after a few hours in bed Seán's blood was seen under his bed, after going through the mattress. I know that he got blood transfusions but did not respond.

I stayed at home for two weeks to give Micheál a hand to get the one acre of sugarbeet off the rain-washed field before returning to work in Enniscorthy. Páraic was granted time off his work to complete the harvesting, which dragged on to the end of November. It was a disasterous harvest, and some crops were left uncut in the fields. The corn that Seán had grown for his own benefit, cleared the ground rent, the seed and manure, but did not cover the labour input. The sugar beet returns were even worse than the corn results. Some farmers got a bill to pay after seed, manure and carriage had been paid for out of the beet returns. My return home for the Christmas of 1954 brought back sad and happy memories of our days in the choir, singing Christmas hymns. I had to thank God that he gave Seán time to receive the Sacrament of the Dying while he was still conscious. That had taken a big end of the sting off the tragedy. All in all we had a pretty good Christmas in 1954.

During my holidays, I was asked if I would like to stay at home and help out on the farm. After a little thought, I decided that I must help out at home. I gave my boss in Enniscorthy two week's notice on my return after holidays. He understood my situation, and wished me well in life before my departure. Having said farewell to my friends and girlfriend, I left Enniscorthy on Sunday, 11th January, 1955, on a very cold, but dry day. On my journey by bus from Dublin to Navan, I noticed snow in the fields, and hard packed snow on the road from Blanchardstown on. I felt a wee bit astray farming for a while, but soon got the hang of things. Micheál looked after the dairy, while I did the tractor work. Ploughing with a three sod plough gave me a bit of a problem for the first few days.

I was finding it difficult to finish the furrows properly. Páraic gave me a hand in the evenings until I got the run of things. We were not too keen on the combine and sold it for £900. It just cleared itself for that unfortunate year, and Ma was delighted to see it go. I am not going into farming details but I will write a short chapter on the more interesting parts that I experienced in my eleven years farming.

CHAPTER X

I was very fortunate starting, as all the bull-work had already been completed, thanks to Da and Seán. All the sheds were of stone or concrete, and well plastered. The only yellow clay building was the dwelling house, but most of the rooms were newly floored and smoothly plastered. The aga cooker, now about fifteen years old, was as good as new. Apart from the two ton of anthracite for the cooker, the only other fuel required was an odd bag of coal for the parlour fire, which was only lit on special occasions and during frosty and snowy weather. Water was laid on to the house and sheds, which was a big improvement from my younger days. All the land was in good heart and all but eight acres in grass. The machinery was in first class condition as the tractor, three sod plough, combine seed, manure sower and buck-rake had been bought new the previous spring. The disc-harrow discs were so worn that Seán had been on the look-out for a good second-hand one. Our disc harrow was all of thirty years of age. I saw an advertisement in the *Meath Chronicle* for two very good second-hand disc harrows, one a Denning and the other a Pierce. A man called Guy Rooney from near Dunshaughlin owned them and was getting out of tillage. It was no wonder after all the rain in 1954, which put some farmers on the road. There was no messing about the price of the disc harrows with Mr. Guy Rooney. Forty Two pounds each was his price, and forty two pounds he had to get. I chose the Pierce machine and was delighted to get it for forty two pounds as the harrow was only one year old. He gave me two pounds luck for myself. I brought it home that very same day as I had the tractor with me. It was a bitter cold day and it snowed all the way home. Mick and Ma were well satisfied with my purchase. Séamus Boccán set five acres of stubble ground to me for a corn crop. I got my seed and manure on a six month credit basis. I chose a wheat crop, because the ground was of high quality.

The summer of 1955 was a lovely one and crops which had been sown early were looking great. I bought a new mower, a Busatus to suit the David Brown 30D tractor. Three minutes attached the mower in working position, and three minutes took it off. I also got a new Remmy Martin side delivery rake for the sum of fifty-five pounds from Leonards' Hardware in Trim. These two machines left the hay-making a more manageable task, but were far removed from the hay-making machinery available in the 1990's. I went into a big field to mow in the middle of July or later, and my heart was broken trying to keep the mowing bar clear. The present day rotary mowers are a hay maker's dream. In my young days, farmers did not cut a meadow until it was ripe, as they put it. All the grasses were gone to seed, and more than half of them would have lost the seed as well. Good barley straw with a bit of greenery through it would have been better feeding. Hay was all cocked in the forties and fifties, except for about 5% of it. Those people that baled hay that time, left it on the ground for a couple of days after cocking time, thus the feeding value was greatly lowered. Swop help was on the way out, so every farmer had to do with his own manpower. New machinery was responsible for this change in country lifestyle, and with the advent of much better combine harvesters doing most of the harvest, the old style threshings died away. It is probably true to say that 90% of farmers' sons under the age of 25 in 1990 never say a field of sheaves, stooks or hand-stacks. Hitler's army was not as well lined up as a field of stooks. Good hand-stacking was a sight to behold, and perfected only by a few. We made a sum up at home in the late forties, and found out that for every click the reaper and binder made in casting out a sheaf of a good crop of wheat, 9d was registered.

It took me a while to adjust to country life again. Living down a half-mile laneway was far removed from the bright lively streets of Enniscorthy. We had no car, and it was my intention to buy a good second-hand one out of my corn profits. I got it combined and had a yield of twenty two barrells to the Irish acre, which was

2 ton 15cwt in weight. Attle wheat, which was the best spring wheat at that time was not nearly as good a yielder as present day varieties of wheat. I had a net profit of £90 on the five acres. Ma was agreeable to help in the purchase of a car. Myself, and two of my neighbours who knew a few garages in Dublin city, went up on speculation. Our fourth garage had a Ford Prefect ZL 7907 for the sum of £165. It was a well-minded car, very roadworthy, and looked sound value for the price.

We had a celebration drink in some back street pub. We tried our hands in a game of rings, which was all the go at that time. The first dart board I ever saw was in Hayes' Pub in Enniscorthy in 1954. There were only three other customers in the pub, and they happened to be three chimney sweeps that had very much the Al Jolson look. They challenged us for a shilling per man and we duly obliged. We were winning a few shillings each and found that our opponents were beginning to get narky and to dispute the correct score. It was beginning to look as if they would fight with us. While the biggest of our men was throwing the rings, the other man went over to the three sweeps and told them to be very careful not to upset the man throwing the rings, as he was the heavyweight champion of Connaught! Right enough he had a western accent, but the same man would not beat a child. This had the desired result, as they started collecting the rings for us, and calling the so-called champ "Sir". We often had a good laugh over that same event in later years.

On summer evenings, I played football and tennis, and finished up with two to three pints of stout in Dunderry, Navan or Bohermeen. Micheál went for a drink every night as well. Rings were the only pub game played then, and two teams of four, five or six a side got a great kick out of playing for 100-1 for a few coppers stake. Sometimes on a bank holiday, or the weekend, a sing-song would take place with the accompaniment of an accordion. I did no reading, except for the *Farmer's Journal* and the daily newspaper. It was hard to sit at home looking into a fire. Ma was the only one I could have a bit of a chat with, as my eldest sister was not much of a talker. No one could sit talking to their Ma from 6 o'clock to 11 o'clock on a winter's night for four or five months of the year. After some time I could not stay at home, not even for one night of the week, as we had no telly which was now to be seen in all pubs. A few years previous to this (about 1952-3) there was only the one pub in the town of Mullingar with a television. Now and again three or four horse races would be televised. Eight of the smart punters made use of this one telly to great advantage for a while. With a relay of hand and foot signs they were able to signal the winner of one particular horse race to a man standing at the door of a bookmaker's office within a couple of seconds of the result. This bookie's office was a full half mile from the pub with the telly, so no suspicion was cast on the man that put on the bet. They were clever enough to back some losers as well. Finally after two months they overdid the winnings with one large bet that brought in a large win. It was a very cold spell of weather and they went to a party in one of the lad's houses with one dozen large bottles of rum. Their system of winning leaked out and found its way to the bookies involved. They were marked men after that and lost their right to bet in some bookies' offices.

In 1956 I bought three pure bred Fresian heifers in calf, one with the registered certificate. They were bought from a Captain Eccles from Dunderry, who was retiring from farming. They cost me seventy pounds each, less two pound luck penny. I had to join the British Fresian Cattle Society , Rickmansworth, Herts., for an annual fee of five pounds, in order to be eligible to register newly born calves. They sent me a journal every two months. One page of every journal gave the number of registered farmers in each of the thirty two counties. I was the third farmer to be registered in Co. Meath. At that time, five or six was the number registered in 90% of the counties, with the exception of Co. Cork and the six northern counties, which averaged about eighty registered farmers. The AI station had a few well bred and proven Fresian bulls, so I had no bother in breeding good milking strain calves from the three Fresians. I was very keen on the Fresians for quantity of milk, as Seán had bought one five years previously and she was a wonderful milker. She was a Dutch Fresian and much smaller than a British Fresian. One thing about the Fresian cattle was their great appetite. With their thin silkish skin, it took more food to maintain them in cold weather than other common Irish breeds. The Fresian calves were great at lowering the milk, unlike some white-headed sucks that seemed to take in two mouthfulls and then let one mouthfull back into the bucket again!

Boring you with no more minor farming details, which you all know, I will say that there is no better place to bring up a family of young children, than on a farm. They have a better chance to develope their muscles, and if they have to ride a bicycle two or three miles to school and back home again in the evening, all the better for them. The two and three-year-old children running after fowl, calves and lambs! The four and five-year-olds jumping ditches, climbing small trees, helping to round up cattle and sheep, going through the fields with their Ma on a summer's evening as she collected the churn sweetening plants, sorel and watercress plants or wild flowers for home decoration, picking spuds, collecting eggs, jumping windrows and wrestling in them during the hay season, left them in no need of a lullaby to help them to sleep! On the farm, they got a gradual feed of the facts of life, as they asked their elders about the mating of fowl and animals that they happened to see. They see the little chicks leave their shells, the cows calving and the sheep having their lambs. Before I knew the full facts of life, I got a detailed account from my younger sister, Áine, which Ma had responsibly told her the previous day. I think I knew the whole lot after that.

During my farming years, my eldest sister had to be hospitalised for a few months. Seán's death seemed to take all the good humour out of her, and just like myself and Micheál, she took to heavy smoking. With the help of God, none of us will die with cancer of the lungs, which we are giving every chance.

One summer's morning about the year 1957, Ma came up to my bedroom at 8a.m., and told me she had slipped and broken her arm in the fall. I rushed her to hospital, where she was kept for about three months. It was a bad break and was slow to mend. She was home three days when Maggie called to tell me, as I reaped corn in St. Martha's College, that Ma had broken her arm again as she tried to lift a bucket of milk. On her second return home from hospital, she took a good holiday for two weeks, and the arm troubled her no more. From my nightly drinking, unknown to myself I was getting fond of the booze. I was now drinking for a few hours when I went shopping to Navan. At that time, I always put the blame on someone I would happen to meet, instead of blaming myself. There was no trouble in getting farming company in any of the pubs near Laughrans' Corner. Apart from these day-time drinkings, which could occur about three times a month, I looked after the farm to the best of my ability. There were often times during the summer, when I would be working until 11.30p.m. during the hay and harvest seasons, especially before a spill of rain, as there would be no dew on the grass. Like many other farmers' sons, I was restricted in my farm capabilities, in that Ma held the purse strings. She was by no means mean, but if I were to put on the full quota of manure required each year, she might get a desperate fright when the account would arrive. I was putting on about one third of the required amount. Once, my older brother Páraic made a remark to me about all the cocks of hay my Da had in the Cock Park, which is the name of one of our fields, compared with what was on it, one of the summers I was farming it. He did not know that unlike me, Da had the use of all the money he required. There are thousands of young Irish farmers in the same predicament as I was, since 75% of the farms are owned by men over sixty years of age, who will not change their old ways, and widowed women. I had a few pints with my next door neighbour the evening of the day Páraic passed the remark about the cocks of hay in Cock Park, and told him the story. He gave me great consolation when he told me not to mind Páraic, that he was what you call a "weekend farmer" and that the country was full of the same blokes. I had a lot of good outings with the same neighbour at dinner dances, and I shared my one and only visit to Lough Derg with him.

From a visit I had to Grange, Warrenstown, I formed the opinion of which every man is entitled to that 75% of Irish farmers had twice too much land. With the full requirement of lime, phosphate, potash and three annual dressings of 1-cwt of nitrogen per acre, production on the farm would more than double in my eleven years of farming. With only half the farm to work, they would be much nearer to their work and having the other half sold, they would get a nice little annual cheque for interest on capital invested and they would be an inspiration to their new farming neighbours. "GREEN" would shoot me down on that type of farming enterprise, as it upsets the balance of nature, with bad results on fish, birds, insects and animal life. Holland and Denmark, who farmed in that style, are getting negative effects now. They have, as well, a huge pile of slurry and farmyard manure, with nowhere to dispose of it. There is no such thing as a weed, as we know it. It is a plant of yet unknown quality, that is growing in the wrong place. Wheat stocks in a crop of beet could be called weeds.

I did a two year course in a winter farming school. It was one half-day per week for twenty four weeks each year. Two items I found most informative were to do with machinery and animal feeding. The first demonstration was how to take the back wheel off a tractor, mend a tube, and replace it in fifty minutes. It was first shown by a local garage man, and then repeated by one of the students in the fifty minutes flat. All that was needed was a proper fitting wrench for back wheel studs, with an extension tube, a basin of suddy water to be thrown about the tyre where it meets the wheel rimming, two wooden wedges, and a lump-hammer to put down the tyre, and two proper tyre levers. With these implements it was possible to take off the wheel and get out the tube in eighteen minutes, fourteen minutes mended the tube and eighteen minutes replaced the fully fixed wheel. I am talking about twenty-eight years ago. Nowadays, in the 1990's, with modern rolling levers, the story is quiet different. I once spent half-a-day mending a back tractor wheel!

A warning about tractor driving was given to us, and God knows how many thousands that were killed under overturned tractors worldwide! One black spot for this accident is turning off a main road to go into a laneway that runs at right angles to it. What every farmer, especially young farmers, should know is that a tractor is not on springs. Because of this, if a tractor has cause to raise a back wheel, unlike a car on springs, it will go all the way over. Another black spot is registered when a tractor is pulling a heavy lorry or even a fully loaded trailer that has got bogged down, and a tractor is called on to pull out another tractor with a strong rope or chain. If the tow-rope or chain is connected to the tractor that is called to help too high up on the back of that tractor, when the clutch is released, that tractor will rear up on its front wheels and all the way over. There would be no time to disengage the clutch, unless a man knew the danger and released his foot from the clutch very, very slowly. The right thing to do is join the tow-rope or chain as low as possible. One other thing that can happen a tractor and cause death, is for the tractor to start with the engine running the reverse way to the normal. I have never heard of an accident happening this way, but it is a possibility. If this happens to a tractor, all the forward gears would be reverse gears and the reverse gears would be forward gears. Think of a man standing at the back of a machine being pulled by a tractor that had the engine running the wrong way! When the tractor driver raised the foot of the clutch to go forward, it is back the tractor would go to the surprise of the man standing there. The man standing behind a sower could easily be crossed over. I have started a couple of diesel engines that were driving cement mixers, and they started off in the wrong cycle. Of course, everyone knows the danger of the unguarded power drive-shaft, but just like the man working on a saw the more familiar they are with it, the more likely they are to be caught out. The second item of major interest, the feeding of farm animals, was made very clear and distinct to us. Now, one fodder unit is the equivalent of 1-lb of good barley. A table of the feed value from other farm feeds, such as oats, silage, hay, straw, turnips, mangle, beet, fodder beet, etc, can be got from any farm instructor, showing what weight of these feeds is required to equal 1-lb of barley. 7-lbs of barley, or to use the right term, 7 fodder units, are required to mantain the average cow or bullock of two years. They will drink 1 gallon of water per 1-cwt of their weight. In addition to that, a cow requires three-and-a-half fodder units per gallon of milk, and a two-year-old heifer or bullock requires three-and-a-half fodder units per 1-lb weight gain. I will do three simple sums from the above information.

(1) 40 cows averaging 2 gallons of milk daily over one year require 14 fodder units daily each.

20 cows averaging 4 gallons daily over one year require 21 fodder units daily.

Now, you will have the same milk cheque out of 20 cows as 40 cows. As well as that, the 40 cows require 560 fodder units per day, while 420 will do the 20 cows per day. This is possible with a start of about five very good Fresian milkers, good breeding, good husbandry and culling over about ten years. Nowadays, the computer could help out at that as well as doing the feed costings.

(2) Now, taking three and a half fodder units for 1-lb daily weight gain:

50 cattle feed over the winter months and getting 7 fodder units daily. No weight gain.

25 cattle feed 14 fodder units daily over the same period. 50-lb daily weight gain.

Thus for the same amount of feed, the 25 cattle excel the 50 by 50-lbs daily. Add to this gain the interest on the price of 25 cattle.

(3) The same applies to sheep and pigs. It is much better to have 25 well fed sheep, than 50 with twine lamp disease for equal feeding. It is easier to farm on paper than on the land itself as it is a "hurler on the ditch" act. In my farming years, i.e. late fifties early sixties, these feeding theories did not always work to a more profitable conclusion. Young cattle of about four cwt. could be bought in at about £6 per cwt. in the late autumn and sold around May day at about £9 per cwt. and sometimes up to the ten or eleven pound mark. Thus, double the number of cattle that just maintained their weight over the winter and early spring months probably paid better than half the number well fed. It is a different story now in the 1990's, as cattle are more or less at static prices all the year round.

A Department veterinary surgeon gave us a couple of hourly lessons on animal ailments. At the end of each lesson, he took questions freely for about fifteen minutes. He probably left us with more knowledge than our local vets would like us to know. One very useful hint that he gave us was, that when a ruminating animal is sick, instead of chewing the cud for about fifty to sixty mouth twists, it will only perform this for ten to twenty turns before letting it down into the lower stomach. Another hint he gave us that is useful to know, is that when the slime coming from a heifer or cow is a strawish colour, that animal is within two hours of calving.

Looking back on my farming days, I think I would have made more profit by doubling the cow numbers from twenty to forty, and cutting out the hire work. Micheál did not like the dairy ever, and ever since Seán's death he suffered from slight depression and was very easily upset. He loved working when he had company, which managing twenty cows on his own, denied him of. He was able to smoke up to sixty cigarettes a day and was getting fond of the drink, just like myself.

One job I loved was the care of breeding ewes. I once wintered ninety ewes, thirty of them being hoggets and got one hundred and thirty healthy lambs from them. My very first year, I had only twenty ewes and three of them got twine lamb disease, which taught me a life-long lesson on the value of good feeding. My vet, Joseph Clarke of Dunderry Stud, who went to the same school as I, namely St Pat's in Navan, instilled the value of feeding of breeding ewes, in- calf heifers and cows. Joe, as we called him, had a 100% clear sheet with all his visits to our farm, a few of them very urgent cases. He never leaned too hard on the pen either. In my school days, gymkhanas were a popular race meeting for ponies. Joe Clarke had two ponies, which he always rode himself, and had more victories than defeats with them within a fifty mile radius of Navan. "Hello Paddy", a piebald, was the more popular of the two with racegoers. The bookies showed their respect for him, and apart from his first few victories, they chalked him as favourite at very short odds. "Late For School" was the name of the second pony, and he too made his stamp in pony racing to a lessor extent. "Hello Paddy" lived to the ripe old age of twenty-nine.

One night at 12 o'clock, a cow that had got milk fever on two previous occasions after calving, and whom I watched very closely as a result, lay stretched out in the field. I immediately rushed up to Clarkes and met Joe's wife. Joe had a bout of flu and was confined to his bed. From his bed he gave instructions to his wife, who came out to me with two five-noggin bottles of a liquid to be injected under the skin of the animal's neck. On my return home, the cow looked very distressed and had a heavy, slow grunting. I started injecting with my 20cc syringe, and it took me almost half an hour to inject the two bottles. I left her, and I had no much hope of seeing her alive in the morning. I looked out my bedroom window at 8a.m. the next day, and to my great joy, heading the grazing herd was my darling patient! I said a short prayer that God would give Joe many more years of work with his gentle healing animal hands. Patrick Hilliard, who was married to my Aunt Mary had the real old method of curing milk fever. I once saw him in action. With the rear end of a cow raised with a bundle of straw, he pumped air into the cow's paps with a bicycle pump. It worked, and from what I was told after, it never failed to get him a positive result. This art was used for hundreds of years, just like the "charge" that was made for the repair of broken animal bones. Pat Hilliard was a well known, honest cow dealer, who died a very happy death, and by no means a millionaire. He was the last milk cow dealer on the open Dublin market which terminated with his death. He lived in Gainstown, Navan.

To get back to the sheep, which I have strayed from, I fully agree that they are not very intelligent. Instead of heading into a hail or rain storm, they head for the worst possible hedge in a field for shelter. This is the reason that they are caught in snow drifts during wintry weather. One month of March when I was farming there came a few weeks of harsh drying wind. I noticed the wool of the sheep getting a blackish taint. I began to wonder if they were getting any water. There was water in the ditches, but I never saw any of them coming up from the drinking place there. I brought out 2 five-gallon cans of water and put them into the feeding troughs. I called the sheep and was delighted to see them empty the troughs in a very short time. I had to bring out about 4 more five-gallon cans to the eighty sheep or thereabouts. As long as the drying wind lasted I kept up the same practice with great results. It is not every ditch that a ewe will go into and unless they are getting a lot of turnips or kale while suckling lambs, a supply of water is most important. The same watering would have to be exercised during a spell of dry black frost. The most pathetic sight I ever saw, animal wise, was two four-week old lambs beside their dead mother sheep, whose body was still warm. One of the lambs had his two legs up on her body as he scraped with one of them, that looked to be an effort to get her up so that they could suckle her. Their bulging eyes showed great fear, just as the lambs on a third story of a lorry stopped at the traffic lights of a big town. The two lambs instilled a desperate picture of a household of young children, whose mother has had a sudden death. Think of the plight of the poor husband. The lambs on top of the lorry remind me of a telly news item I saw one night. I saw South African police lashing out at young black boys in their teens, and then throwing them into the back of a guarded lorry. It was pathetic to see the frightened faces of them as they looked down at their crying and waving mothers. Another news item I read on the same subject was that of six black boys that were taken out of a bunch of about twenty and put on the back of a flat-bodied lorry. They were driven round the same housing block seven times, as the big dogs stood towering over and biting at the boys limbs in full view of the comrades they had been taken from!

I learned my sheep shearing from a next door neighbour, and it took me about two hours to shear the first one. Micheál shouted half time after one hour, and indeed the poor ewe could have done with a ten minute break! That same next door neighbour had two poems, one each for two different occasions. The first one was used when he had shaved and dressed for his nightcap in the local. It went thus:

"Here's to those that stay at home
And with their parents dwell,
But why should I just stay at home,
When ramblers do so well!"

He used the second one when I would make my entry into the local:

"Brady and Brandy differ by one letter,
So why shouldn't Brady love Brandy the better!"

That same gentleman always brought home a good parcel of meat after a fair or mart, as was customary with almost all farmers. After all, there is no point in selling five or six hundred pounds of meat, which is the equivalent of one beast, if you are not able to eat one lb of it yourself! He would fry this meat himself on the open fire, and nearly always managed to set the pan ablaze. Off with the pan and on to the floor of the kitchen, he would then put the blaze out with vigorous shaking strokes of his hat. When the wife made a sigh of disapproval, he would say "This is part of the grilling process that only a few top class chefs know about."

I quickly learned, with practice, and with an electric machine which Seán had made by converting a hand-twist one, I was capable of shearing eighty sheep a day. This was far from the Meath Champ of my farming days "The Red Dowd" from Dunderry, who could shear a ewe in two-and-a-half minutes. He is the grandfather of the present Thomas Dowd, who plays a forward with the Meath Senior team and being the chief engineer of the golden goal that crucified Dublin on the final match of four in 1991, has a great future ahead of him. I took my annual holidays of two weeks, and used it shearing sheep on hire for neighbouring farmers. At 2/6 in old money, at the time it was possible to make up to £10 per day, which was the weekly wage for a farm labourer at that time.

Like 80% of cattle skullers and sheep shearers I used all my holiday money for drink. Ma used to say to me "Easy got, easy gone". Cheviot sheep and Suffolk x Galway crossbreds were much more hardy to winter weather than the pure Galway sheep. The year 1958, which was probably as wet a summer and autumn period as 1954, killed about 25% of the country's sheep population with fluke. One of my next door neighbours lost his entire flock of twenty ewes to leave a very lonesome Suffolk ram on his own. I had dosed all my ewes with a fluke dose that was known locally as the "Kells Dose". Out of sixty ewes I had, I did not lose one as a result of fluke. The Kells Dose for fluke was compounded by a Mr.

Kelly MRCVS, who had his practice in Railway St., Kells. The year 1958 was another disastrous harvest year that is better forgotten!

Another bad result of the wet years 1954 and 1958, which were so close together, was that the constant weight of heavy thatch on the roofs of thatched cottages caused some of the roof rafters to crack, or almost completely break about two foot up from the wall-plate. All rafters had a class of dry rot, and most of the houses were up to 300 years old. Four of the rafters on the roof of our house broke and caused wall damage, which I did not see in time because of the extension building at the back of the house. I had to get an emergency asbestos roof on half the house until I slated the entire house in a much better summer. These two wet summers were responsible for the wholesale pulling down of thatched roofs in the years following close to 1954 and 1958.

The best summer weather-wise was 1959. The spring that supplied our house failed for the first time in my life and it never failed in Da's life either. Another cattle-drinking well in one of the field's ditches failed in 1959. I was told by Da that it, too, had never failed in his lifetime, and he was born in 1892. I worked hard on the farm, and had a happy life on it. I had some good outings during my eleven years working there, but my drinking gradually progressed, often leaving me in depressed moods, and I suffered greatly from an inferiority complex. Of all my pals on the football, tennis and hurling teams, I was the only outcast. Of course, I was definitely the black sheep, rake, ram or anything else you care to call me in a fairly respectable family. I would have been much better at these sports but for my drinking. Boyerstown had a hurling team with a unique record. In its two years of existence, in which they must have played thirty matches, they never won a single match! Our tennis team was more successful in that we had a player in Michael Buchannon, that was the best in Meath, and who won over one hundred cups and trophies in tournaments throughout

Meath, Louth and Westmeath. He was a very successful badminton player as well. But for the club we formed on his father's farm, Michael might have missed out on all the great enjoyment he got. The land supplied was free gratis.

I went to a good few dances, but there had to be a bar attached, or a shebeen close by. Unlike Navan, whose publicans were well to do, there were always three or four publicans in Trim only too glad to oblige thirsty men during illegal hours. One of these was right in front of the dance hall. Three raps of a penny on the window brought a sure reply to the door in two minutes or less. When you got into this very homely candlelight pub, you were asked "Did you see any cops around?". From what I heard in the pub, there were some guards devils, and the rest were old gentlemen! It was never raided on my visits there, and from the pubs location in the early sixties, the poor publican who had a family to rear, would have needed the extra trade. As the small bar ran alongside the street, it was a "speak very low" pub. All went in little groups at a time half an hour before the end of the dance. I once went to the dance in that hall in Trim to see *The Dubliners*. On going into that same pub, I was in the company of that gifted band. I had a warm handshake from both Ronnie Drew, and poor Luke Kelly.

In later years, these shebeen pubs were not prepared to take chances as the penalties were too heavy. I then reverted to Navan Rugby Club dances, and on an odd occasion Bellinter Golf Club dances, where there was always an unending supply of booze. Women in those mentioned years had no time for a drinking man. Thus is my present state of bachelorhood for which I have no regrets. All things told, people behaved themselves pretty well then. Broken marriages were a very rare occurence. I should not say this, but I have had occasion to visit a heavy whiskey drinker's bedroom since I gave up drink, and if I were his wife I would not sleep with him. The man I speak about is a long time divorced, for which I do not wonder.

Micheál and I had a great day trip excursion by train to Belfast in 1957. We had the pleasure of going all through the Harland and Wolfe ship-building yard, and were astonished to see the size of these monsters, when nearing completion in dry dock. We were on our way out of the yard, when questioned by a groundsman looking for an invitation card. On getting a negative response, he pointed to the exit and told us to get out of the place as fast as we could. We also got a visit to the Belfast City Hall, which was well worth visiting. The red and cream buses, powered by the overhead electric cables were also new to us.

I had a most enjoyable holiday in Ballybunion in 1962, accompanied by Páraic and three of our neighbouring friends. There was no scarcity of drink in that Las Vegas of the Kerry kingdom. During my farming years, I went to all the football and hurling Senior Championship Finals. Cork and Wexford in the 1955 final, is the hurling match that sticks out in my memory. When Christy Ring sent in the ball from the Cusack stand and canal corner in the dying seconds of the match, and Artie Foley came out with the ball rivetted to his hand from that Ring stinger, a roar erupted in Croke Park that was never heard since! Before that Foley stepping out, 90% of spectators did not know whether the ball was in Foley's hand or the back of the net! The final whistle blew, and the Rackards chaired Christy Ring across the field in admiration for him. Wexford had won by one or two points.

After the 1956 hurling final, which Wexford again won, myself and two butties of mine had the pleasure of meeting Willie Rackard and Séamus Ahern in Dolans' pub in Marlborough Street. They wondered why Nicky Rackard was not down to celebrate with them. On reading Nicky's life story after, this was a day that he broke out after a long abstinence, and wandered off on his own. One of my pals got me to stand back-to-back with Willie Rackard, and he told me that I would fit into him very handy! I am five foot, eleven-and-a-half inches tall, and by no means a narrow man, but these three Rackard brothers had physique unique to very few brothers. I had another great day at a Munster final between Cork and Tipperary in Limerick, when Christy Ring was at his brilliant best. Limerick was the Croke Park of the south, and every square foot of the ground had a pair of shoes and the palm trees had their flying supporters as well. We had a good after-the-match party, and had a lovely trip around the town in a jaunting car, to view places and monuments of note, among them the one of Sarsfield Treaty Stone.

One other hurling match I never forgot was a national league final between Wexford and Tipperary in Croke Park on a windy day. Tipperary were leading by 19 points at half time, but Wexford came out and beat them by four points in the end. My only recollection of Mick Mackey was listening to the wireless when I was about four years of age. Was he as good as Christy Ring? Some people will dare to answer, but my verdict from all I have heard is that it is similar to judging a beauty queen, which neither of those two lads were!

Our school teachers taught us to be faithful to our grace before and after meals. Surely there are better occasions for these two thanksgiving prayers, than before and after belly-feed time. I said mine before and after Meath's two great victories in 1987 and 1988 All-Ireland finals, and it was well rewarded. Similarly, looking back at Jack Charlton's charges beating Maggie Thatchers charges in England and Northern Ireland was an occasion for similar thanksgiving prayers. I only have to look back at my own Da, who used raise the delph off the kitchen table with his fist hammering, when Meath played Louth in three games to beat Louth by one point in the 1949 Leinster championship, all games which were broadcast on the radio. I dread to imagine what would have happened if he had to be looking at a 28 inch colour television picture of the three same games, or better still, Meath's miraculous one-point win over Dublin in the first round Senior Football Championship of Leinster in 1991, after three replays, two of which were extra time or a total of 340 minutes.

Da's first cousin Séamus Boccán died in the year 1960. Now I had to do extra work for his widowed wife, which gave me more money for drink! My Uncle Jack died one year later, and as a result, Aunt Rose had to be hospitalised. Ma got two small farms as a result of these tragedies, which left us with four small scattered parcels of land.

During my farming years, I had three brushes with the law. After a dance in Skerries one summer's night, my pals who were in the car with me, kept hooting the horn of the car at good-looking lassies that were passing. This noise brought a young Garda over to the car. I was caught for not having a driver's licence, which was four weeks out of date. I was summonsed, and got the benefit of the Probation Act. The second offence was for being in a council field at the back of Jim Kearney's pub in Railway Street, Navan, at 12.30a.m. with two friends. The three of us were summonsed for being on licensed premises during forbidden hours. One solicitor was hired to answer for the three of us. He put up the case that we could have been buying cattle when we were on the council field behind the bar that night! We were guilty, of course, but after good laughter in the court, which was packed with farmers who were charged with blocking the road, the case was dismissed.

The third case was a simple slip-up that turned out very sour for me. It was the year 1963, in which I had almost all of one of the farms, about thirty -three acres, in wheat and barley. As it was sown pretty late, I decided to reap the barley in August, and wheat in September, for fear the ground would get too wet to carry a combine harvester. As the weather turned out, I took the right decision and had all the corn hand-stacked in early October. As this was almost five days threshing, and the land was five miles from our house, I decided to get the men's dinners in Reillys' Arcadian Cafe, Trimgate St., Navan, which was only two miles from the place we were threshing. After a hard bargain with Mr. Thomas Reilly he did the dinners for four shillings a head. Ma was delighted with this arrangement as she was getting on in years by then. The arrangement worked to perfection, and the men left the cafe very well satisfied with the quality and quantity of the meal served. I think that threshing would have been very near the last big threshing in Co. Meath. About one month later, I went to settle up with the threshing contractors, about one mile from the bog cross on the main Navan to Athboy road. I paid the man forty pounds for the five day's threshing, and as he had no change he got me to drive him the two-and-a-half miles to Finnegans' of Greetiagh. On getting change in Johnny Finnegans, the contractor handed me a five pound luck penny and ordered two half ones. We fell into the company of a few farmers, and time slipped by very quickly. We left the pub at about 6p.m. and brought back one dozen of stout for a few lads that were with the threshing mill. On our way back, we noticed a bag of meal at the bog cross, and I, thinking it must belong to the Garrys, whose threshing had been done, put the bag of meal in the back of the car. There was a man with a horse and dray collecting empty milk cans at the cross at that time, and he spoke to the man that was with me. When we arrived at Garrys, all the lads had gone home and the man of the house brought us into the house for tea. We brought in the dozen of stout and tackled it after tea. I enquired if the meal was for this farmplace, and was informed that it wasn't. The fireplace was the turf on the hearth type with the big black swinging crane to hold up the kettle and pots. The pot oven sat on a hob one side of the fireplace, ever ready to make more golden wheaten bread.

Now I was about to leave back the bag of meal, but my friend told me to do so in the morning, when I would be leaving the milk up to Clarke's Cross, as his very old father would be worrying about him. I saw his point and left him home. I had to have another tea in his house, so it was about 9p.m. when I got home. I went to Navan that night and while talking to a friend, I told him about the bag of meal that I had to leave back in the morning. He told me to leave it back that night, and how right he was. My brother Micheál got up the next morning, and took out the meal to leave room for the milk cans. He put the meal into the meal store, thinking that it was for the farm use as he had often done before. I was up a bit late that morning, and as I had pigs and calves to feed and cattle and sheep to look after, I intended leaving the meal back first thing after dinner.

At about 2p.m. there was a knock at the door, and I went out to answer it. It was two Athboy guards, one a sergeant, and the first thing I said to them was "Are you looking for a bag of meal". They came into the meal store and brought the untouched bag out to their car. I gave them a full statement and signed it. The sergeant, in particular, went off a very happy man, and I knew now that I was in trouble. I went to my neighbouring guard and told him my trouble. The first thing he asked me was did I make a statement, and on answering, he told me that I should not have made one. All of this guard's four sons had gone to St. Pats secondary school with me, and played football on the same Boyerstown football team as well. He tried everything in the trade, including a trip to the Superintendent in Kells, all to no avail. Another neighbour of mine brought me to that great Fianna Fail T.D., Marty Johnston, from Slane. He was a large farmer and publican and the father of The Johnstons, the singing sisters of great fame, who were once in partnership with Paul Brady, another present day great. He gave me great hopes of success, but about two weeks later I got a letter with a harp signed by a very influential man, that regretted he could do nothing about the case as it was now sub-judice.

Just as I had thought about Seán's death first thing every morning for months, this happening was haunting me in just as bad a way. I was kicking football one Sunday just before the court case, and kicked four very easy frees wide from about twenty one yards. My thoughts were a hundred miles away from the game. I never thought of getting my parish priest or curate to try to use their good influence. I collected the oats for them from three townlands every year, and knew them well to talk to from their visits for the house stations. My solicitor told me not to be worrying over the thing, which was a very simple charge. The guard that brought out the summons asked me did I get hungry or what?. I happened to have a few good nights with the same guard who had some liking to drink as myself. He retired from the force, and got a great job as a car salesman a couple of years later. My summons for a court hearing was adjourned on the first appointed date to attend. I don't know why this adjournment took place. It appeared on the Meath Chronicle, giving my name and why I was charged. There was a neighbour's funeral between the first adjournment and the proper case, which I attended, and if I were given the choice I might have swapped with the body in the coffin. I had four good witnesses, as well as my brother Micheál, that I could have summoned to the court, but knew nothing about this at the time. When the case was called, the judge asked me if I would prefer a trial by a court with a jury. My first reaction to this was the thought that this was as bad as a murder case. My solicitor answered that I would go ahead with the case. The sergeant, when called, made a great-looking case for a conviction, telling the truth as he saw it. My solicitor put up a great fight, telling the judge that he played football on the same team as I and that he was quite sure it was a bit of carelessness over a lot of drink. The judge gave his verdict, "I have grave doubt over this case, but I must give the defendant the benefit of the doubt". That was a day I spent in court and which coincided with my half day in the winter farming school.

My next worry was to get the *Meath Chronicle* before Ma, and take out the page with the court report in it. I had a chat with James Lawlor, a member of the great Lawlors Bakery firm of Trimgate St., Navan, who was an inlaw to some of the proprietors of the *Meath Chronicle*. I still have a good mental picture of the same James Lawlor warding off wasps with a swipe of his hands as they hovered around his head while putting twine round a parcel of bread. The same wasps sucked away at cream and jam on top of the sweet cakes and buns in the glass cabinet. The same buns which had a lovely fresh smell would put a desperate yearning on me, as my dinner awaited me at home. All I could afford at that time would be a 1d toffee, a 1d lucky package, an apple or an orange. I often had a quiet drink with that gentleman, and having told him my story, I asked him to use his influence to try to get the report on the sports page off the paper. Right enough it was a two columned half page report on a single sport's page, with the judge's verdict in bold print at the top. I didn't feel as bad now as between the first adjourned case and the proper court case. I was relieved to have the damn thing finalised. Ma had a slight suspicion there was something wrong, because one day I was on my way to Navan with her, I pulled up at the neighbouring guard's house for something to know about the case. On my return out to the car she said, "I hope you are not in any trouble". It was about three months later when she bumped into our C.C. in the town of Navan. He told her in good faith not to mind the write-up that I got in the local paper, and let the cat out of the bag in doing so! All Ma ever said to me in a quiet way was "You let us down".

The whole thing that annoyed me after, was that distant cousins of ours, who were very good friends of ours, stopped sending Christmas cards, attending future funerals and the wedding reception exchanges came to an end also. Why my poor Ma, that had such trouble throughout her life, should be penalised for a foul act of mine I found hard to understand. I'll say one good thing that happened, it did not affect the hospitality of my maternal first cousins, my many friends in Navan, the Commons, Dunderry or Bohermeen. I allege here now, from what I was told by the owner of the bag of meal, that the taking of the meal into my car was reported by the man who saw me putting it into the car or one of his family. This was because I had refused to take five pound shares in the foundation of the Athboy Creamery, because I was getting full milk price from Merville Daries, who were a highly held company. I forgot to mention that the owner of the bag of meal went to great pains to get me out of the trouble, but to no success. "Case Closed".

As a result of that lesson and experience I went through, I would like to make a special appeal to any guard or sergeant who reads this book. Think twice before bringing any person to court for their first offence, through the abuse of drugs, alcohol or anything else, unless it is a Bonny and Clyde act. It is the father, mother and other members of the family who have to suffer too. If it is a young person, let them off with a strict warning, telling their parents and the shame it would bring on the household. That should give a positive result. A short time after my mishap, two of my neighbour's houses were broken into. One was only an attempted break-in, and the other was a case in which forty pounds was taken from a teapot that lay on top of a kitchen dresser. Both these events were later solved, but until they were I was told by both householders that the Navan guards had me down as a strong suspect. They asked Mrs. Buccán, one of the owners affected, where I got the money for drink. I asked her what reply she gave him. It was a Kerryman's answer. She asked the guard where did he get money from! Robbing orchards in my younger days, I always had two guard's sons with me and felt very safe.

As time went by, I drank more and more. My brother Páraic gave me the use of his almost new Volkswagen car, while he was at university in Columbus, Ohio, for one year. On the bank holiday of Easter Monday that same year, I had a head on collision while driving that car and was very lucky there was no-one killed or seriously injured. My passenger, whom I was leaving home, came out the worst of all of us. He was flung out the passenger front door after bursting it open. He was hospitalised for three weeks, with his teeth caged up for resetting as some of them were very loose. The man's wife and two-year old child in the other car were only slightly injured. Lucky enough the young woman was not pregnant. A sister of my passenger was a nurse in the hospital, and told enquiring guards that we were too ill to be interrogated that night. I got a note from the guards of their intention to prosecute, but for lack of any evidence or witnesses there was never anything more about it. Who was at fault, I will never know, but I was very grateful to God that no-one was killed. Both vehicles were insured and the due compensation paid out. I only claimed for the car, as I was not injured too much. My passenger, who invested his money from the accident to buy cattle, had great luck with them and is a wealthy man now. He had a good job at the time, and was a very correct type of man. My brother Páraic got his Master's Degree in science for his year's study in the USA. He was a bit annoyed over his lovely car, as it was his first Volkswagen, and as he put it "There will never be another you". Its registered number was ZN 3948. I'll have to give credit to Páraic here for taking the accident in the manner that he did.

I had a lot of new grass on the thirty-three acres of cornground I had sown in the spring of 1963. As there was no baler in the neighbourhood, I decided to buy a New Holland baler in the spring of 1964, and bale all the new meadow hay. I knew that cocking hay was on the way out, and that there would be plenty of hire work to be done as well. The baler cost £600 and at 6d per bale, it was possible to earn up to £50 for a good day's baling. Once I baled a little over 3000 bales in a long day from 10a.m. to 11p.m. The hay was in great form, nicely put into very tidy and nicely sized wind-rows. I earned a little over £75 for that day's work. Most baling days only last from about 12 noon to about 9pm, as in good weather the dew would be down by then. Unlike a combine harvester that worked for only seven or eight weeks of the year, the baler was a machine that could work all year round. The hay and straw baling pickup season lasted for at least three months. There was another few weeks to be worked baling field hay-cocks.

During the winter months, for a man that would have time, there was good money to be earned by buying pikes of hay or even a link of hay in a hay barn at a keen price, and selling it by the bale. With shear bolts in the main drive and knotter drive, as well as slip clutches, there was very little to go wrong with a properly greased baler, that was well housed when not in use. I often wondered how a bullet-shaped 4"piping about 18" long, fixed to the very centre of the compressor ram face, would work in a baler. I don't think it would interfere with the take-in forks or the knotter drive. If it did interfere with either of the drives, very little adjustment of the timing of the three drives would have to be made. If that idea allowed a good medium sized bale to be made without distorting the bale shape and endurance, there should be a passage for free air to go right through the bale centre, allowing the hay to be baled much sooner, thus improving the protein content of the hay, which is the dearest component in all bought food mixtures.

I was now thirty-two years of age, in the year 1965, and as I had two sisters, as well as Micheál and Ma in the family unit, I thought it was time for some kind of family settlement to be made. Ma, just like every mother, thought I was only a youngster, but agreed to have a chat with all members of the family about some class of a settlement. It was coming up to Christmas, so we agreed to let the matter lie until after Christmas.

During my drinking bouts, I had slept out under the skys five times in as many years. After a football match in Croke Park one Sunday, I over-did it with the drink, missed my lift home, and went to O' Donoghues' singing pub until closing time. My only chance of a sure lift home was with our milk collector in the mid-morning. I had a light meal, and walked all the way to Merville Dairies in Santry. I was told there that the milk lorry that collected our milk would be starting out on its round at 4 o'clock in the morning. I lay down on a bank in front of the dairy, which lucky enough was bone dry, tried to get a bit of sleep and not to miss the lorry on any account. The dread of missing the lorry left me without any shut-eye. On the dot of 4a.m., out came the lorry I had been waiting for, and Charlie, the driver, copped my raised hand across the road. "Where in the name of God were you?", he asked, as I dragged myself up into the lorry. On telling him my story, I lay down on the cushions and had a badly needed three hours' sleep, as Charlie hauled in the full cans of milk onto the lorry, after leaving down as many empty ones.

Another Saturday night, after a swim in Bettystown, a friend and I had a drinking session in The Northlands, a hotel between Drogheda and Bettystown. It was after one of the hottest days in that year. I decided to have a sleep somewhere before the long journey home. We went back out to Bettystown, and lay down on the car rug on the golf course. I was awakened at 7a.m. with the noise of the swish of a golf club and the whizz of a ball, as it rocketed past me. I woke up my sleeping partner who enquired "Where in the name of God are we". We had a swim, got a light meal in a Drogheda restaurant, and went to Mass in St. Peter's. On coming out, I saw my pal's brother with the fag in the side of his mouth, and he taking some great whiffs out of it. I sensed trouble. We spun a lie which is a drunkard's "true" story, that the car broke down and we had to wait until morning to get it rectified. Home I went, and as Micheál had the milk delivered by means of the tractor, Ma knew nothing about the happening. To satisfy my drinking, I ran a sort of illegal hackney service from the pub each night. If it was a wet night, bicycles would be left in the pub yard. Three or four men would get into my car, and I would leave them home. Mostly, it would be on my way home, but occasionally it would be in the reverse direction. I often ran out of petrol as a result of this, by taking pot luck. These lads were quite generous and would always buy a good drink the following night, if not the night I left them home. They would bunce up and collect 10/- for the petrol expenses, which would buy two gallons at that time, even though the detour might only take a half gallon extra.

Talk came up in a Navan pub one day about swimming. The question came up about who among us could swim. None but I could answer this positively. I was challenged about that act, and a farmer bet me ten pounds that I could not swim. The publican took the ten pounds and put ten pounds along with it for the winner. I happened to have my towel and togs in the back of the car. "How will we prove it", asked my challenger. "Come on with me", I said. I drove him down to the river Boyne, which was only a quarter of a mile away. I dived in, and to give my friend a fright I swam underwater for as long as I could. When I came up, he was yelling for help, thinking I was drowning. It being the end of September, the water was on the cold side, but it was well worth doing, as ten pounds would buy eighty pints of beer at that time!

I won another ten pound bet on the query "What length of rope would you give to an ass tied to an ESB pole in the middle of a large field, so that he grazed one acre only?". I had no bother winning the bet. I always overdid the drinking at the dozen wedding receptions I attended. It took me three full days to recover after one of these outings.

Páraic got married in the spring of 1965, and I was best man. I did the best I could do at the ceremony, and got by with a pass. With the hard hat and white gloves in my hand, I did not feel as much at home with them as Fred Astaire. Going away from Dubliin airport on his honeymoon, Páraic did not offer me his car until his return!

In the end of January, 1966, I brought up the question of a family settlement again. After a few night's discussion and thought on all aspects of the problem, all were willing to give me the twenty six acres of land that Seán had bought some twenty-eight years previously. With the acreage we had, I was very pleased with the settlement. Thus I made my exit from a happy eleven years farming, before the entry of the powered zig-zag harrow, the round-bale baler, silage made in bags, rotary mowers, brucelosis testing, milk quotas, marginal land grants, etc. All these changes were far removed from the days of skulling by hobbles, pulling thistles with a tongs, cooling milk in a river, broadcasting seed and manure by hand, the clod-crusher for finishing the tillage ground, etc.

CHAPTER XI

There was a pub for sale in the town of Athboy in the month of March, 1966, a pub I had often drunk in. It was always known as Cullens' pub from the days that a Mr. Cullen and a Mr. Smith, two Cavan men, bought it in the 1920's. In the days of the railway in Athboy, it wa known as the Railway Hotel, as it had six bedrooms, dining room, bar and lounge and a big spacious kitchen. In those early years, that house catered for wedding receptions, as about twenty people was the number at the average wedding. One of my next door neighbours in Boyerstown told me that he had his wedding reception there. As my sister, Áine, had several years' experience in the bar trade, I thought that that pub might be a good investment. She was willing to work in the pub. Her boyfriend Frank was willing to join forces with me in the buying of the pub on a 50-50 basis. We bought the pub for £7,000, so my share of the input was £3,500. This money was not available to me for some months until the sale of my land, for which I got £5,400. It was the end of May when we finally got the key of the place. We spent three weeks painting the entire pub and lounge, while all shelving was empty. We opened up on a Friday evening in early June, and had a packed house, even though an awful lot of Athboy people went to Kinnegad the same night, where a very popular Athboy man, Jack Mc Elhinney, was opening a pub he had bought in that town. Let me say from the start, that my buying of the pub was a huge success in that it was a partial failure. The reason for this failure was that none of us were born to that type of life and we were not a Tony O'Reilly - Dennis Guiney partnership. We had five years of a happy life there, and met good life-long friends from all around Athboy and Rathcarn districts. A great place to cure a sick man after a feed of drink would be a couple of laps of one of the fields on the "Hill of Ward" on a sharp, crisp, frosty morning. I did not mind doing the pub in the daytime for the first two years, but it became a bit of a bore after that. I got a job doing a bit of work baling, and jumped to it. It was a gift to be back out in the open land again. I suppose a man who is born into the bar business and starts work there with his father, becomes institutionalised to it. It was a very lazy type of life for me, and Frank was not too fond of the day-time work there either.

Frank married my sister Áine in June, 1966. As we had four bedrooms set on a weekly rent, Áine had enough to do keeping the place clean, getting our meals, and giving a hand in the bar from 6p.m. to closing time. When all were gone at night, the place had to be left ready for the following day's opening. It took time to clean the bar, lounge, get the empties out to the yard, bring in the cases of drink from the store, pack up the shelves, and clean and shine all empty glasses and tumblers. It was always after 1a.m. before we could get to retire for the night.

Bar work was very different from the hardware business I had served my time at. In the hardware job you took your order, parcelled it up, gave it to the customer, collected the money, gave out the change and that was that. In the bar you had to be in good humour all the time. You had to be a good listener, even though it might be some dry yarn being told to you for the tenth time since morning, from the same three-quarters-shot customer. You had to be alert to the heated arguments and tone them down before they got out of hand. When almost 99% of workers were free from Friday evening until Monday morning, the bar took in about 65% of its weekly turnover. On a Saturday, the shelves had to be repacked and empties left out at about 3pm, as well as Saturday night. I heard a good joke on RTE1 radio chat show a few weeks past. This is a true story and happened in a Dublin city pub. In the ladies' toilet there was a little brass statue of a man who was naked, except for an olive leaf covering where it mattered. When a lady went to the toilet from the lounge, the boys weighed her up and had their little private, illegal bets as to would she or would she not lift up the olive leaf. There was then a great air of excitement among the lads, as they waited for the toilet door to open, and the lady to come out or a little bell to ring in the lounge. The olive leaf acted as an electrical switch, that turned on the circuit of current to the little bell when raised. It was a 50/50 chance bet, with no tax, V.A.T., etc, and gave a great bit of enjoyment to the lads as they became merry!

That bar life did not improve my efforts to cut down on the drink. After five continuous days at work there, when one was released for a day off, you felt like a calf leaving a dark shed to go out to graze grass for the first time on a lovely sunny early summer's day. The first place I headed for was to a neighbouring bar. I can't confirm it, but I would safely say that at least one third of the country's publicans are alcoholics. The more shrewd, good business-like publican has his breaks at playing golf, pitch and putt, fishing or shooting and perhaps two of those pastimes.

I once went to Bellewstown races, a meeting I had never missed when farming, had a fierce session of drink after a successful day's backing winners, and finished up sleeping on a lovely pitch and putt course in the village of Duleek. When I awoke, I was minus my shoes, and had to go up to Owens' pub in my stocking feet. There was a good laugh in that pub that morning after the previous day's racing. The publican said he heard of a lad losing his shirt at the races, but never his shoes! I had a few fast pints to fill up the vacuums in my stomach, before phoning up my brother-in-law in Athboy to come to Duleek and bring me home. One thing I have not mentioned is that there was horse racing in Boyerstown, Navan, up to the year 1933. Da attended many meetings there in his youth.

My best friend and I went to his first cousin's wedding which was in the town of Trim. We were waiting for the bride's arrival in St. Patrick's Church, when our patience ran out. Down to Michael Leonard's pub we went, three of us, a brother of the groom, and the two of us. We had one round of large whiskeys i.e. six half ones each. The ceremony was well advanced on our return to the church. After the ceremony, we waited for a long ten minutes, hoping the bride and groom would make their appearance soon. Patience got the better of us again, and we tip-toed from the back, and down to Leonard's again. This time we had six large whiskeys before returning to the church yard, and finding out that all had gone to Fays' Hotel which was only a few hundred yards away. We had time for one bottle of ale each before the grub. Half ways through the meal my friend got an awful pain in his stomach. I tried to retain him until the meal ended, but he had to go. I stayed on for the speeches, and joined in the merryment that followed. I have no recollection of the last half of that day. I woke up in the Garda barracks, and told the first guard that came in to me that I wanted a drink badly. He gave me a cup of strong tea and a sandwich, and told me it was 10p.m. Having given me a summons for a day about three weeks away and directions to the nearest pub, he told me to take it handy on the drink. I met a friend of mine from Trim, who put me up for the night. On my return to Athboy the next day, I found that my starting off pal at the wedding was in Navan hospital getting pumped out. The summons did not worry me unduly, but I gave it to a friend who said he would look after it. I said nothing to him until three days before the court. On asking him, he told me to forget about it. As I had been at a wedding reception, the case was struck out. During our time in Athboy, we had to eject four men, on four occasions to prevent a major row. We can face those men today and laugh about those happenings, and not one of them had any hard feelings about it.

One man I had great respect for was a James Kane from Rathcarn. He was one of about twelve men who were moved from Rosmuck, Co. Galway to a new house, and a small farm of land per man with the promotion of the Irish language in mind in the early thirties. Looking at Rathcarn at the present time, with their own chapel, primary school, secondary school, hall and public house, I deem the experiment to have been a success. Bus loads arrive there from Dublin for Irish speaking summer weekends, and plenty of ceili dancing. I remember Jim Kane, as he was known by, from my very young years as we came home from Boyerstown national school. During the war years, he drove a few cart loads of turf from Bohermeen Bog to the town of Navan every week. His starting point from Rathcarn was a good eight miles from Navan. He had a long day, as he had to fill the cart on his way, as well as selling the turf on his arrival in Navan. We would meet him at 3.30p.m. on our way from school. He would always stop to talk to us, know our first names, would ask us what we learned during the day, all in Irish. He would always send us off laughing after spinning a yarn. His son Mick was a well known heavyweight boxer, who had a boxing match with Martin Thornton from Spiddal. Mick Kane once went to the blacksmith in Athboy to collect the wheel of a dray. He tried for half an hour to find some way to get it the two and a half miles home. Failing to get any means, he loaded the wheel on his shoulder, up on his bike, climbed the Hill of Ward and did not get off the bicycle until he landed in his yard!

A strange story happened about that same feat of strength. I was in a pub a couple of years back, and was having a chat about strong men. I listened to all that everyone there had said on the subject, and then told them the story of Mick Kane and the cart wheel. This was the first time I had mentioned Mick's name since I was in Athboy, which was about eighteen years before. Looking at the deaths on the following morning's paper, I saw Mick's death in it. I showed it to the publican who had heard the chat the previous day, and just like myself, he was very surprised.

The Rathcarn people were very hospitable, and they were always game for a game of "25". You would be only in the door, when you would be offered a strong, hot, colourless drink that would warm the cockles of your heart on a cold night!

Frank was a devil at playing tricks on customers. One grand summer's night, a bunch of young lads were chatting outside the pub door, wondering would they go to Navan or Trim to a dance.

It was about 10.30 on a Sunday night. "Watch this", said Frank to me, and upstairs he went with a full bucket of water. The curses and threats from the half drowned lads wasn't good to hear. They had played a trick on Frank that night and many a night before, and he told me he was a long time waiting for that opportunity. The give and take attitude was all taken in the right spirit.

We had an annual visit from the Meath branch of the Comortas Ceoltoire na h-Eireann groups and they were great social outings under the great master of ceremonies P.J. Fallon, a Roscommon man. He always had a few new jokes that went down well with everyone present. I love ceili music. My favourite tune is a reel called *The Foxhunter*. I love listening to Seán Ó Rioda, who is the best Irish singer I ever heard. The McKennas' from Trim and the Fitzsimmons's from Kilbride were two of the more talented groups that entertained that night. I love Irish poetry, as well as the music. I would love to have a record of Benedict Kiely reciting *Roisín Dubh, Fáinne Geal an Lae* and *Bán Cnuic Eireann O!* Every man that drinks has one song he loves to sing or hear when he is from half way to full drunkeness. My song when I was in that mood was *Irene Good Night*, which was fairly appropriate for the occasion. The reason for my liking of that song, apart from the good music and lyrics, was that it brought me back to the happy days of Navan carnival, in whose marquee I first heard that song. My present days pick of three songs in the 1990's are *Don't Cry for Me, Argentina, The Fields of Athenry,* and *Mull of Kintyre.* In the classical music, I have a great liking for *Golden Wing* from Verdi's opera *Le Buccu, The Drinking Song* from Verdi's *La Traviata* and *The Song for the Hebrew Slaves.*

I have happy memories of a holiday Ma spent with us in Athboy. After closing the pub at night Frank and Áine left everything spick and span for the following morning's opening. I would have two pints before retiring for the night. In the five years we were in the pub business, which was called "Failte", I drank during working hours about ten times. Nine of those times was on days approaching the Christmas, when at that time I was often feeling depressed. The 10th occasion was a Sunday evening on which day Meath and Offaly were playing a championship match in Tullamore. Frank and Áine went to the match. It had been their Sunday afternoon off. At around 6 o'clock in the evening I had about the usual number of customers for that time of day, which was about twenty. By 7 o'clock there must have been one hundred and twenty, as the bar, lounge and even the sitting room were full of customers. They were people returning from the match to Navan, Dunderry, Bohermeen and Boyerstown areas, most of whom I knew well. I had no help and was managing the bar as well as I could, when the lounge bells started ringing fairly frequently. I went into the lounge, took one large order, while four or five were shouting their orders at the one time. I brought the tray of four pints and six shorts to the kitchen and told one man who had a little experience at this job to take over. I went back into the kitchen and saying to myself "You can't do the impossible", I started at the tray of drink. When Frank and Áine returned at about 8 o'clock, they took over and I went off to finish up a very drunken man that night!

The nicest crowd to serve drink to was those that drank after Mass on a Sunday up to 2.30p.m. They were all sober, and nearly always had the right money ready for their order. Athboy and the surrounding countryside had lads of talent as regards football and hurling. Unfortunately, some years before our arrival there, there had been a major disagreement among the officers of the club that ran both teams. This resulted in a big split and the formation of two separate clubs, Athboy and Martinstown. Both clubs played football and hurling from their formation. Athboy were now composed of 80% from the town and 20% from the countryside. Martinstown were the pick of Rathcarn, Martinstown, Gilltown and about 20% from the town. Both teams had their victories in junior and senior grade. Athboy had a few senior hurling championship victories, while Martinstown had victories in the lower graded football championships finals. Victory celebrations were a noisy affair, as a result of the split, and took on something of the "Orange Day" parade style, marching behind a band the full length of Athboy's one street. There were never any fights over the split, but a certain amount of slagging was engaged in. The teams and supporters had their separate drinking houses. We did not get involved in this childish enemity, and our customers came from both camps. I often told that fine Limerick man, Dan Prendergast, that as things were, they would not win the amount of victories that it was possible to win if the two clubs were amalgamated. Athboy needed a few Martinstown hurlers, and Martinstown needed a few Athboy footballers to achieve great resulting victories. Dan thoroughly agreed with me, and told me he tried on numerous occasions to bring the two clubs together again to no avail. As the life span of a hurler or footballer is only about fifteen years, both sets of teams would soon rue the folly of the split. Now twenty years later three quarters of the men that formed the committees of both clubs are gone to their eternal rest. I am not too sure, but I think there was a coming together of the two clubs in the late eighties.

It was the year 1970 that we had a serious chat about pub life. As none of us liked that style of life, we decided to sell the pub. Áine did not like living in the town and was much more at home living in the country. She is a keen gardener and takes a keen interest in flowers. The pub was sold during a bank strike and the highest bid was £9,000. We let it go at that price. There arose some complication over the sale, and an alleged accusation on us for giving false account figures on the yearly turnover of the pub, and it went to the High Courts. It transpired that the information read out to prospective buyers by the auctioneer before the sale had been the correct information, so we won the case. It resulted in nearly a two-year delay in a second sale, as the terms of the first sale had not been honoured. It was another strange coincidence that the day we sold the pub Jack Mc Elhinney's pub in Kinnegad was burnt to the ground. That was the pub I have already mentioned that opened up the same Friday night as our pub opened!

I took a job with four local lads felling trees, cutting them into one foot rings and lorrying them to a Dublin city yard where they were blocked and bagged, and sold around the city for fuel. These trees were on the farm of a race horse owner and trainer, so there were always a few horses to be seen not too far from where we were working. Three chainsaws working at the same time kept one wide awake. I mostly gave a hand with the tractor and trailer, bringing the rings of cut tree to fill the lorry that would be parked on drier ground or on the roadside if the land were too wet. Occasionally, I relieved one of the lads on the saw. It took about six trailer loads to fill the lorry, which brought three loads to Dublin weekly. Ninety per cent of lorry loads went to the yard of a Mr. McCloud near Ballymun. I always went on the lorry deliveries, and enjoyed the run immensely. Not being the driver, I had a full view of the countryside, and the goings-on there. In the timber yard, the two of us threw down the load in about twenty-five minutes, at our ease. In the yard there were up to a dozen young lads blocking the timber and putting it into bags. Four Clydesdale-type horses were engaged for trailering the bags of timber from door to door around the city streets and outer built-up areas. It was a thriving little industry and gave good employment.

On our way back from Dublin, we always pulled up at P.J. McMahons pub in Warrenstown for a few pints of beer. The woods that we worked in were alive with grey squirrels. The agility of these little creatures is astonishing. I was once asked why a squirrel swam on his back. Failing to answer, I was told that he does not like getting his nuts wet! I was told by a very knowledgeable nature-study man that a squirrel did not swim, only in an emergency. The animal, he told me gets a piece of the bark of a tree, brings it to the water's edge, mounts it and uses his tail as a sail with great precision, to cross the water to the other side! There was no way I could contradict that honourable gentleman.

After about eighteen months at the timber, it was getting harder to sell lorryloads of it. There were new sellers coming on the market, and Bord na Mona briquettes were getting very popular. It was with regret that all of us became redundant.

I wasn't idle for long before a large farmer, Brendan Lynch, from Lombay asked me to give him a hand with the harvest. I was delighted to help this man out, as he was a very valued customer of ours in Athboy. He is one of the cleverest men I have ever met, a great native speaker and a true Irishman to the bone. He was married with bad luck and lost his first wife on the birth of their first baby boy. Picking himself up again, with that great fighting spirit he has, he married a second time to a beautiful girl from Rathcarn. They were a very united couple and reared five children from that marriage. It was lovely to hear Brendan give out the angelus in Irish and the family answer the response in their native tongue. It was a great house for Irish stew, my favourite dinner. I started at the barley, giving a hand to put the grain on the loft and the baled straw in the hay barn. After that we piked a lot of good hay in a sheltered corner of a field, as the hay barn was already full of good baled hay. All was now ready for tackling the forty acres of potatoes on all rented ground. He had a contract for the entire crop with the sugar company. The weather was very pleasant, and the ground was in perfect condition for getting the potatoes out. Brendan had spent long days spraying the crops against blight. He had covered that forty acres four times with the sprayer, three times with a blight spray, and once to kill off the stalks and weeds. He and three of his sons planted the entire crop. His sons ranged in age from seven to twelve, and they were the best-mannered children I ever came across. Like ourselves at home in our younger days, they had to work hard during the school holidays and after school in the evening. I saw two of them tackle the milking of twenty big Frisian cows with a milking machine, and they were no more than ten and eleven years of age! They were able to handle the four-gallon units of milk and empty them when full into the strainer, fixed on top of the twelve gallon cans without spilling one drop! They worked on the back of the potato harvester, taking potatoes off the main conveyor belt on to the bagger belt. They were not too heavy, and as they were nimble with their fingers, they suited the job very well. The eldest girl who was about thirteen, helped at the work as well. Brendan said that working on the back of the potato harvester was great practice for a pickpocket. From the bit of work I did on the back of the machine, I agreed with him. It took seven to take the potatoes off the main belt in a good fruitful crop. One man did the bagging, which was my job, and I was stretched to the limits to keep them bagged and tied in more than half the acreage. Filling the 1 cwt bags for the sugar company wasn't too bad but filling the four stone paper bags was a horse of a different colour! In a drill of 130 yards long, I filled sixteen four stone bags, and tied them as well. This was the first time I used or saw a hand machine for twisting the tying wire around the neck of the filled bags. One little slip- up, and I had to shout stop to the tractor driver who was Brendan himself, and as he was slightly over-charged with doing the job as fast and right as possible, I dared not stop him. The previous year the sugar company had paid much better than the potato merchants, but it would be Brendan's bad luck as the gods had never showered gold ingots on him, that the reverse situation ruled that particular year that I helped him. The merchants were paying 30% more than the sugar company. It was no wonder that he sent a few lorry loads to the merchants. I will never forget the loading of the sugar company's lorry. One ton on the lorry looked like a grain of sugar in a 2-lb bag of sugar! I and another man from Rathcarn spent most of a day putting on 60 ton which was about four acres of an average crop of spuds. We drank some pints of beer that night!

While we worked at that job, we always finished up in a pub on Friday evening, as Brendan had to get change to pay the wages. When we were working near Kildalkey, we finished the day in Miggin's thatched pub that always had a good turf fire in the bar. As the December evenings were getting colder, this fire was more than welcome. We had three meals of tea and sandwiches during the day, and got a good dinner from Mrs. Lynch in the evening. Kildalkey is a village about which is said that the traveller that walked the whole of Ireland, on coming to Kildalkey he ran through it! I often drank in it and found the locals there great, hospitable, sporting people. I do once remember playing a Kildalkey team at football and found them a wee bit careless with the boot! One thing that happened during the "Potatoe Expedition" was that one morning as four of us strolled into the field one hour late, Brendan started roaring at us while we were still 100 yards away from him. "Do you think you are in Butlin's holiday camp, or what?" We had a few strong words now and then, but always finished up the best of friends at the end of the day. I have very happy memories of my time working with Brendan, and we often laugh over little incidences that happened while on that work. Kildalkey is easily the best countryside for pheasants I ever saw, as you would almost trip across them there.

During the two years I worked at the timber and potatoes, I drank an awful lot. I went to a Fleadh Cheoil in Kells one Sunday night and finished up sleeping in a graveyard. It was during the warm weather and the devil a harm it did to me. It was a small Church of Ireland graveyard not too far from the Catholic church. The bell for 8a.m. mass woke me up. I went to Mass, got a breakfast and wash in a restaurant, and kept a good watch for an open pub. I had around eight pints in about three hours and headed back to Athboy. I was now at a dead end as regards work, as I waited for the resale of the pub. The drink pulled me down, and I had to be hospitalised at St. Loman's, Mullingar. About half the patients that came into the admission wards were suffering from depression after drink or drugs. Deep depression is an overdose of self pity that can come about by too much alcoholic drink, drugs, a business failure or sudden death of a close relative or very good friend. The opposite to a person with bad depression is the man or woman that, as well as doing their own work well, they will jump to the help of a neighbour if there is the slightest hint that there is something wrong with them. There is no danger of Mother Theresa getting depressed! She is the mother of thousands, not in the true sense, but a very good mother to thousands in every other good sense.

The rest of the patients were naturally depressed, finding the world too hard to cope with, sometimes after a sudden death of a relative. It was possible to get permission to go to town after the evening tea, but you had to be back before 9p.m. Television or a game of "25" passed the time until the stage to retire. One lesson I learnt about the game of "Poker" is, never play it when you have drink taken! You might not think it, but you will do all the wrong things that play into a sober man's hands. Everything was spick and span in the admission wards and dormitories, and the food was first class. There was a recreation building nearby, where cards, snooker and draughts were played. There was a coffee and mineral bar in that same building also. A grocery, sweet and fruit shop was situated in a central position to the rest of the hospital buildings. Two churches, a Catholic and Church of Ireland, looked after the spiritual needs of all there. The present auxiliary bishop of Meath, Dr. Michael Smith was the chaplin of the hospital at that time, and was a great source of comfort to all patients there. He got to know the names of every patient there, some eighteen hundred in all! After about an eight week stay there, I went back to Athboy in fairly good form.

After the court case in the Four Courts, we sold the pub for £9,000. It took a few months for the sale to be completed, and the money to be released. During that period, I was living and drinking on borrowed money. As I was doing no work, I became very depressed again, and decided to go back to St. Loman's hospital. I was so depressed that I asked myself "Will I ever see outside these walls again?". This was all a result of no work, too much drink, an irregular lifestyle and a temporary lapse in my Faith, as I missed Mass a few Sundays, and actually stayed away for a full six months at one period. However, I always had it in the back of my mind that I would rectify that when I was feeling better.

One day, as I was on my way back to the hospital after a few pints in Mullingar, a car pulled up alongside me. Who was it, but three of my neighbours from Boyerstown whom I had socialised with during their dancing years, and whose weddings I had the pleasure of attending. I even had three adventurous days with them in Lough Derg. I was a wee bit improved at this time, and tried to put up some sort of a spirited show to them. I often wondered what they thought of me that day, as I was for sure in the doldrums. I phased down on my drinking, and made my peace with God. After being away from Confession for a long time, it was then I felt the true value of the Gospel reading "Come all ye who labour and are burdened, and I will refresh you!" At the present time, I would be very much happier doing very laborious work with a clear conscience, than having a holiday with a guilty conscience.

I was now improving every week and doing some work around the hospital grounds. They tried me in the shop, which was a very busy place, between the wants of the nurses as well as the patients. On telling them it did not suit me, I was granted pardon from that work. That shop did a better trade than any of its sort in the town of Mullingar. The ice cream van called every day, but the shop was always cleared of ice cream at the end of any hot summer's day. I got a small wage for the work I did in the hospital grounds, and had a few pints after the evening tea. A job myself and another man did was to mow the graveyard with two scythes. It was about three statute acres in size. All the graves, about four thousand of them, were single graves and had a small iron cross at their head. We took our time, as it was during a heat wave, but had the job finished in about two weeks. Another man painted all the crosses, each of which was numbered for identification purposes. A Dr. Finnegan and his wife, who had been attached to the medical staff of St. Loman's, chose to be buried in the middle of this graveyard. Sometimes I stayed drinking too long after tea, and had to tell a lie to the doctor the following morning. The usual excuse was that I met up with neighbours from near home, which was quite a permissible excuse. He told me one morning that I had more neighbours than he who was born in the city had.

After about one year, my health improved immensely, and I was sent out to plant gardens, mow lawns and do fencing around lawns or gardens. I got well paid for this work and often stole a march for a quick pint, saying I was going for cigarettes. I got my meals whereever I was working. This lifestyle, with its certain amount of restriction, suited me down to the ground, and I had no worries. If the money I was now earning wasn't enough to keep me happy, I had money from the sale of the pub sent to me in the quantity as requested by phone, to a certain place in the town for my collection. I began to do a small bet on the horses every day, a 10p yankee. On Saturdays I spent the last half of the day looking and betting on the televised races and drinking pints. Sometimes I would dine out in the evening, and drink on until 8.45p.m. There was always a plentiful supply of daily papers in each ward at 8a.m. I was now in a ward where all patients went out to work each morning. A hospital van dispatched each person to his place of work, collected them in the evening and brought them into tea. The meals for these workers was as good as any hotel, as the patients were paying well out of their wages for them. The ward for these workers was a good lively one with plenty of card games, and pleasant nurses over us.

Pat Collins and his four umpires were among some of the male nurses that supervised us. They were a grand lot of lads, who were good footballers in their younger days, and they talked a lot about football games. Pat Collins was born and reared in Athboy, Co. Meath, my home county. In the year of 1972, the steward in St. Finian's College came into the hospital looking for a couple of farm workers. I was chosen along with another farmer's son from Moate. The steward asked me to work on a permanent basis and I agreed.

With about forty acres the college had rented, there were about 120 statute acres in all to be farmed. A milk dairy of about twenty cows supplied the entire milk requirements for the teaching staff and about one hundred and twenty boarders. All the meat requirements were brought in from a local butcher, who supplied full half-sides of cattle ready for the deep freeze. Incidentally now twenty years later, the reverse procedure is implemented. All the milk is being bought in and the meat requirements are coming from the college farm. Mick Flynn, the steward, looked after the cows all on his own, as well as stewarding and helping with the rest of the work. He was a great man to get through a lot of work in an orderly manner, was always up to date with the work and was very understanding with the workers. On my arrival at 8.30a.m., Mick would have all the cows milked. My first duty was the bringing of about thirty gallons of milk in a trolley up to the fridge in the store-room adjoining the kitchen. On my return journey, I brought back a barrowful of food collected from the kitchen, which helped to feed about twenty store pigs and two sows.

I mucked out the cows and pigs each morning, as Mick looked after about ninety cattle equivalents apart from the dairy cows. We both did the tractor work. One of the fields I ploughed was on a hillside, and it was very rocky. Westmeath land is very stoney compared to Meath land. I had to be very careful, holding the tractor steering wheel very tightly, as going down a hill when ploughing I would come to a sudden dead stop, as the plough point met the edge of a huge rock. One could very easily get chest damage by being suddenly thrown forward. It was on this farm I saw my last vision of the reaper and binder in action. It was a crop of oats that grew a full 7ft. in height, and it was cut fairly green so that it would not be flattened by an autumn storm. Oats, unlike other grain crops, rippens in the stook. I once saw a crop of oats being combined that was yielding fourteen barrels of grain in one round of a field! Sometime around the year 1960, a storm that was named Debbie came on a Saturday morning, and when the combine started in the afternoon, the yield dropped to two barrels to the round of the field, the rest having been threshed with the storm and lying on the ground. It was a big loss to the man who paid a big rent for that field. Two old men in their seventies worked that reaper and binder to perfection. I admired the grand easy-going style of life they held on to. There was plenty of time for a chat and bull-driving did not enter their heads.

On the college farm, about eight acres of corn for animal feeding, six acres of potatoes all for college use, and about two acres of vegetables were grown. Three 1cwt. bags of cabbage, or one barrowfull of turnips were delivered to the kitchen each day. One nun and about six good-looking girls looked after the cooking and the dining rooms. Another nun looked after the dormitories, and being a nursing sister she looked after sick students. Cabbage planting took place five times beween the months of March and October. About four thousand plants were planted at any one time, and were put into the soil with a "Dipper Stick", which was a pointed, one foot length of shovel, spade or fork handle. Previous to this, I always used a spade when planting cabbage plants. This planting took about two days to complete. All the hay was baled before mid June. As there were about eighty ton of potatoes to be picked, a gang of about thirty students were chosen to help out from 3.30p.m. to 6.30p.m. for about two weeks around the end of September. They were marshalled by the president, Fr. Duignan, who conveyed them to the field in the college van. The boys wore their football boots and stockings, which were drawn over the legs of their trousers.

The potato stalks were burnt off by spraying a few weeks before digging, which left the drills very clean. The old type spinner digger dug out three drills at one time in three different parts of the crop. This kept the boys going with a plentiful supply of potatoes to pick. The president gave a hand picking also, for what Cavan man wouldn't know how to pick spuds! I need not tell you there was a small amount of potato throwing, for boys will always be boys. A shout from the steward and an odd look up by the president, who gave the blind eye to what he would see, kept things in their proper perspective. Fr. Greham, the farm manager, would arrive at about 5p.m., with huge pots of good strong tea and about twenty jam-rolls. The lads enjoyed the picnic, and took photos of groups and individuals. Ten minutes loaded the trailer with half the bags of potatoes picked with the good help, before the boys went back to college. The other load was picked up the following morning, leaving a clean sheet for that evening.

When all the potatoes were housed, I spent about three weeks with the help of two other men, sorting out the eating, seed potatoes and the poreens for animal feeding. I had a machine for doing that work and enjoyed doing it in the mid-autumn.

One man was employed as a kitchen helper. He got the vegetables, cleaned and trimmed them, and washed them, leaving them ready for the boiler. He also brought in the potatoes, washed and peeled them with a machine that peeled a handy bucketfull at a time. He also gave a hand in the dormitories and classrooms if any furniture needed shifting. He is part of the furniture himself, being all of about thirty years employed there. He gave a hand at the hay in the summer, mostly at drawing in the bales. I worked there for two years and only knew him by the name "Owen". I never heard or enquired about his surname. He was the strongest man I ever met and handled the bales of hay as if they were bales of sponge!

The meals I got in St. Finian's were every bit as good as I got in the Castle Hotel in Dublin. The farm workers were given the same menu as the priests so a full four course dinner was served. I had a tea- break at 11a.m. and 3.30p.m. I finished work for the day at 5.30p.m., at which time the hospital van collected me on the dot. For hay-making and potato-planting, a few extra hands were hired for a few days. The army supplied the requirements here. One day in the mid-summer, there landed eighty new mattresses, and Owen and I had to carry them up to the second and third stories of the main building. This was a very leg-tiring exercise on a scorching hot day! One of the kind sisters brought out a couple of lagers, each fresh from the fridge, and boy, did we not relish them! They, being single bed mattresses, we carried them the Asian way, on top of the head, with the two hands free to keep them there. I thought on my way up with the mattresses, of the time my poor Da, who was now a few years along with twenty dead, gave me the grinds in history to try to get me a scholarship to this college. I now think I was better off biking my way through the wide open countryside to St. Pat's in Navan. The supplier of the mattresses, a good order, was an Oldcastle man with the trade name of "Castle Beddings", who had attended the college a few years previously. That is what you could call making use of your education.

Every year around the 10th of December, the feast day of St. Finian, the students were given a few days off, after a good meal of turkey and plum pudding. The college priest, invited guests (the bishop among them), had their own little celebration. Before this outing, as before the retreats and conferences, we, the farm hands had to have the playground, the pitch and putt course, lawns, football pitch and the college grounds in top class form. We were treated well during these periods. The girls in the kitchens were very pleasant and the crack at meal times was good. They backed horses, and were forever looking for a tip. Before the Grand National in Aintree, they persuaded one of the nuns to have a flutter. After a lot of persuasion, the good sister resurrected a 10p piece and asked me to name the winner. I told her Red Rum, a horse I did not back myself. I was watching the race with them when the mighty horse, Red Rum, came home an easy winner for the second time! The shouting of us at that finish was never heard in that college before! As regards the other nun, no one would pick up that much courage to ask her to have a bet. If perhaps they did, the answer, as well as her looks would most definitely be in the negative.

Reverend sisters have come a long way forward, sportswise, since then, for only about sixteen years later, in 1989, Trim Annual Festival had a race, yes, a full horse race, with nuns in the saddle! Bookies took bets, as in any horse race, and I am almost sure the favourite won. There was no inquiry over excessive use of the whip, by any jockeys or stewards inquiry, as everything was above board. I am prepared to bet that Michael Regan, the Trim solicitor, was at the bottom of that great enjoyable event. Perhaps they will have the male Reverends doing jockey at the next festival, and the nuns in the wheelbarrow race! It wasn't the first first for Trim, as they were first in Meath to win the great Tidy Towns competition!

I was two-and-a-half years in the college when I put my foot over the traces. On a Saturday afternoon, I drank poteen and I failed to go back to the hospital at 9p.m. I had a tip for a local dog, and went down to the dog track. The dog won, so I spent all my time in the course bar, having only the one winning bet. When the dogs were over, I stayed on drinking in the town until midnight. The next morning, I had to answer a charge of coming into the hospital at 1am blind drunk. I was ordered off any outdoor work around the town of Mullingar. I had to go back working in the hospital grounds, and was forbidden to go to town for a few months. As I was a voluntary patient, I was going to leave the hospital, but on the advice of a very sound nurse, I stayed. There was one nurse in the hospital who took and supervised about ten men at the making of lawns, landscaping, farm work, etc. He was a man called Barney Smith, and casually one day, I asked him was there any chance of getting on his team. He had a chat with some of his superiors, and got me named as one of his understudies. We were brought to our place of employment each morning in the hospital van, which was driven by Barney. A large box of ham and salad sandwiches was brought in the van with us, as well as a small gas fire to boil up the small galvanise boiler of water for tea-making. We had three tea-breaks, and the usual four course dinner on our arrival back in the evening. Our work could be anywhere within fifteen miles of

Mullingar. We always had a few pints of beer between the finish of our work in the evening, and our arrival in to our dinner. I was delighted with this new job, as it gave me a chance to get a few pints in the evening since I was not allowed to go to town.

Barney was a typical country man from Longford, and spoke in a lovely soft, slow style, and he came out with some very unique statements. One of the first jokes I heard in that hospital was about Barney. The story went that Barney attended a very posh wedding. The following morning he was describing all the good things about that wedding. When he was talking for a couple of minutes, one of the young nurses shot out the question "Barney, was there any serviettes at it?". "Would you stop", was the reply, "we ate them till they came out our ears!" I enjoyed that joke, but from what I knew of Barney, he was a lot more clever than the chap that asked the question. Perhaps that question was asked, and that reply given, but if it did it was heard in the wrong context. Barney was a fully qualified carpenter and electrician. There was the same solution to any problem that arose in the hospital buildings, be it chapel wards, dormitories, or toilets and that was "Get Barney to repair it".

During that restricted four months of my going to town, I had four Sunday excursions to football matches, a Sunday trip to Lough Key and a trip to Knock. On these excursions, our meals and a few pints were paid for out of the "Bingo" profits. The bingo was held every Friday, and something in the region of 2,500 attended it. I tried it a few times without any luck. While I was restricted, I sent money for a baby power and two stouts, with one of the patients going to town. I only once failed to get them. On that occasion, the patient came back in great form. I asked him for my drink and he told me to "f--- off". What could I do about that? I was properly blackmailed and no drink or money came back. So you see what looked like a very black few months, turned out to be alright.

CHAPTER IX

In the month of Sept 1974, I got a chance of starting a permanent job with a firm called Midland Concrete Products. It was situated in Robinstown, Mullingar, and was about two miles from the town centre on the Castlepollard road. It was a new business to Mullingar, and had been two years in production before I joined the forces there. The boss, his father-in-law and brother-in-law were the complete work force there. The latter two came to work by car all the way from Rhode, Co. Offaly, a total daily journey of forty six miles or thereabouts. At that time, the boss supplied three tea breaks with ham and cornbeef sandwiches on alternative days. We manufactured window cills, three different sizes of 3ft long kerbing, pier caps in four different sizes, wall capping in three sizes, 8ft paling posts, 6ft. 6in. paling posts, standard size security posts, clothes line posts, the stay posts for all the posts mentioned, king posts for them, gate posts, 2ft. x 2ft. paving slabs in a smooth finish, or with the chippings exposed, graveside kerbing, and the corner pillars for them. Lintels were bought in wholesale and sold retail, as we had no means of making them at that time. As there was no competition within twenty miles of Mullingar, business grew rapidly from month to month. I had good money at this work, which increased my Guinness intake. I went out every night after tea and drank for three hours. I would bring back a baby power and three stouts for drinking between 9p.m. and midnight. I used to hide that nightcap on the front lawn under a certain tree. While playing a game of "25", I would go out to the toilet, slip out to the lawn, have a slug at the baby power and one bottle of stout before returning to the game of cards. I repeated this act three times per night until all the drink was gone, the game of cards was over, and then I hopped off to bed. I was a fully seasoned drinker by now, and did not come under observation as a result. Saturday was again my danger day. I worked the first half day, had a good dinner, and off to town at 2p.m. I rarely went into my tea at 5p.m., but I would have a good meal in town. I was then free to drink until 8.45p.m. My absence from tea would be noted in the day book by some of the nurses, but when queried by a doctor the following morning, I always told lies. I used say I met someone from home and they treated me to an evening tea. I did meet lads from Navan and Athboy, but it was not a meal I got, it was extra porter!

Somebody of note among the hospital staff got to know about my heavy drinking, because I was put on anti-booze tablets. I was warned that if I drank more than four pints, I would become very sick and become a class of disabled for a few hours, as a result of taking two of these tablets in the morning. Some mornings I went unnoticed to work without the tablet. There was one nurse, a fellow county man of my own, who insisted I get them every morning when he, a deputy charge nurse, was on duty. I got to know two men that were on anti-booze tablets and I found out from them that what the nurses told me about taking the tablets was true. The tablets were given out to the patients during the breakfast so I knew exactly when it was near my turn. I put a small bit of paper into my mouth just before I got mine and on getting the tablets into my mouth, I used put them into the paper with my tongue immediately as they were very soluble. I would then push the parcel to the very corner of one side of my mouth. I made a swallow of fresh air in front of the nurse, and off to work I went. The very first chance I got, I got rid of the paper and tablets. I had no ill effects from drinking heavy, as a result, which puzzled that nurse who was hell bent on downing me with the tablets. He changed his tactics, so did I. He put the tablets into glass of orange juice, stirred them thoroughly for about a minute, and then got me to swallow it all. I carried a small bottle of cod-liver oil, which I fully knew would upset my stomach. On my way to the van that brought me to work, I would go to a toilet, take a small amount of the cod-liver oil, do a few bends up and down, and the orange juice plus the cod-liver oil

came up my throat, to be disposed of in the toilet, which I immediately flushed. Cod-liver oil always had the effect of sickening me, even before I took my first alcoholic drink. It wasn't too hard to upset one's stomach after drinking about twelve pints the night before while chain-smoking. I was careful with the drink for a while, until I was certain I would have no ill effects from the tablets in the drink. Gradually, I increased it and found no ill effects even after about fourteen pints.

Talking about tablets reminds me of the grow young tablets. An Irishman who worked in New York for over twenty years got his mother to send on her photo with the next letter. This she gladly did, but the resulting aged photo shocked her son. He knew of tablets the Yankees had for growing younger looking. He sent a box of them to his mother, with the recommended dosage, and told her he would be home in four months. The old lady did as told, and was finding good results. On the return of the excited Irishman to their thatched cottage done a laneway, he met a woman wheeling a pram a couple of hundred yards away from the house. After a while, he recognised his mother, and was delighted with the result of the tablets. Looking into the pram at a baby boy he said to his mother, "I didn't think the tablets would put you in child bearing condition again". "Ah", said she, "do you not know your own poor Daddy? He took an overdose one night!"

That joke reminds me of one night I was drinking in Dunderry during a bad flu epidemic. This poor man in his sixties who would be after walking two miles to the pub after a severe bout of flu looked very shook. His own best friend was delighted to see him again, and bought him a drink. When the drink was put up, he looked very close at the convalesing man and said "God, Ben, you will want to die in the peak of you health, or you will make a very shook looking corpse!"

I was only four months in my new job, when I overdid the Saturday drinking again. I got a half bottle of poteen from a friend

and a good tip for a horse. I had only the one bet as a result and the horse won at 14 to 1. I had ten pounds on the horse, the largest bet I had since or before. I got a good feed of T-bone steak and onions, and drank up to 7.30p.m. I then went to the dogs and won more money there. I was in great form going back to my town pub at 10p.m. I drank up to 11.30p.m. and then went to a house party. It was about 3a.m. when I got to the hospital for my night's sleep. Next morning I knew I was in serious trouble, because the nurse that tried to down me with the anti-booze tablets came on duty at 8a.m. All the rest of the nurses would try to soften the blow, when I would be confronted by a doctor, but this nurse for sure would hang me. I saw him talking to the doctor in the ward office, and the doctor throwing an odd eye down at me. I wasn't even called in to answer my case which puzzled me at the time. When the doctor left, the nurse came straight down to me, told me to pack my belongings and leave the hospital at 10a.m. that Sunday morning. Thus ended about four years of another chapter of my life.

CHAPTER XII

I had a few hundred pounds saved out of my wages and insurance money from the time I worked in the hospital grounds, and for Barney Smith's work around the town. I asked the nurse to get me that money, but as it was a Sunday morning, the head office was closed so there was no hope of getting the money. I went into town and got a badly needed four pints of beer. I knew now that I had to stand on my own two feet, as if I ever went back to that hospital, they would literally run me out again. This to me was quite understandable, as I had abused the privileges given to voluntary patients.

I drank all day that Sunday, and settled for bed and breakfast in Broders' Hotel that night. I went to work on Monday morning and explained my plight to my boss. He come with me that evening to look for a flat. Flats were very hard to come by in Mullingar at that time. However, we struck oil in the second place we tried. The rent in 1975 was £7 per week. I had my own bedroom, a shared kitchen, sitting room, bathroom and toilet. Now I had all the freedom in the world to do as I pleased, and knowing this well, I watched my drinking for a while. The landlady, her husband and four more flat dwellers lived in this large house that was the Central Hotel at one time. I got a lift to work each morning with the lads from Rhode, and a lift back to my flat in the evening, as they passed my door. This was my first taste of flat life so cooking, washing up the delph, keeping the place tidy and washing my own clothes was a bit strange to me for a while. I also had to do my own shopping, a job that I enjoyed. I always grubbed well, and was determined to keep it that way. A gas cooker did my cooking, and there was always a fire in the sitting room which any of the tenants could use.

After a short time, I was delighted with flat life. Two of the tenants were elderly retired country folk, and as I had a lot in common with them, we had some great chats. My landlady's husband was very fond of the drink and I often had the pleasure of his company. He originated from Athboy, and he knew all the people that I knew there. He told me a few great yarns about some of the hard-cores from there. I was about nine months in that flat when one Sunday morning about 4a.m., I was awakened by my landlady who shouted "Is there a fire in your room?". I told her there was not, but that the room was full of smoke. I put on my clothes as fast as possible, and rushed down stairs, while firemen rushed up the stairs past me. The next thing I saw was the firemen coming down with a smouldering mattress and a bundle of blankets also belching smoke from them. Yes, it was the morning after the night before, and it was my bed that had caught fire. Now I was in the wars over the drink again. I paid for the mattress and the blankets and sheets, and told the landlady that smoking in my bedroom was finished for all time. She told me I would have to deal with her husband as regards staying on in the flat. This brought me some hope, as I woud meet him in his usual pub that evening and get him a few half-ones to soften him up. This, I did and after a reluctant type of start, he decided to give me another chance. Mullingar was now starving as regards flat accomodation, as there was a factory, with a force of over 400 men needed, about to open. I was counting myself very lucky to be left on there at all.

I was a total of about two-and-a-half years in that flat, when the whole place came under the hammer. We were all given six weeks to find new accommodation. Actually, it was that landlady that put me into my next place of rest. I was now living in Belvedere Place, almost in front of the dog track. I brought one of the two old gentlemen in my first place of accomodation with me to the new flats, as there were two single beds in one large bedroom. My first impressions of this new place were not too good. We landed into the place on a dark evening, but when we switched on the lights, there was no response. A lassie came down from upstairs and told us that the meter required more money. It transpired that there were three lassies upstairs in flats also, who cooked on an electric cooker, and used two electric heaters. The one hall meter metered the whole house. I put in three 10p pieces into the meter and got light straight away. I got my tea and then went to see the landlady about the metering situation. To my joy, she told me that the three lassies upstairs were leaving that weekend. When they went, two lads came in their place who used gas for cooking, and briquettes for fire fuel the same as ourselves. So all rolled on smoothly again.

The move to a new part of town meant a change of pub for me, as I always drank in the nearest pub to my place of rest. The man that was sleeping in my bedroom was fond of a few drinks and enjoyed a game of darts and the card game "25". We made many new friends in our new pub, and like myself, they were all working class lads. A large number of farmers from the Tullamore side of the town drank in this pub also. It was owned and personally managed by a very respectable man, a James McCormack from Mount Street, Mullingar. Sometimes, for a matter of change, we drank in another pub right opposite this one, owned by a famous Westmeath lake fisherman, Lawrence Caffrey. He was a sharp-shooter with a gun, and a great supporter of clay pidgeon shooting club competitions. I was only a few days in my new flat when a lad in one of the pubs asked me where I was staying. To my surprise he told me that a dead baby had been found under the floor boards of a room there a few weeks before. I said to him I hope God shows mercy to the soul that was responsible for that happening. He asked me would I not be afraid to stay there, to which I replied that I had never heard of a baby ghost appearing to anybody yet. There were now four men in the place, and I never told any of them about what I had heard. I found out after that what I heard was true, as there was a court case relating to the alleged mother a few months later.

Ma used to call over four or five times a year to see me, as well as my younger sister Maggie who drove her over. We would have a few drinks, a very good meal, and a drive to Lough Ennell, Lough Owel or perhaps the Multifarnan Friary. We always had Ma's age to be the same as the Queen Mother, but as it transpired later, she was one year older, as she was born in the last year of the last century. Every year told on Ma, who was now in her eighties. She took a couple of brandies, since a doctor told her they would do her good. She was a pioneer all her life, until she came to her 65th year. She sold a small parcel of land and got £25,000 for it. She took a few continental holidays, Rome and Lourdes among them. Having mentioned Rome there reminds me of the Pope's visit in 1979. I had the pleasure of seeing him in the Phoenix Park. There were two old ladies by the name Stapleton that lived down a lane-way on the Commons Road, Navan, who did not bother keeping up with the Joneses. They had no E.S.B., telly or any other of the modern-style cleaning and cooking instruments of today. Their house was a thatched cottage which they kept very well by the stone aged methods. Young lads, their near neighbours rigged up a battery telly, for the old ladies to watch and follow the Pope's visit. They were well rewarded when some of them walked in during a programme on the event and found the two ladies on their knees with eyes glued to the telly and Rosaries in their hands! Ma had a great fear of telephones, and never used one in her life. When it came to boarding a plane it gave her no problem. After rearing seven of us, with the likes of me among them, and burying a son at the age of twenty-five, she was well entitled to enjoy her autumn years!

My place of employment was getting to be a big concern from its humble beginnings. By the year 1980, it was giving work to ten men. There was a lintel manufacturing bed erected at a large amount of money. It was forty yards long, had one length of 9" lintel, one of 6" lintel, and six of 4" lintels. One coil of wire that sufficed for filling the entire lintel bed seventeen times, cost in the region of £1,500. A Swedish hydraulic jack was capable of stretching the forty yard run of wire 1ft. There was a protective steel cage at each end of the lintel bed. This was for human protection, in case the wire should break or slip from its anchors at either end. I was told by a man from the west of Ireland that he knew of a place where they made lintels, and when one of the lengths of wire was being stressed, it slipped from the anchors at one end and split an animal in two that had been grazing in an adjoining field. I always had a certain amount of fear when using it after hearing that story.

A lorry was now employed almost full-time, making deliveries of bought produce. House building was in its glory, and as many as ten houses per week on a few occasions were supplied with cills and lintels. Although we were two miles out from the centre of Mullingar, there was a furniture factory, a Board of Works office and repair yard and an archaeological branch office all within arm's reach of us. Down the years, we all got to know each other and always joined forces for a Christmas party. I always got a good whiskey treat in the Board of Works on my return after the Christmas holidays. A couple of mechanics and machinery maintenance men had their headquarters there. I was now helping to give a hand in the yard of my employment, serving customers. It's many a time I saw as many as seven lorries and pick-up vans collecting some of our goods for immediate use. It took a bit of time to put up about twelve sills on the fork-lift and leave them on the lorry. When that was done, the lintels had to be loaded on the forklift and up on a lorry as well. Sometimes, some or all of the lintels might have to be cut out of the lentil bed. A docket had then to be written out and all the prices made out. We were lucky in that, if the yard was really busy with a lot of customers, there were four of us ready to look after them, although it took us off the production line for a while.

After one-and-a-half years in my second flat, the landlady sold it to a private house buyer. We got two week's notice only, but I was very lucky to get a lovely flat on the main street, right beside the railway station. My new drinking pub was next door to my flat, which was just as well, with the amount of drink I now took on Saturdays. I missed about six days in the year from work, entirely due to drink. My boss, knowing my plight, never reduced my weekly wage packet over these missed days. It was always on a Monday, and from sheer depression and disgust, I would decide to lie on and get a good healer later on. When I got my two weeks summer holidays, I always went back to work after one week, thoroughly fed up with drinking and to save me from more depression.

Sometime in the spring of 1983, on a Saturday night, I fell over a chair in the kitchen of my flat and broke a large window on to the street. My landlady told me to get other accommodation. This I got after a few days, and it was not too far away from the flat I was leaving. It was a place called Brewery Yard which was a suitable name for an address that I would be going to live in. It was at the entrance to the Mullingar livestock salesyard. The Brewery Yard was a store yard for barrells of Guinness beer in the time of canal and railway transport. There was one man in this new flat that had a whiskey drinking problem. We were lucky enough in that when I came in drunk, he would be sober and vice versa. We grew to be the best of friends and he always had my dinner ready after work in the evening as he finished at 4.30p.m.

My Ma had a stroke in the autumn of 1983, but made a very good recovery after a few months. She had a second stroke in the summer of 1984 during a heatwave, and slowly went downhill all the time. I called a couple of days before she died to bid my last farewell to her. The heart finally came to a stop, but all that time she suffered very little pain. I always said for a few years leading up to her death, that I would say thanks be to God when she would finally die, as she was very feeble for the last few years of her life, and her poor old head was not the best. I kept to my word when I got the news while working on a scorching hot July day. She was eighty-five years of age, left three men and three women behind her as well as five grandchildren. She herself was the last of a family of seven.

The recession had by now brought the construction work to a crawling pace. Building contractors were winding up their businesses, going to Saudi Arabia, Canada, the United States and some to England. Our work force was now down to three full-time and one part-time. My boss bought a new semi-automatic mixer in almost new condition. This machine took a lot of bull-work out of the job. It was now possible to put up five barrowfulls of perfectly mixed concrete ready for the dumper in three minutes. The dumper was used for bringing concrete close to the moulds that required filling. It was unfortunate that the building trade took a turn for the worse when we only had the mixer for one year.

In the month of September, 1984, a good customer of the business I was working in gave me a tip of £10, and told me to give a couple of drinks that evening to one of my workmates and keep the rest myself. That evening, I went into Aidan Moore's pub on the Green Bridge to drink the £10 along with my friend. I had been drinking there for the past few years, as it was closest to my last flat. This is one of the last old-fashioned pubs left in the town of Mullingar. It is very well known for tobacco and smoking pipes. There, you can buy anything from a clay pipe to an Indian peace pipe. The only drawback about this pub, is that you might get the bite of a greyhound as it is a famous doggy pub! The talk there most of the time is about time, for all you will hear is 19.30, 30.30, 33.45, etc. The rest of the while is all about sires, dams, sire's dam, dam's sire, sire's sire, and dam's dam! Lame dogs were walked up and down the full length of the shop under Aidan's sharp eye. Toe nails were examined . Home-made lubricants were given to owners with strict instructions. Secret dose bottles were given to owners of dogs going for a big-timer and this man's dog knowledge puts Dinny the Glenroe man in the halfpenny place! Anything wrong that might escape Aidan Moore's eye would surely be diagnosed by either Sunny Mullen, James Farrell or Johnny Boyle, three men with x-ray eyes as regards greyhounds. Aidan Moore himself is a great doggy man. He sold some good pups in his time. The best of them was a dog called Lomonds Lad that won the Caesarwich Cup in Navan at the price of 16/1. I didn't go to work for two days after that win. He was owned by Ambrose Harte, Mullingar.

To get back on course again, we had the ten pounds drunk in about an hour. This was the first time I drank with this workmate of mine, so we were now settled down for the whole evening's drinking. When we were too full of pint drinking, we turned to whiskey. How I got to bed that night after climbing the stairs I will never know, but how I left my bed at 3.30a.m. that same morning I will never forget. At that very time I woke, I saw a few blankets almost in flames and the room full of smoke. I shouted at the man that was staying with me "Fire, get up at once", as I banged on his door. I went to fill a basin with water, but feeling the fumes of the smoke too strong, I bolted downstairs with the other man as fast as possible. I got no time to put clothes on, so I had to run about 200 yards in my vest and underpants to the nearest public telephone. The other man got his trousers on, but had to leave his coat behind him. He had £260 in that coat, as he had received his monthly army pension cheque the previous day and had changed it!

On getting downstairs and into the yard, I looked back at my bedroom window and saw that the room was now in flames. I sprinted down Patrick St. to the phone, dialed 999, my intercert exam number, and got an immediate response. Having given the details of the disaster, I went back to the house. By now the kitchen had caught fire as well as the two bedrooms. The fire brigade landed in ten minutes, which to me seemed an eternity. As they were rigging up their gear, flames were starting to come out of the roof over my bedroom and were threatening the roof of the adjoining house as well. The firemen had the flames under control in about twenty minutes. Everthing in my possession went up in flames. By this time, there were about fifty onlookers. A kind neighbour got me trousers and a coat to put on as well as a coat for my friend. It was about 7.30a.m. when the brigade had finished their good work. I went back upstairs and lay down on a damp couch in the kitchen for a snooze. A good friend came in at about 10a.m. with a baby Power, a flask of soup, a couple of beef sandwiches and a pair of shoes. This left me in a right state to go down to the pub and out of the way of reporters that might call. Actually, I learned later that they had been there that morning looking for me or my friend. After about six pints I got over the shock of what had happened that morning. I had money left by in such a way that it was not immediately available. I got on the phone to my sister Maggie. The fire was on a Friday morning, and I did not go back to work that day. My boss sent in my wages, so that kept the wolf from my door, if I now had one, for another while. I arranged for bed and breakfast for Friday and Saturday night. I paid £18 for that service in advance, as when one is drinking a lot anything goes! I had good meals that day, and went to bed at 11p.m. as I was badly in need of a good night's sleep. The following morning I was up at 8 o'clock, and took it easy for the first half of the day and got a good dinner. After dinner that Saturday, I backed a few winners of televised races. I had a few whiskeys as a result, and then started drinking pints by the new time. Before I got too drunk, I arranged for one week's full board, starting on Sunday night, to give me time to find another flat. That breathing space of a week took a lot of pressure off me for the immediate future.

I got very drunk that Saturday, and could not find the key of the hotel door where I had booked my bed and breakfast. There I was out in the open at 1a.m. on Sunday morning on a cloudy damp night. I went down under the canal bridge and lay myself down for a sleep. I was on a five foot passway that ran alongside the canal, as cars and an odd lorry roared across that bridge. I managed a few hour's sleep, even though I was lying on the stoney passway, and there was a damp mist blowing through the bridge. This, I thought, would give me a cold if not pneumonia. I thought of the time Ma used make whey for us during a flu epidemic. Whatever way I turned during the night, the seam of the backside of my trousers had a 1ft. rip. Now this was a Sunday morning at 7.30 and it would be only three-quarters of an hour until a lot of people would be using the passway that I lay on, as they took a shortcut to 8.30 Mass in the cathedral close by. It was a must that I be gone before this march of the fresh-looking, well dressed people took place. When I got the road fairly quiet, I walked the thirty yards up to the top of the bridge. I walked sideways nice and slowly along the footpath and crossed the road to a telephone box when there was nobody about. I had a good smoke in there and time to study my next move. I noticed a woman sweeping the footpath in front of her house, a woman I often bid the time of day to while waiting to be collected for work in the morning. I immediately seized this opportunity to lighten my plight if at all possible. Going over to the lady, I asked her for a drink of water. She brought me in and I told the true story to her. She knew that I was involved in a house fire a few days ago, and made a good breakfast for me. I got a needle and thread from her, went to the toilet and mended my trousers. I had a razor in my pocket, and had a good shave and went to Mass at 8.30. I went for a walk after drinking a large bottle of milk to fill a few holes until the pubs would be opened.

I had slept out five or six times before on good summer's nights, but that damp autumn night under the bridge was a self-inflicted, cruel, sobering experience. I never went to bed after that, without saying one Hail Mary for anybody sleeping out all over the world, and expecially the Irish lads in New York, London and even Dublin. I found the key in one of my pockets that Sunday, the key that was the cause of me sleeping out, and duly left it back. The receptionist gave me a £5 refund, as I had not used my bedroom or got my breakfast which I had paid for.

The same Sunday during the 2.30p.m. to 4p.m. pub closing period, I was standing on the Green Bridge over which I had slept that night, and looking down towards the railway station. In the background as I looked towards the right is an elevated acreage of land on which is a lovely little hillock. It immediately reminded me of the hill of Calvary, and Christ dying for every man in the world, which included a drunk like me. I thought to myself What a bloke to loose one's life over! If I had been burnt to death in either of the bed fires, I would have sentenced myself to hell fire for eternity! I used to go to Confessions about once a month, and it was the one old story every time, 99% of my sins as a result of drink and breaking the commands of the 6th and 9th commandments. They all go together like sister and brother to a carefree single man. I had fairly well mastered the 6th and 9th commandments after stooping to the lowest of the low. I was now determined to do the same with the drink problem. I had been getting drunk every Saturday, so I told the priest I would not buy a drink after 7p.m. I got around this by firstly, ordering two pints at 6.55p.m. It wasn't long until two pints became three, then four, etc. Who am I fooling, I asked myself? God! Some hope! I there and then decided that since I could not cut down on the drink, I would have to cut it out. So said the RTE 1 advertisement.

I decided that November 1st would be D-day in my life. I got very drunk on October 31st, phoned up Páraic in Navan, and had a row with him on the phone over a very small misunderstanding. I apologised to him two days later, and there were no hard feelings. In my later years drinking whiskey would make me narky, instead of putting me in good form. During my life-long drinking, I had about ten scraps. I would apologise the following day, and thank God I haven't an enemy in the world! A short time before that, I hit a man that had drawn a blow at another man, as there was no one but a young girl in charge of the pub that night. There was a brother of the man I hit in the pub also, and I had overlooked that. The two brothers got at me, one from behind and the other in front, and gave me the most fatherly hiding including two black eyes. There were charges being brought against them by the Gardai, as somebody reported the matter, and I gave a statement that night.

On the pleading of their aged mother, I dropped the charges and there was no more about it. I meet these lads every day of the week, and we are the best of friends. I am very glad that there was no lifelong enmity over the same drunken fights.

Another reason for my stopping drink, was that it was the dying wish of my mother and three next door neighbours of mine in Boyerstown. My Ma left me a few pound and I decided to buy a motorbike to get me out of town in fine weather, especially the weekends and for renewing my friendship with my relations and friends around Boyerstown. There is something in the old saying "Old friends are best", and as I got on in years I had a great desire to meet friends I had ten, twenty and thirty years ago, and to chat about the good old days when life was ticking over at a slow, smooth and contentment-giving pace. My first Christmas on the dry came, and I managed with some God-given grace to master my desire for drink. I enjoyed that Christmas so much that I swore that if I every drank again that I would stay off it for every Christmas at least. I enjoyed that Christmas just as I had enjoyed them when I was a schoolboy. I always took a drink in a pub Christmas morning in Mullingar. One Christmas I was caught along with about twenty others by the Gardai. I gave my name in Irish and heard no more about it. All the other lads were summonsed and fined £5 each. During my thirty three years of drinking, I surely drank an average of three pints per night. This comes to 1095 pints per year which is 137 gallons per year and 4521 gallons during a life's drinking! At £1.50 per pint that comes to £54,252! Add to that £10,000 for whiskey drinking, as I always started drinking with one small whiskey before the pints of beer, and the total comes to £64,252! As I smoke 30 cigarettes per day, this comes to £21 per week or £1,092 per year or £43,680 for my forty years smoking! End result is £107,932 at present day prices, for my life's smoking and drinking, and I am not finished yet in the year 1990! That figure is a very conservative one, as anyone that knows me can tell. The only visible bad effects of all that drinking and smoking are in my jaws or cheeks, but there is nothing there that a couple of pounds of pollyfilla wouldn't rectify!

One abiding memory of Christmas that I never forget is my Ma bringing the turkey over burning newspapers in the middle of the kitchen floor, and my Da telling her that she will burn the house down! Ma would not give him his way in this matter, saying this is the way her mother and grandmother did it and she was not going to change that custom now. She would then tell some of us to put another sheet of paper on or it would go out.

During those past few months in 1984, I had been staying since the fire in my flat, in another flat owned by Mrs. Camilla Duncan in Patrick St., Mullingar. This lady is known all over Leinster and a couple of the western counties for her great Plant hire work which comprises land reclamation, site clearing and levelling, and even bog draining. You could see her dressed like a film star at any particular time, and one hour later togged out in her working clothes driving a large low-loader with a caterpillar tractor aboard when she was on her way to work herself on some job or other. She was a lady to deal with as regards rent collecting, and always gave me a great Christmas. She is over twenty years at that work now and people have great praise for her.

In the month of April, 1985, I had an operation for a hernia. It was on my lower stomach and the operation was a minor one. I went into hospital on a Friday morning, fasting, and the operation was performed in three hours after my arrival. I was allowed out the following Tuesday. In between, an event was televised that half the world watched. I watched it from my bed, as did the rest of the patients in the ward, and two good-looking female nurses sitting on my bed. It was, of course, the "Battle of the Black Ball" between Denis Taylor and Steve Davis. That game must have been the most nail-biting game of snooker ever played for onlookers. What condition must the two giants have been in? That game of snooker was on a par with Darby's goal against Kerry in the last seconds of the game, or Devon Lough's fall on the flat when in the lead in the Aintree Grand National and only yards to the winning post. The only major difference in the latter two from the first, is that the snooker was played in slow motion compared to the other two events.

My Ma's money was slow coming, and I had to wait until September, 1985, to purchase my new motorbike. I chose a Suzuki GS125S model. I paid £1,500 cash for it and got a £50 helmet for luck out of the deal. I bought it off Joseph Murray, Green Bridge, Mullingar, a next door neighbour, so that I could have first-class service at my door-step. Joe was brought over to the Suzuki factory in Japan for a four week educational course in all their motorcycles, all expenses paid. I felt very proud of the bike, and looked forward to learning all the works of it, and then learning to drive it. Even though the place I bought it was only about 100 yards from the yard of my flat, I knew so little about the machine that I had to get it delivered. I got an owner's manual to bring with me. This showed all the controls in detail and in pictures. My first education was to familiarise myself thoroughly with these controls. Having done this to perfection, my next work was to mount the machine and get it in motion, which was difficult as I only had 30 yards of a runway in the yard of my flat. Take-off in first gear gave me my hardest act to get right, until I got the feel of the clutch. I remember having the same trouble learning to drive a car. The press button engine start gave my bike a status above the kick-start machines. I drove a lot of cars in my time including a Jaguar, but I was getting much more satisfaction in learning to ride my motorbike. The big difference in it and a car, as regards controls, was that the clutch and acceleration in the car were foot controlled, while on the motorbike they were hand controlled. I don't know what my neighbours thought of my learning endeavours, with all the sudden cut-outs and jumpy starts, but I was not worried. In about three weeks' time, I considered myself roadworthy for a trial. I got my driver's licence, year's tax £11, and £89 for a year's insurance.

When first I put on the helmet, I thought I would never feel at home in it. I had familiarised myself with it during my practise runs, so that it was to my head as gloves are to the hand.

I decided that 3p.m. on a Sunday was the slackest time on the roads, and chose it for the take-off time. I now had my bike on the road, I mounted it and the engine warmed up. I was now feeling as good as any pilot in a cock-pit set for his first solo run. I took off up Patrick St. in first gear until I got out of the town. I then got it into second, third and fourth and was travelling at 35m.p.h. Now, I was more than delighted with my performance. I did not use fifth gear that first day. My nervous start was probably similiar to a young swallow on the top edge of its nest as it prepared for its first flight. I did not stop on the road until I came to Lough Ennell at Ladenstown, which is one-and-a-half miles off the Athlone road. It was terrific to see the vast lake, on which there were a lot of fishing boats, skiers behind speed boats, people wind-surfing, row boats and paddle canoes. It was my first time to see water skiers or wind surfers in action except on Hawaii 50 or telly advertisments, and this was all going on beside me for over twenty years. I got an offer of a trip in a speed boat and jumped to it, but was a bit scared when I saw the speedometer hand at 90m.p.h. and I with no life-jacket on! I spent four hours at the lake that lovely sunny autumn day. It was that day that I felt the true meaning of the phrase "Heaven and earth are full of Your glory". For the past thirty years, my life cycle was work to the bar, sleep, work, the bar, sleep, etc.

By the autumn of 1985, there was only one other man on the concrete works with me and the boss himself. As the two men from Rhode were no longer working with me, the boss came to town to collect me every morning and left me back each evening, a total journey of eight miles. This procedure was going on for a few years now, so my boss was delighted to see me land in on my motorbike on a Monday morning after my first road journey to the lake!

Although I was off the drink, I still went into my usual pub for a game of cards, a look at the daily papers, to watch the 9pm news, sport, Irish dance music and dancing, and to have the crack with the lads, all of whom I knew well by now. I drank minerals, mostly Kaliber Lager, but found the scales index hand rising sharply so I had to cut it out except for a very special occasion.

The autumn of 1985 was quite a busy one for me. I had always wanted a holiday on the continent, so I had booked myself a flight to Lourdes for the end of September at a cost of £295. This holiday cum prayer journey suited me as I knew about ten people from the Mullingar area that were going. The summer of 1985 was not a very good one in Ireland, so I looked forward to the sun in Southern France and I was not disappointed. I enjoyed the trip to Lourdes very much and will always cherish my memories of the baths and the torch-light procession. The night before my return journey, we had a ripping good sing-song in a hotel that caters for the Irish visitors in a big way. All in all, it was great value for the small amount of money invested. One memory I almost by-passed is that of a group of Spanish men and women, who all must have been about eighty years of age. They were on the praying platform the far side of the river reciting the Rosary in their native language, with the help of microphone for the person giving out the Rosary. They all had their Rosary beads in their hands as they fingered the Hail Marys, and from the looks and lines on their faces, I would say they were from a poorish countryside, mountainous area of Spain. Five years later now, I can see those faces, just as clear as I did in reality on that lovely September day.

I was only back from Lourdes, when I had a wedding engagement to fulfil. This was my first wedding on the dry, and I was determined to stay on the dry. I did miss a few drinks in the hotel that morning just for that half hour before the meal. I had gone to about twenty weddings up to my stopping the drink, and finished up drunk at them all. I enjoyed a very good meal and the crack after it. When late in the evening I saw lads that were very full buying more drink for their friends that had three or four pints in front of them, I thanked God that I had given up the drink. Of the seventy, or thereabouts, that were at that wedding, there were about one hundred and fifty untouched pints and shorts on the tables and counter at the finish. I know that because I was one of the last three of the wedding group that left the hotel that night. I enjoyed that day immensely and got up the next morning raring to go to work.

As I write this page, it is Thursday 12th April, Holy Thursday, and I can't but think of the lovely seasonal poem by Katherine Tynan - Sheep and Lambs:-

All in the April evening,
    April airs were abroad,
The sheep with their little lambs
    Passed me by on the road.

The sheep with their little lambs
    Passed me by on the road;
All in the April evening
    I thought on the Lamb of God.

The lambs were weary, and crying
    With a weak, human cry.
I thought on the Lamb of God
    Going meekly to die.

Up in the blue, blue mountains
    Dewy pastures are sweet;
Rest for the little bodies,
    Rest for the little feet.

But for the Lamb of God,
    Up on the hill-top green,
Only a Cross of shame
    Two stark crosses between.

All in the April evening,
    April airs were abroad;
I saw the sheep with their lambs,
    And thought of the Lamb of God.

With motorbike power now, I pay regular visits down the country to my brother Páraic in Navan, and my sister Áine in Rathvale, Athboy. I always stay a few nights in Athboy with Áine and Frank, and use it as a take-off centre for visits to my relations and friends in Boyerstown, Dunderry, the Commons, Bohermeen and Navan. It is very refreshing to get this change of air about six times a year, and at a very low cost thanks to Áine and Frank.

Lough Owel is one and a half miles from Mullingar, but the built-up swimming pool, with its three tier diving board and lay-by are three miles out of town. Five minutes gets me to the swimming pool, which is a great help in knocking off surface fat. There was a time I would dive off the middle board, but now I am quite satisfied to walk in like a four-year-old child. I had missed swimming for over twenty years, but like the bicycle, "once learned never forgotten". I was never a real strong swimmer, but in my own leisurely way, I would manage a few miles with a breast stroke act. On Saturday summer's evenings, I would sometimes have a swim after my tea, and go to Multyfarnham to the 8p.m. vigil Mass, as it was only a couple of miles away from the swimming pool. Mass had a unique dimension there in the stone-walled chapel and large sculptured altar. Franciscan monks and brothers managed this agricultural college where young students from all over Ireland learned good farming on the two hundred acre farm there. The lawns, with their lovely flowers, the slabbed graves of all buried there, the lovely little brook that runs through the wood in the grounds of the monastery and the life-sized Stations of the Cross that are perfectly placed at intervals throughout the entire front grounds, make it a place well worth a visit.

My one and only helicopter flight was over and around Multyfarnham village. Multyfarnham was the tidiest village in the country winner in the late seventies. Looking down from the helicopter, the farm attached to the monastery was a cut above its neighbouring farms, and it was quite easy to see that they stripe-grazed all their pasture land, and the stocking rate seemed to be very high. I wonder will these great farming men go back to organic farming and give the good example that they have given all along? I knew a few Meath men who had a drinking problem and used Multyfarnham to take the pledge for a short period of time or for life. I didn't get there until I was a year off the drink but I suppose it is not a bad place to pray in for the keeping of abstinence.

One pledge I did take was that I would never bring out the motorbike on frosty roads or on night journeys during the autumn when the dead leaves were still on the roads. Drink and a motorbike made a very bad medicine. As a matter of fact, I'd say they are a deadly poison. I would say that if I had a motorbike between my being eighteen and thirty years of age, I would have met the same end as hundreds of young men of that age group did. It is possible to get away with speeding around a corner in a car, but with a motorbike, severe injury or death follows. I always bring the speedometer down to 30m.p.h. when going into a corner of unknown curvature, and even less at a "Very Slow" road warning or black-spot road sign. If I had a son and I had to give him a motorbike or gun choice, I would give him the gun with a few warnings.

A trip I make every year lately, is an excursion by bus to Knock. Apart from the spiritual aspect, the bus is ideal from which to view the autumn countryside when it is looking at its best. It was on my trip to Knock in 1987 that I first noticed that all the elm trees of the country had died. On enquiring into it, I was told that they died from an attack of some woodpest or another. Other people thought it was the result of acid rain. A visit to the museum there in Knock for a fee of £1 is well worth it. You could spend a full hour there to see all the exhibitions. Items that were common enough in my young days are no longer in use, which brought back many happy memories to me and convinced me of my true age. I will never forget that 1987 visit, as it was my last time to have a short chat with my youngest sister Maggie. I told her that day that she had got very thin and did not look too well. She told me that her ulcers, for which she had an operation two years previously, were at her again. In a mere five weeks time I arrived for work at 8.30 to be told by my boss that he had very bad news for me. My first thought was that my job was in jeopardy, but before I had my motorbike parked, he told me that Maggie was dead. It hit me with a bang in the manner it was told to me, but what is the point in beating around the bush! My boss was of great help and assistance to me and Micheál during that period of time. I had heard her first cry of life, but failed to see her candle of life blow out when only a little over half-ways burnt down. That lovliest phrase in any language is not too far out of context here, *Ó eirí na greine go dul fui an ceana.* She had cancer of the pancreas. She had nursed Ma for a good many years and only survived her by a mere three short years. This latest death hit Máire hard, as she had lived with Ma and Maggie and was now on her own in the space of three years. Seán's death at twenty-five hit me so hard that the following four deaths were only minor upsets to me. Ma's Rosary trimmings for a peaceful, and a safeguard against unprovided sudden, death for all of us, was getting a fruitful hearing.

It is very hard to see a young person, be it a close relative or a neighbouring friend, taken away in the prime of life. It is bad enough even to see them emigrate to some distant land with no guarantee of their return. There is no use rearing up against God's wishes, for He knows what is best for us. Everyone has to live out their own lives to the best of their capabilities, for we all come into the world on our own and we will definitely be on our own leaving it. Time is a great healer, and all we can do for our dead friends, which is a big lot, is to remember them with daily prayer.

In the weeks following the August holidays, business came almost to a halt and on the 6th November, 1987, I became redundant. This put me on social welfare for the first time in my life. Now that I was not drinking, I could live quite well with the aid of a rent allowance. It was the depth of winter. I worked out a lifestyle for myself, and it worked out grand. After an 8.30a.m. rise and a good breakfast, I went to church at 10 o'clock for Mass as the church was only about 300 yards away. On my return at 10.30, I had a cup of coffee and two buttered cream crackers. I then did the required shopping, and on my return about noon, I brought my landlady's dog, an Irish terrier, for a good walk. Returning at about 1.30, I got my dinner, and by the time I had washed up after it, it was about 3.30. If there was racing televised, I looked at it on my neighbouring publican's television, after speculating 55p on a 5p yankee. I followed soccer, snooker and tennis that were televised also. I read the daily newspaper in that same pub as well, thus saving about £4 per week. It was now teatime, and I also listened to the 6.30 news on the radio. I washed my clothes myself once a week, and kept the flat as clean as I could. In the long evenings, I would bring the dog for a second walk. I found no trouble putting in the day. During the summer and autumn, I had swimming visits to the lake and fishing in the River Brosna to add to my enjoyment.

In the spring of 1988, I got work with a Dublin firm of construction contractors, who were expanding Quinnsworths' in Mullingar town. The work lasted from mid-March to the end of June. It was a highly paid job, and the work was comparatively easy. We were very lucky weatherwise, as it rained a lot for the first few weeks when we were working indoors, and on our moving to the outdoor work, the weather turned out to be very pleasant. That was my last job, apart from a few two-day a week part-time jobs. I had been suffering from severe chest pains for about three years, and reported the matter to my doctor. I got them about twice a week and they would last for about twenty minutes. He arranged for an urgent x-ray, which I got after a two-week delay. It transpired that I had a hiatus hernia, which was much better than heart trouble. Putting two four-inch bricks under the two head-legs of my bed, put an end to that suffering. I have to be a wee bit careful of what I lift and with my meals. Apart from an odd mild chest pain and varicose veins, I am 100% fit.

One thing I noticed since I gave up drinking, was that everything was done on time by me. Correspondence, phonecalls, clothes washing, and the maintenance check-up on my motorbike were all done on time, and it was a pleasure doing them. When I was drinking, I never bothered writing or phoning my relatives, and washing and housework were always behind time and a bore to do. I blame ten years work behind the counter for my varicose veins. I feel a wee bit leg weary if standing for a long time now. I am going to try elastic stockings, which the doctor tells me will do and prevent the requirement of an operation.

I visit my brother Micheál in hospital fairly often. He is well looked after, and has a visit to town about two nights per week. He also gets to lots of Sunday football matches, especially if Meath are playing. He is as fond of cigarettes and Guinness as ever, but all in all he is enjoying life well, but in a slightly restricted way. It would be much worse if he had taken hard drugs in his younger days.

August, 1988, I got a chance to move to a flat I was once in before and I liked very well but lost it over the drink. The flat is on the Green Bridge next door to the railway station, and next door to my favourite ceili house, Aidan Moore's, the famous bar and tobacconist. During the long winter's nights, I bring in my Irish terrier for company, as I sit by a good turf fire listening to the radio or reading stories in The Readers Digest, of which I have a large number. I still have no liking to start reading books, and my eyesight is not getting any better now. Dog company has the advantage over human company in that if he does something wrong he will not retaliate when chastised. I spent a lot of time teaching him good manners, and how to do a few simple tricks. I find him a most eager student to learn. My landlady's husband, Mr. Michael Reynolds, had two nice-sized farms on either side of Mullingar town. The River Brosna, famous for trout fishing, circles half the perimeter of each of the two farms. I fish a lot on both these farms and manage to catch a good few trout with the humble worm. The dog which I have to keep on a lead until I get to the land, does a great gallop through the fields when released. There are snipe and pheasants on these two farms, and the dog is an ideal beater for gun work. A walk out to one of these farms and around the perimeter, is a distance of about four miles. This is great exercise for a non-working man.

Mr. Michael Reynolds, the owner of the farms, was a staunch GAA man and the key man in the founding of the Mullingar Shamrocks. He had been a great footballer himself. He was a very pleasant man to have a chat with, was highly intelligent, and was handicapped with pains, with which he suffered for a long number of years. This did not interfere with his good humour and he had a new yarn for every day of the week. I will never forget the last one he told me a day before he died. It went like this: "Two elderly farmers had been at a sales to sell their annual amount of fat cattle, and as usual, this was one day in the year that they went to town in a big way. Fully dressed in their very best clothes, they were by evening time, fit for any occasion that came their way. Well lubricted with whiskey and Guinness, they decided to go to a variety show that was on in the town hall. Halfways through the show, one of them wanted to have a slash and made his way out a nearby open side door. A steward outside told him to go in a certain door, take the first turn right and go in the second door on the left. The man got confused, took the first turn left and went in the second door on the right. Here he was in a wooden structure, but saw an opening at one corner. It was out here that he relieved himself. He managed to get back to his friend, who was doubled in two laughing like the rest of the audience. When things returned to near normal, he asked his pal what was the great joke he had missed. The high humoured reply came, 'When you were out, a fellow came up to the gap in the corner of the stage, and pissed down on the lady that was playing the piano!'

Michael was the last blacksmith in Mullingar, and a first class coach builder as well. He was a gifted carpenter, and ironwork man as well. All in all, he would have been a great friend of my Da had they ever the luck to meet. His son, Joseph, built the last trap under the careful eye of his Da, and it took first prize at the Mullingar Show in the autumn of 1989. Joseph is a fully qualified carpenter and is shaping up like a true son of his father, workwise. It came as a great shock to me when I heard that Michael had been killed in a car crash in mid-October, 1989. I had accompanied him to a funeral just a week earlier, and at the finish of it he brought me to his own family burial plot and said to me, "This is where this hurl of bones will rest, sooner or later". He left a good, hard-working wife, and equally hard-working son, and three very good-looking daughters, two of whom are going to university, and the youngest who did her leaving in 1990.

He was only one week dead when I got word that my eldest sister Máire had to have an operation for a brain tumor. It was a success, but she was too far gone to take the treatment that would be required for a cure. As I write these last few pages, she is semi-concious but does not seem to be suffering too much. She is the last of my three sisters to have got this common disease, Maggie having dies from it in 1987, and Áine my younger sister had a very successful operation for cancer of one of her breasts some eight years ago. Máire died on 19th June, 1990.

My religous beliefs are pretty strong, but very simple. It is an act of miraculous mercy that I am alive today to write this story. How I survived the fall from the shed when I was only three years old, my two bad falls off the bicycle, my three encounters with fire, my fall from the trailer to the tractor draw-bar, my car crash and my encounter with a mad heifer after calving, put me on a par with the cat with nine lives. We were well drilled into religion in my younger days. I have fond memories of the one week's mission we had every three years, the Stations of the Cross, and the passion sermon on Holy Thursday nights and the monthly holy hour as the slanting autumn sunlight came in the western windows of Boyerstown church. The humble choir gave of their best, to the music of an antique peddled organ played by our head school teacher. Funerals in my young days were seen from the playground of Boyerstown national school. The bell that rang one single peal every twenty seconds, and the hearse that was powered by two jet black horses, and steered by a man dressed in all black with a tall bowler black hat and a long black whip, all added up to a very sad and partly frightening-looking occasion. We did say a silent prayer for the dead person that was about to be buried.

I like to visit the church once a day now, as I am only a few hundred yards away from it. I say a few small prayers every night and morning. God helps those that help themselves, and this I found to be very true. He was 99.999% responsible for my stopping of drink and the writing of this book, my humble contribution being .001%. I always say the hymn *Soul of my Saviour* after Communion, for it is to me the passion personified. I have huge faith in God's forgiveness, and if He has forgiven me, which I know He has, there is no trouble in anyone else getting forgiveness. It is only a matter of asking for it. He who cannot be condemned by his own conscience, hath no need fearing meeting the Lord in judgement. This consoling truth leaves us all the complete masters of our own destination. A small time back, I made a good general Confession in Knock by telling all the sins of my entire life. To make sure I told them all, I wrote them down on paper. I asked my Confessor was it all right for me to read them out to him as I took out the list and my spectacles. Certainly, he replied. I left Confession a very happy man, made a bee-line to the gents' toilets while holding on to the list with a firm grip for fear it might fall out of my pocket on that very windy day. I burned the list and flushed the ashes down the toilet. The pleasure I got from that fire more than compensated for the three fires in which I nearly lost my life. If they finished up in a river, I hope no trout got a taste of the ashes as they would surely be toxic!

The funny thing about my night prayers is that I was walking the dog along a path in town, when he picked up a yellow two-page leaflet. Not being able to read without my glasses, I brought it to my flat for examination. There in front of me was a few prayers which I say every night, and feel I have something useful done for sick people, and down and outs, a member of which I was for a long

number of years. I feel it would be a sin for me not to make use of
this book without writing down these prayers which go as follows:

Watch, dear Lord, with those who wake or watch or weep tonight
and give your angels charge over these who sleep.
Tend your sick ones, Lord Jesus Christ, rest your weary ones,
bless your dying ones, shield your joyous ones, and all for your
loves sake. Amen.

May the Lord support us all the day long,
till the shades lengthen and the evening comes,
and the busy world is hushed,
and the fever of life is over and our work is done.
Then, in His mercy, may God give us a safe lodging,
a holy rest and peace at the last.

Mary, mother of the sick, watch over all the sickbeds on this earth,
over those who at this moment are losing conciousness and are dying.
Over those who lie in struggle with death,
Over those who have no hope of cure,
Over those who will be sleepless this night,
Over those who will lie restless on their bed of pain.

Stay with us Lord, for night is at hand and day has passed,
Stay with us with your grace and goodness,
With your consolation and blessing.
Stay with us when night comes over us, the night of suffering
and doubt, the night of bitter death.
Stay with us Lord in time and in eternity.

May we cherish the bread while we still have some,
respect each other for what we are,
and love each other for who we are,
while we still have time.

If I have wounded anyone today, if I have caused one soul
to go astray,
If I have walked in my own willful way,
Dear Lord forgive me.
If I have uttered idle words or vain,
If I've turned aside from want or pain,
Lest I myself should suffer strain,
Dear Lord forgive me.
If I have been perverse or cold,
If I've longed for shelter in the fold,
Forgive the sins I have confessed,
Forgive the sins I see no more,
Forgive me for what I was and for what I failed to be.

Father, at the end of the day,
I want to thank You for your blessings,

Thank you for today's gift of life,
(Here give thanks for today's blessings),
I need your help, so that I will become aware of my failures to see
you.
In particular, I ask you to heal me of fears and worries.
Forgive me for letting doubt take over when I was sad or worried,
Give me tonight restful sleep and the peace of heart which comes
from knowing that I am always in the hands of a loving father.

Family Prayer

We, as a family, come before You, Lord, with our prayer at the end of this day. We pray for all who feel crucified like Your son. We pray for all who feel forsaken, for all who suffer and cannot see why. We pray for all who have no earthly beauty, for those who cannot keep up with others. We pray for unhappy children, and for their families, for all who are handicapped and for those who are incurably ill. We pray for those who will go on living after death of a partner and for those who mourn the death of a child and for all who have suffered unspeakable loss.

Lord bless the darkening earth, bless the city and the town. Bless the countryside and the rich so that they may have compassion, the poor so that they may grow in respect for each other. We pray for all who will not pray to You this night. We pray for all who feel love for You no more. We offer this night prayer for this family, that their lives will be fuller and happier.

The nice thing about these prayers is that they are so unselfish. It takes three and a half minutes to say these prayers, which is a very small part of twenty four hours or 1440 minutes. It is no harm at night to remember that tomorrow is a great day in your life since it is "the first day in the rest of your life". These great days don't last forever and are deminishing by the day.

CHAPTER XIII

Brothers and sisters, friends and foe, I am delighted you are still with me! This concluding short chapter to my script is a sort of a mixed grill chapter. It takes in little items from my first script which I completed on Easter Saturday, 1989, and has been omitted in my second script which I had to do in more presentable writing. It also takes an account of some good and bad news items of interest that have happened up to this present day, Monday, 28th September, 1992.

Firstly I have to apologise to two saints, Fr. Thomas O'Keeffe and Fr. McLoughlin of whom I have been a wee bit critical. I gave my impression of them as I saw at the time when I was a boy. My present impression of them is one of admiration and if the two of them are not in heaven, we may as well throw away all our religious beliefs!

I have made a small public confession of some of my sins and I find this good for my soul. At the opening prayers at Mass nowadays don't we all confess our sins to one another when we say "I have sinned in my thoughts; words; deeds and omissions?" Three church hymns of classical music, that elevate my spirits greatly when sung by the "Boys Cantorri Choirsters" in Mullingar Cathedral at the Sunday 10 o'clock Mass are: *Panis Angelicus; Piae Jesu and The Lord is my Shepherd. Amazing Grace* is another of my favourites.

I hope this story will be a little help to keep some of our youth from becoming miserable alcoholics, Would they could experience the misery I went through after a few days heavy drinking in comparision to my joy on fine summer days since my conversion to sobriety. It is amazing the help God can give to a person that makes a small effort.

276

Since I first started this book I have lost an awful lot of great friends who were about my own age, both here in Mullingar and my home county, Meath. Máire died in the summer of 1990. I brought poor Páraic to the chapel on Christmas Eve, 1991 and buried him on St. Stephen's Day. He had been a very good brother to all of us and I had been looking forward to his comments on this book. My good neighbour in Boyerstown, Matthew Rogers, ex-Meath Senior Footballer, died this summer, 1992.

Other bad news on this last weekend of September, 1992, are the civil war in Yugoslavia and the horrific famine in Somalia. It never should happen and warnings were given about eighteen months ago. I'm thinking that if the pictures of that famine as shown on television were of animals dying with protruding bones, instead of humans, there would be a greater public outcry! What about the food piles in intervention and it is not that millionaires have too much money, but that money has too much of the millionaires! As they speculate on the floors of the "Money Exchange Market", the demons of greed and impurity are doing a merry dance along side them.

I give my heartiest Ole-Ole-Oles to the superb Donegal Senior Football team that brought the Sam Maguire Cup to the hills of Donegal for the very first time. All credit to Clare for their great display against Dublin in the semi-final. Earlier this summer of 1992, two young Irish boxers did great work in the Barcelona Olympics, Mick Carruth brought back the first gold medal since Ronnie Delaney in 1956. A badly injured last round finalist, Wayne McCullough, brought back a silver medal.

On the same day that a Skryne martyr, Margaret Ball was beatified, Skryne won their first Meath County Senior Football Championship in twenty eight years. Colm O'Rourke receives his first County Senior Football medal and young Giles who is only 17 years of age, got another to add to his All-Ireland Minor Football medal, just one week ago. It was on the last Sunday of September,

1992, also that Mullingar Shamrocks took the Westmeath Senior Football Championship with the assistance of Bernard Flynn the great Meath marksman who scored six points. What a great weekend of sport, that was for on the previous Saturday night Ireland's greatest greyhound trainer Mick O'Sullivan from Tipperary, saddled Manx Treasure to win the Irish 1992 *Respond Puppy Dog Derby*. Although a wee bit lame from an old injury he went into trap in splendid form.

Hundreds of books are written by Irish authors every year, so I won't get a swelled head over this book. I have one big advantage over writers who read a lot and who I feel would be inclined to quote phrases from their readings, in that I have read almost nothing. I am a great believer in the saying "Call a spade a spade", so I pulled no punches.

My first script was all written during the season of Lent, 1989. It was my penance for Lent, the first penance I ever did and what a penance it was! I must have asked myself one hundred times "What were you doing letting yourself into this for?" I was even tempted to put the whole lot into the fire on a few occasions, especially when I would read my day's work each night and from the bad writing, I knew I would have to rewrite all again. All I had to guide me was loose pages of little instances that happened during my lifetime from the age of two years. These were taken during my work and pleasure time over a period of four years.

No note was taken unless it led to a story that I would love to read about myself, if I did not know what I knew about the same story and having experienced it. My age was put over each of these notes as well as one of the letterings A.B.C.D. depending on the season of the year in which they happened.

After putting all these happenings in their proper sequence I was ready to start my script properly. The biggest work then was bridging in the extended details after each happening. Chapterizing the script gave me least trouble.

I made a few changes in my second script and tried to improve my writing. It was then I thought of a school comrade by the name of William Dowdall who now lives in Mullhuddart. I defy any man in the whole of Ireland to write as clear and perfect as he can. He is another product of Saint Patrick's classical school, Navan and brother of the great exemplary farming Dowdall Bros., Knockcumber, Navan, Co. Meath.

The second script lay dormant until April, 1991, almost two years. On the *Mike Murphy Art Show* programme one evening I heard of *Kells Publishing Company Ltd.*, John Street, Kells. It is managed by Jack Fitzsimons, a well known and highly rated architect. From my very first meeting with him, he gave me great encouragement and all the advice cum help I needed. His secretary, Fiona, has the patience of Job! There must be an awful lot of beauty queens in Kells or is it that the boys are slipping up? Writing for long hours is very boring and a very lonesome occupation on your own in a flat. My poor little Irish terrier did not like it either, as he would put his two paws on my lap, look me straight in the face as much as to say "What in the name of God are you doing?" Once I watched an old dog and a pup and got the real meaning of "The old dog for the hard road, the pup for the path". It was at home on the farm that I watched a pup spend ten minutes burying a bone while the old dog lay asleep with his head resting on his two front paws. When the pup was gone away satisfied that his bone was safe, up gets the old dog and walks straight over to the buried bone some thrity yards away! As I write these last few lines it is 12.30 a.m., Wednesday, 30th September, 1992.

The World I Live In.

Running streamlets, bubbling brooks,
Singing birds, and cawing rooks,
Chattering magpies, twittering wrens,
Quacking ducks and clucking hens,
Neighing horses, lowing cows,
Squealing pigs and snorting sows,
Barking dogs and mewing cats, stealing after mice and rats.
Oh, what a noise and what a din, is the world that I live in!

AN CRÍOCH